Cambridge Studies in Chinese History, Literature and Institut
General Editors
Patrick Hanan & Denis Twitchett

T'AO YÜAN-MING
HIS WORKS AND THEIR MEANING

Volume II   Additional Commentary, Notes and Biography

T'ao Yüan-ming

(AD 365–427)

HIS WORKS AND THEIR MEANING

A.R. DAVIS

Professor of Oriental Studies
University of Sydney

Volume II   Additional Commentary, Notes and Biography

CAMBRIDGE UNIVERSITY PRESS
CAMBRIDGE
LONDON   NEW YORK   NEW ROCHELLE
MELBOURNE   SYDNEY

CAMBRIDGE UNIVERSITY PRESS
Cambridge, New York, Melbourne, Madrid, Cape Town, Singapore, São Paulo, Delhi

Cambridge University Press
The Edinburgh Building, Cambridge CB2 8RU, UK

Published in the United States of America by Cambridge University Press, New York

www.cambridge.org
Information on this title: www.cambridge.org/9780521104531

First published 1983
This digitally printed version 2009

A catalogue record for this publication is available from the British Library

Library of Congress Catalogue Card Number: 82-22092

ISBN 978-0-521-23616-4 hardback
ISBN 978-0-521-10453-1 paperback

In memory of
G.H. and A.D.W.

CONTENTS

Volume II

Volume I

PREFATORY NOTE

This second volume contains the text of T'ao Yüan-ming's works which my translation in Volume 1 renders, together with additional commentaries and notes and a composite version with text, translation and discussion of the traditional biographies of the poet.

The text of T'ao's works printed here has been chosen, character by character, from the various texts which I have been able to see in the course of this study. Thus it does not follow exactly any one text hitherto printed, without of course differing very widely from other modern texts of the works, which generally follow that printed by T'ao Shu in his *Ching-chieh hsien-sheng chi.* Already in the Southern Sung editions of the works, variant readings are noted, but it has not seemed worthwhile to me to present these and the variants of later editions in an attempt at a 'critical apparatus.' So much of the information could not be truly firsthand, and while the choice between variants can sometimes be defended on logical grounds and 'objective' criteria such as graphic confusions or taboo substitutions can be adduced, all too often the basis of selection seems to be due to what I should like to call an 'educated subjectivity.' Professor Wang Shu-min in his *T'ao Yüan-ming shih chien-cheng kao* seems to me to have given a fine display of this 'educated subjectivity', and I have very seldom in fact gone against his decisions in choosing my text.

I have therefore only noted the more major departures of other critics and myself from the general readings accepted in the Southern Sung texts. Since, as I have said, T'ao Shu's has become the most common text of the works, I have especially noted my departures from it. I have made my annotations in the usual Chinese *chiao-k'an chi* form. On the editions of T'ao's works the studies by Hashikawa Tokio and Kuo Shao-yü are to be commended.

In the case of my composite biography I am attempting something rather different and in comparing related but separate texts it has seemed to me important to note all the variations between them. Since it would have been more cumbersome to present this in the Chinese *chiao-k'an chi* style, I hope that the form I have adopted (explained in the introduction to the Biography) may be acceptable.

THE FOUR-WORD POEMS

1 HANGING CLOUDS

停 雲

序　停雲，思親友也。罇湛新醪，園列初榮。願言不從，歎
息彌襟。

I

靄靄停雲	靜寄東軒
濛濛時雨	春醪獨撫
八表同昏	良朋悠邈
平路伊阻 4	搔首延佇 8

II

停雲靄靄	有酒有酒
時雨濛濛	閒飲東牕
八表同昏	願言懷人
平陸成江 4	舟車靡從 8

III

東園之樹	人亦有言
枝條載榮	日月于征
競用新好	安得促席
以招余情 4	說彼平生 8

IV

翩翩飛鳥　　　　　　　豈無他人
息我庭柯　　　　　　　念子實多
斂翮閒止　　　　　　　願言不獲
好聲相和　　　　　　　抱恨如何

4   8

Additional Notes

PREFACE. T'ao here and in II, 7 and IV, 7 uses 言 in imitation of the *Songs*. In the *Songs* 言 is actually a conjunctive particle (cf. 焉, 云, 曰) but the Mao-Cheng Hsüan interpretation of it is as the first person pronoun. It is hard to say whether or not T'ao is following this 'incorrect' understanding, because his examples like those in the *Songs* are susceptible of either interpretation.

I, 8. Adapted from *Song* 42. 1: 愛而不見, 搔首踟蹰 'I love her but do not go to see her;/I scratch my head and hesitate.'

III, 5. This line occurs five times in the *Ta-ya* section of the *Songs* (255, 8; 256, 1; 257, 9; 260, 5&6).

III, 7. The expression *ts'u hsi* perhaps derives immediately from Tso Ssu's *Shu-tu fu* (*Wen-hsüan* 4, 29b): 合樽促席 'Place side by side the wine-jars and set close the mats.' There is, however, a much earlier occurrence in the *Liu-yen shih* of Tung-fang Shuo (quoted in Li Shan commentary, ibid.).

IV, 5. This line occurs in *Songs* 87, 1&2; 119, 1&2; 120, 1&2. It is probably *Song* 120 which T'ao had in mind. There the following lines are respectively: 維子之故 'It is only with you that I have an old friendship' and 維子之好 'It is only you that I love.'

IV, 7. This line had been used by Hsi K'ang (*Tseng Hsiu-ts'ai ju-chün shih* 贈秀才入軍詩 III; *Wen-hsüan* 24, 11a) and Chang Heng (see Li Shan commentary, ibid.).

2   THE REVOLUTION OF THE SEASONS

時　運

序　時運，游暮春也。春服既成，景物斯和，偶景獨遊，欣
慨交心。

I

邁 邁 時 運	山 滌 餘 靄
穆 穆 良 朝	宇 曖 微 霄
襲 我 春 服	有 風 自 南
4　薄 言 東 郊	翼 彼 新 苗　　8

II

洋 洋 平 津	人 亦 有 言
乃 漱 乃 濯	稱 心 易 足 *
邈 邈 遐 景	揮 茲 一 觴
4　載 欣 載 矚	陶 然 自 樂　　8

* 此句曾集本作稱心而言，人亦易足，註云一作人亦有言，稱心易足。今從之。

III

延 目 中 流	我 愛 其 靜
悠 想 清 沂 *	寤 寐 交 揮
童 冠 齊 業	但 恨 殊 世
4　閒 詠 以 歸	邈 不 可 追　　8

* 悠想，曾集本作悠悠，註云一作悠想。今從之。

IV

斯 晨 斯 夕	清 琴 橫 牀
言 息 其 廬	濁 酒 半 壺
花 藥 分 列	黃 唐 莫 逮
4　林 竹 翳 如	慨 獨 在 余　　8

Additional Notes

I, 1. The *locus classicus* of the reduplicated compound *mai-mai* is in *Song* 229, 5 where it is defined by the Mao commentary as 不說 'with displeasure' (cf. Karlgren's discussion under gloss 726). In view of the close imitation of the *Songs* in T'ao's four-word poems, he might be expected to use the compound in this sense. From the context, however, he seems to have formed a compound in the sense of the simple character as used, e.g. in *Song* 114, 2: 日月其邁 'the days and months, how they pass!'

I, 4. *Po yen*, see Additional Note to *Hanging Clouds*, preface, for discussion of *yen*. Mao (*Song* 8) explains *po* as a particle, whereas Cheng Hsüan (*Song* 273) interprets it as 'for the first time'. The relatively weak meaning of both interpretations would make it difficult in any case to say whether T'ao and others were following either, but I suspect that they in fact treated *po yen* as a unit without analysis and used it for its sound and archaic flavour.

I, 7–8. These lines are founded on *Song* 32, 1: 凱風自南，吹彼棘心 'The joyful wind comes from the south;/It blows on the heart of that jujube tree.' The word *i* is no doubt descriptive of the wind blowing over the young shoots, but it does not seem proper to give it the meaning of 'cause to wave' (披拂) as Ting Fu-pao does. Particularly in view of the underlying *Song* reference to a loving mother, there is good reason to understand it in its common meaning of 'aid', 'protect.'

II, 5. See note to *Hanging Clouds*, III, 5.

II, 7. *Hui* has a literal meaning of 'shake out the drops from a wine-cup.'

III, 6. *Wu-mei* 'waking or sleeping' is a cliché of the *Songs*, see Nos. 1 and 145. The expression *chiao hui* presents some difficulty. Suzuki Torao has an apparently neat explanation that it signifies 'an exchange of wine-cups'. He thus makes *hui* a nominal form with a sense derived from its use in II, 7 above. There are, however, two examples of *chiao hui* in the *Wen-hsüan* (34, 28a, Ts'ao Chih, *Ch'i ch'i* 七啟 and 57, 5b P'an Yüeh, *Hsia-hou ch'ang-shih lei* 夏侯常侍誄). In these examples ('lutes and citherns are played together' and 'floods of tears are poured out in confusion') *chiao* is adverb and *hui* verb. The present example would then require an analogous translation.

III, 7–8. These lines may be reminiscent of *Ch'u-tz'u* 4, 21a (*Chiu-chang*, *Huai-sha*, st. 13) 古固有不並兮，豈知其故也，湯禹久遠兮，邈不可慕也 'From of old truly there have been those not in accord with their age./How can we know why it is so?/T'ang and Yü are remote in time,/Far off and not to be longed for.'

IV, 7. Cf. last note.

3 THE TREE IN BLOSSOM

榮 木

序　榮木，念將老也。日月推遷，已復九夏。總角聞道，白首無成。

I

采采榮木
結根于茲
晨耀其華
夕已喪之
人生若寄
顦顇有時
靜言孔念
中心悵而

II

采采榮木
于茲託根
繁華朝起
慨暮不存
貞脆由人
禍福無門
匪道曷依
匪善奚敦

III

嗟予小子
稟茲固陋
徂年既流
業不增舊
志彼不舍
安此日富
我之懷矣
怛焉內疚

IV

先師遺訓
余豈云墜
四十無聞
斯不足畏
脂我名車
策我名驥
千里雖遙
孰敢不至

Additional Notes

TITLE. Ku Chih identified the tree (or shrub) of the title as the *mu-chin* 木堇 (also written as 木槿), the hibiscus, noting that *Li-chi*, *Yüeh-ling* (= 5, 13a) states that the hibiscus is in bloom in the middle summer month (fifth month), which agrees with T'ao's preface, and also that *Shuo-wen* sub *shun* 蕣 (= p. 21) states that the hibiscus comes out in the morning and drops in the evening, which agrees with ll.3–4 of T'ao's first stanza. While Ku might even be literally correct that the hibiscus was in bloom in T'ao's garden, I doubt whether the poet intended to be so categorical. *Jung* ('blossom') with its metaphorical meaning of 'glory' and its immediately suggested antonym of 'fading' ('decline') was very much to his purpose.

PREFACE. The use of *chiu-hsia* as an expression for 'summer' (cf. *chiu-ch'un* 九春 = 'spring') arises from a season having ninety (nine periods of ten) days.

I, 1. 'Luxuriant' follows the definition of the Mao commentary to *Song* 129, 3 (= 萋萋).

I, 2. *Chieh-ken* ('planted its roots') may be a reminiscence of *Old Poem*, VIII, 1–2: 冉冉孤生竹, 結根泰山阿 'Bending is the solitary growing bamboo;/It has planted its roots on a slope of T'ai-shan.'

I, 5. The oldest extant example of this frequently expressed sentiment appears to be in a fragment of the third century BC philosophical work *Shih-tzu* (ap. Li Shan commentary to *Wen-hsüan* 29, 2b): 老來子曰人生於天地 之間寄也 'Lao-lai-tzu said: "Man's life between Heaven and Earth is like a sojourning."' It occurs in *Old Poem*, XIII, 1.13: 人生忽如寄, but the source which may have been uppermost in the poet's mind is Wei Wen-ti (Ts'ao P'i) whose *Shan-tsai hsing* 善哉行 (*Wen-hsüan* 27, 25a–b), a poem generally reminiscent of the *Nineteen Old Poems* and in intention different from T'ao's, provides a closely parallel expression here in 人生如寄, 多憂何爲 'Man's life is like a sojourning;/Why has he many cares?' and also in 策我良馬 'I whip up my excellent horses' one for line 6 of T'ao's fourth stanza.

I, 7–8. These lines are modelled on *Song* 58, 5: 靜言思之, 躬自悼矣 'Quietly I brood over it;/I grieve for myself.' *Erh* is a suffix here like 然, 如.

II, 6. is a quotation from *Tso-chuan*, Hsiang twenty-third year 禍福無門, 唯人所召 'For ill or good fortune there are no gates; they are invited in by man.'

III, 1. Suzuki Torao suggests (and several subsequent Japanese commentators have followed him) that T'ao used the expression *hsiao-tzu* in the sense of 'disciple' *vis-à-vis* Confucius, the 'former master' of the fourth stanza, but the whole line is a cliché of self-depreciation in the four-word poems of the period so that it is probably unnecessary to make this connection.

III, 5. The possibility of a sort of pun between the two references of *pu she* 'not ceasing' has been discussed in the commentary to the poem. The existence of a variant reading 忘 for 志, although it might simply be the result of graphic confusion, seems more likely to have come from an editor who took the reference to be to *Lun-yü* 9, 16 and thus thought 志 an inappropriate verb.

III, 6. 'Daily growing richer' is derived from *Song* 196, 2: 人之齊聖, 飲酒溫克,

彼昏不知，壹醉日富 'Men who are correct and wise/Are mild and restrained in drinking wine/Those stupid and ignorant men,/When once they are drunk, think themselves daily growing richer.' Most commentators have seen the reference of this allusion as being to drinking, thus interpreting the line as 'I remain content with getting drunk.' This seems to me to be inadequate to the context and to take little account of the moral exhortation of the original *Song*. It seems more likely that T'ao is using the allusion to criticize himself for foolish self-satisfaction and self-deception.

III, 7. This line is taken from *Song* 33, 1: 我之懷矣，自詒伊阻 'Oh, you whom I cherish,/You have given me this trouble.' Its reading has to be slightly adapted to T'ao's context.

III, 8. Underlying the expression *nei-chiu* is probably *Lun-yü* 12, 4: 內省不疚, 夫何憂何懼 'If he searches into himself and finds no sickness, at what should he be troubled, what should he fear?'

IV, 3–4. The full quotation of *Lun-yü* 9, 22 which T'ao abbreviates to fit his line is: 四十五十而無聞焉斯亦不足畏也已.

4　TO MY GRANDFATHER'S COUSIN THE DUKE OF CH'ANG-SHA

贈長沙公族祖*

序　余族，長沙公爲族祖⁺，同出大司馬，昭穆既遠，以爲
　　路人。經過潯陽，臨別贈此。

I

同源分流	禮服遂悠
人易世疏	歲月眇徂
慨然寤歎	感彼行路
念茲厥初	眷然躊躇

4　　　　　　　　　　　　　　　　　　　　　　　　　　8

* 各本作贈長沙公族祖，陶注本刪族祖。
⁺ 序各本作長沙公於余爲族祖，或又云一作余於長沙公爲族祖，今改余於作余族。

II

於穆令族　　　　　　　　　　爰采春花
允構斯堂　　　　　　　　　　載警秋霜
諧氣冬暄　　　　　　　　　　我曰欽哉
映懷圭璋　　　　　　　　　　實宗之光

III

伊余云邁　　　　　　　　　　遙遙三湘
在長忘同　　　　　　　　　　滔滔九江
笑言未久　　　　　　　　　　山川阻遠
逝焉西東　　　　　　　　　　行李時通

IV

何以寫心　　　　　　　　　　敬哉離人
貽茲話言　　　　　　　　　　臨路悽然
進簣雖微　　　　　　　　　　款襟或遼
終焉爲山　　　　　　　　　　音問其先

Additional Commentary

The text of the preface, as transmitted appears in two versions: 余於長沙 [some add 公] 爲族祖, which is the reading of the partially preserved early T'ang anthology *Wen-kuan tz'u-lin* (AD 658) chapter 152, 8b and which is noted as a variant in the Southern Sung editions of the collected works; and 長沙公於余爲族祖, which is the reading of the Southern Sung editions. The title of the poem appears in all early editions as 贈長沙公族祖.

Wu Jen-chieh (sub Yüan-chia 2) adopted the first alternative for the preface and proposed that the title should be emended to 贈長沙公族孫. Wu believed that the Duke of Ch'ang-sha, thus designated, was the grandson of the third duke Ch'o-chih. His conception of the relationship would have been:

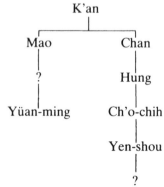

(For the descent of the Dukes of Ch'ang-sha from T'ao K'an, see *Chin shu* 66, 10b).

The name of this supposed grandson of Ch'o-chih is unknown and such a person could not legitimately have been addressed as 'Ch'ang-sha', since the family's hereditary title was reduced at the beginning of Sung, while still held by Yen-shou, to that of Marquis of Li-ling hsien 醴陵縣侯 (*Sung shu* 3, 2a; *Chin shu* 66, 10b. has Marquis of Wu-ch'ang 吳昌侯). Wu thought that Yüan-ming was continuing to use the Chin title. His argument thus rests on two unsupported beliefs, viz. that there was a son of Yen-shou, who would fit the description of the poem and that the poet would have overtly shown hostility to the Sung by using a Chin title. It is not clear why he chose 425 as a date for the poem.

Wu's hypothesis did not find favour and an alternative proposal was made by Chang Yin 張縯 in his critique of Wu's *nien-p'u* (*nien-p'u pien-cheng* 年譜辨證, quoted in Li Kung-huan's commentary to this poem) that the first sentence of the preface ends at 族, i.e. 'I am a kinsman of the Duke of Ch'ang-sha' or 'the Duke of Ch'ang-sha is a kinsman of mine' (with such punctuation the reading ceases to be important). This view has been widely adopted, and it has been further generally held that the 族祖 of the title is an interpolation which should be removed.

Here there is a good example of the weakness of traditional Chinese scholarship in some aspects of textual criticism. As is suggested elsewhere in this study, Chinese scholars seem often to overlook the probability that substantial text variants have a relationship of which one ought to attempt an explanation. Thus one cannot proceed as if the variants offered an entirely free choice to the editor. While one might argue, in the present case, that the 族祖 in the title is an interpolation by someone who misunderstood a text reading 長沙公於余爲族祖, if one does so, one leaves the appearance of the reading 余於長沙[公]爲族祖 wholly unexplained. For a serious text critic this is not permissible. If indeed the relationship of the variant readings to each other and to the title is considered, then the probability will be that the reading 余於長沙[公]爲族祖 is the earlier and the reading 長沙公於余爲族祖 is the later, since the latter could have arisen from an editorial attempt to achieve congruity between preface and title, whereas the former could not. By the same reasoning the words 族祖 in the title would have stood there *before* the appearance of the reading 長沙公於余爲族祖. Thus the common view that 族祖 is an interpolation into the title from the reading 長沙公於余爲族祖 is unlikely and it is reasonable to conclude that at an earlier stage the text read:

(Title) 贈長沙公族祖
(Preface) 余於長沙[公]爲族祖

This is the actual reading of the *Wen-kuan tz'u-lin* version (without 公 in the preface) and of course an apparently unintelligible reading. Nevertheless, it is this reading that should be the starting point for a solution of the problem.

An ingenious solution was offered by the Japanese scholar Matsuzaki Meifuku in the postface to his edition of T'ao's works (also quoted in Hashikawa Tokio, *T'ao-chi pan-pen yüan-liu k'ao*, 26a–b). Matsuzaki believed that if the intended meaning of the title was 'To My Grandfather's Cousin the Duke of Ch'ang-sha', the order of words was incorrect. He suggested, therefore, that the poem's title 贈長沙公 had originally been followed, after an appropriate space, by 族祖淵明, i.e. To the Duke of Ch'ang-sha . . . by his grandfather's cousin Yüan-ming. Later compilers accidentally omitted 淵明, and 族祖 became joined to the title. While Matsuzaki's observation of the word order of such titles is generally accurate, I can cite at least one other example from the period, which matches the present case. In the same chapter of *Wen-kuan tz'u-lin* (ch. 152) that contains *To the Duke of Ch'ang-sha* there is also a poem by Hsiao T'ung, the compiler of the *Wen-hsüan*, *To My Younger Brother the Governor of Hsü-chou* 示徐 州弟. Thus Matsuzaki's objection to the word order of the title is not conclusive. Besides, in the matter of the identity of the addressee he returns to the unsatisfactory proposal of Wu Jen-chieh.

My own attempt at a solution is very simple, although its acceptance would imply that T'ao K'an was not the poet's great-grandfather but his great-great-grandfather on the paternal side. I suggest that the title 贈長沙公族祖 and the reading of the preface 余於長沙[公]爲族祖 can be made congruent by the emendation of 於 to 族. The corruption of 族 to 於 would account satisfactorily for the subsequent incorrect editorial activity. If we thus take the title as it appears in every early edition to be correct, it follows that T'ao Yüan-ming's grandfather was a grandson, not a son of T'ao K'an. For, if the descent of the Dukes of Ch'ang-sha given in *Chin shu* 66, 10b is correct, only if this were the case, could any of them stand in *tsu-tsu* relationship to Yüan-ming and he would have to be T'ao Hung. When one considers that one hundred and six years separate the birth of K'an (259) and Yüan-ming (365), it is by no means impossible for the latter to have been a fourth rather than a third generation descendant of K'an on the paternal side. Nor need this conflict with his being a third generation descendant on the maternal side (for which we have his own statement in his biography of Meng Chia, see p.145), if we bear in mind the great size and probable time spread of T'ao K'an's family of seventeen sons and at least ten daughters. If T'ao Mao, Yüan-ming's grandfather, was a grandson, not a son of K'an, this also can clear away a long-debated problem (see pp. 176–77).

Additional Notes

I, 1. This line appears first in Pan Ku's *Yu-t'ung fu* 幽通賦 (*Wen-hsüan* 14,

21b): 術同源而分流 'Methods [of cultivating the Way] have a common source but proceed in different directions.' Pan Chao comments: 'Like rivers which have a common source but flow in different directions.'

I, 3. 'I lie awake and sigh': a *Shih* expression, see *Songs* 203 and 153 (in the latter written 寤嘆).

II, 1. The form of expression in *wu mu ling tsu* no doubt ultimately goes back to *Song* 266: 於穆清廟 'Oh, majestic is the pure temple.' It is, however, very common in the four-word 'address and response' poems of the third to sixth centuries, applied eulogistically to relatives or friends, e.g. Lu Chi, *In Reply to P'an Ni*: 於穆同心, 'Oh, admirable is my comrade.' (*Lu Shih-heng shih chu*, p. 84.)

II, 2. *Kou ssu t'ang* is an allusion to *Shu, Ta-kao*: 若考作室, 既底法, 厥子乃 弗肯堂, 矧肯構 'If a father begins a house, and, when the foundations have been planned, his son is unwilling to build the hall, how much less will he be willing to roof it.' This is intended as an expression of praise for the Duke. T'ao Shu took this line as referring to the building of a shrine for T'ao K'an at Hsün-yang. Yet if this were the case, it is likely that some mention would have been made in the preface of the poem. The same allusion is made by Lu Chi in his four-word poem to his younger brother Yün: 俯慙堂構, 仰懍先靈 'On the one hand I am ashamed over the roofing of the hall,/On the other I have failed my ancestors.' (*Lu Shih-heng shih chu*, p. 81.)

II, 3. 'Sunshine in winter'. The earliest example of this figure seems to be in *Teng-hsi-tzu*, chapter 1, p. 8: 爲君當若冬日之陽, 夏日之陰 'He who is a ruler must be like sunshine on a winter day, like shade on a summer day'.

II, 4. *Kuei-chang*, originally two kinds of jade sceptre, symbolizes authority, cf. *Songs* 252, 6; 254, 6 如圭如璋 (如璋如圭).

II, 5–6. There has been a tendency among the later commentators, under the influence of T'ao Shu's idea that the Duke had visited Hsün-yang to build a shrine to T'ao K'an, to refer these lines to the performance of sacrificial rites. Ting Fu-pao cites *Li-chi* 24 (14, 5b): 霜露既降, 君子履之, 必有悽愴之心, 非其寒之謂也. 春雨露既濡, 君子履之, 必有怵惕之心, 如將見之 'When the rimy dew descends, the gentleman, as he treads it, must have a sorrowful heart, which is not concerned with the cold. When the wet dew of spring soaks the ground, the gentleman, as he treads it, must have a timorous heart, as if he were about to see them [i.e. the ancestors].' I would suggest that 'the spring flowers' and 'autumn frosts' refer rather to the passing of the Duke's life. One may compare Lu Chi, *To Feng Wen-p'i on His Being Transferred to the Magistracy of Ch'ih-ch'iu* 贈馮文羆遷斥丘令: 及子春華, 後爾秋暉 'I equalled your spring flowers,/But I fall behind your autumn radiance.' (*Lu Shih-heng shih chu*, p. 74); cf. also *San-kuo chih*, *Wei shu*, 12, 12b quoted in Discussion of Biography, note 18, p. 181.

II, 7. The form of words is based on *Shu*, *Yao-tien* (final sentence).

III, 2. Many commentators have followed Wang T'ang 王棠 (ap. Wu Chan-t'ai) in reading the character 長 as *chang* and understanding it as referring to Yüan-ming's seniority in age. With my understanding of the title of the poem this is impossible.

III, 3. *Hsiao-yen* derives from *Song* 58, 2.

III, 5. *San Hsiang* (The Three Hsiang) is here simply a periphrasis (to balance the 'Nine Chiang' of the next line) for the Hsiang River, cf. the similar use by T'ao's friend Yen Yen-chih in his *Written when Climbing the Tower on the Pa-ling Wall with Governor Chang of Hsiang-chou, while Returning from Shih-an Commandery to the Capital* 始安郡還都與張湘州登巴陵城樓作 (*Wen-hsüan* 27, 3b): 三湘淪洞庭 'The Three Hsiang sink into Tung-t'ing.' There is disagreement over which three confluents of the Hsiang are embraced by this expression, but this is of no importance in such a context as this.

III, 6. This line is a reminiscence of *Song* 204, 6: 浩浩江漢 'Broadly flow the Chiang and Han.'

III, 7. This line is a slight variation upon *Song* 232, 1&2: 山川悠遠 'Hills and streams stretch far.'

III, 8. The *locus classicus* for the term *hsing-li* is *Tso-chuan*, Hsi thirtieth year.

IV, 1. The poet adapts here the line 我心寫兮 which occurs in *Songs* 173, 1; 214, 1 and 218, 4. Each of the *Songs* treats a happy meeting. Relying on the obvious reference to the *Songs*, T'ao certainly intended his line to mean: 'How has he relieved my heart?' Wang Yao, quite clearly, and perhaps other of the Chinese commentators have missed this point and thus misconstrued the first four lines of this stanza.

IV, 2. *Hua-yen* is from *Song* 256, 9. The Mao gloss reads: 古之善言也 'the excellent words of the ancients'.

IV, 3–4. The full text of *Lun-yü* 9, 18 which T'ao adapts is: 譬如爲山，未成一簣，止吾止也，譬如平地，雖覆一簣，進吾往也 'One may take the example of making a mound. If one does not complete it by one basketful, the stopping is one's own stopping. One may take the example of levelling ground. Although one has overturned but one basketful, the going forward is one's own going.'

IV, 5. *Ching tsai* is a common *Shu* expression.

5 IN RETURN FOR A POEM FROM TING CH'AI-SANG

酬丁柴桑

I

有客有客　　　　　　　于惠百里　　　4
爰來爰止　　　　　　　飡勝如歸
秉直司聰　　　　　　　聆善若始

II

匪惟諧也　　　　　　　放歡一遇
屢有良由　　　　　　　既醉還休
載言載眺　　　　　　　實欣心期
4　以寫我憂　　　　　　　方從我游　　　8

Additional Commentary

Li Ch'en-tung (p. 10) placed this poem in 403, saying that while it is not certain that it was written in that year, it was certainly written while T'ao Yüan-ming was living in Ch'ai-sang (in his view until 409). But it cannot be said that the text of the poem positively requires this. Wang Yao, on the other hand, placed the poem provisionally in 418 (he believes that T'ao returned to live in Ch'ai-sang in 417). He makes a composite reading of the *Sung shu* biography 'at the end of the I-hsi period he was called to the post of Assistant Archivist but did not accept', and the *Chin shu* biography 'when he had given up ceremonial calls upon the officials of the province and the commandery, his fellow-villager Chang Yeh and his boon companions Yang Sung-ling and P'ang Tsun sometimes, when they had wine, invited him...' (see p. 171) and concludes that T'ao's relations with Magistrate Ting must have been at the end of the I-hsi period. Apart from the questionable way in which he handles the biographies in the histories, Wang Yao seems to have begun with an initial presumption that the poem belongs to the post-405 period. This also is hard to justify. Wang Yao, at least, qualified his dating as 'provisional', but Ōyane Bunjirō (p. 652) and Young Yong (*Chiao-chien*, p. 452) in following him treat it as definite.

Additional Notes

I, 1. From *Song* 284, 1.

I, 3. *Ssu-ts'ung* derives from *Tso-chuan*, Chao ninth year: 女爲君耳，將司聰也 'You are your prince's ears and are to perform the office of sharp hearing.'

I, 4. 'A hundred *li*' indicates the area of a magistrate's district (hsien), cf. Lu Chi's *To Feng Wen-p'i on his Being Transferred to the Magistracy of Ch'ih-ch'iu* 贈馮文羆遷斥丘令 (*Wen-hsüan* 24, 18b; *Lu Shih-heng shih chu*, p. 73): 我求明德，肆于百里 'We seek bright virtue/And spread it over a hundred *li*.'

II, 2. 由 the reading of the Tseng Chi and other Southern Sung texts has generally been understood in the sense of 游, which these texts note as a variant, by those commentators who have not adopted 游 as the correct reading. Ku Chih gives examples of the ancient interchange of these two characters.

II, 4. This line occurs in *Songs* 39, 4 and 59, 4.

6 IN REPLY TO AIDE P'ANG

答龐參軍

序　龐爲衞軍參軍，從江陵使上都，過潯陽見贈。

I

衡門之下	豈無他好
有琴有書	樂是幽居
載彈載詠	朝爲灌園
4　爰得我娛	夕偃蓬廬　8

II

人之所寶	我求良友
尚或未珍	實覯懷人
不有同愛	歡心孔洽
4　云胡以親	棟宇惟鄰　8

III

伊余懷人　　　　　乃陳好言
欣德孜孜　　　　　乃著新詩
我有旨酒　　　　　一日不見
4　與汝樂之　　　　　如何不思　8

IV

嘉遊未斁　　　　　依依舊楚
誓將離分　　　　　邈邈西雲
送爾于路　　　　　之子之遠
4　銜觴無欣　　　　　良話曷聞　8

V

昔我云別　　　　　大藩有命
倉庚載鳴　　　　　作使上京
今也遇之　　　　　豈忘宴安
4　霰雪飄零　　　　　王事靡寧　8

VI

慘慘寒日　　　　　勗哉征人
肅肅其風　　　　　在始思終
翩彼方舟　　　　　敬茲良辰
4　容裔江中　　　　　以保爾躬　8

Additional Commentary

The idea that Aide P'ang was the friend P'ang T'ung-chih of the *Sung shu*
biography of T'ao (see p. 172) was put forward by Wu Shih-tao (1283–1344)
in his *Wu Li-pu shih-hua*, 3b. Wu also suggested that Registrar P'ang of the
Resentful Poem might be the same person. Li Kung-huan, in his edition of the
works, gave the personal name of Registrar P'ang as Tsun, thus identifying
him with the friend P'ang Tsun of the *Chin shu* biography of the poet (see
p. 171). T'ao Shu in his *nien-p'u k'ao-i*, sub Yüan-hsi 1, expressed the view
that P'ang Tsun and P'ang T'ung-chih in the biographies were the same
person, it being a case of the alternate use of personal name (Tsun) and
courtesy name (T'ung-chih). While, however, accepting that P'ang Tsun
(T'ung-chih) is the Registrar P'ang of the *Resentful Poem*, he argued that

Aide P'ang was a separate person. He commented that though Aide and Registrar are both subordinate posts, they could not be held in plurality. His second argument was that from the content of the three poems T'ao's friendship with Aide P'ang was new while that with Registrar P'ang was of long standing. The majority of modern writers, especially those who accept the traditional date for T'ao's birth, have followed this opinion of T'ao Shu that Aide P'ang is not Registrar P'ang Tsun, but they have been less wary than T'ao Shu and have ignored the problem of the dating of the *Resentful Poem* (see also Commentary, vol. 1, p. 59). Thus Wang Yao (p. 78), Ōyane Bunjirō (p. 654) and Young Yong (*Chiao-chien*, p. 451) all continue to date it in 418 in spite of the fact that the passage from the *Sung shu* (64, 5a) which all quote to identify P'ang Tsun as *ssu-t'u chu-pu* (Registrar to the Prime Minister) relates to 426. All fail to identify the Prime Minister as Wang Hung who received this office in the first month of 426 (*Sung shu* 5, 2a) and would therefore have appointed P'ang Tsun in the same year.

Those who have followed Liang Ch'i-ch'ao's dating of T'ao's birth in 372 have had a greater impetus towards regarding Aide P'ang and Registrar P'ang as the same person. For by Liang's dating, if one takes the $6 \times 9 = 54$ years of line 4 of the *Resentful Poem* as a direct statement of age (as I do not), then that poem will come from 425. Liang, himself, who dated the poems to Aide P'ang, whom he took as P'ang T'ung-chih, in 411 (p. 82), did not actually say who he thought Registrar P'ang was (p. 93). Li Ch'en-tung, however, dates the poems to Aide P'ang whom he refers to as P'ang Tsun in 422 (five-word) and 424 (four-word) (p. 24) and when he follows Liang in placing the *Resentful Poem* in 425 speaks of P'ang Tsun as being promoted to Registrar. P'ang Tsun, however, was not *ssu-t'u chu-pu* in 425. Again there is a failure to identify the *ssu-t'u* as Wang Hung.

One of the few modern writers to take note of this important connection with Wang Hung is Lu Ch'in-li who dates the *Resentful Poem* in 426 (p. 246). He, however, does not identify Registrar P'ang with Aide P'ang, nor does he think that Aide P'ang was on the staff of Wang Hung. Because of the fact that Aide P'ang started out from Chiang-ling, he thinks that he must have been on the staff of the Governor of Ching-chou, and since the governor in question had to have the rank of Guard General, he is forced to choose Hsieh Hui 謝晦 who replaced the Prince of I-tu as Governor of Ching-chou, when the latter became emperor, and who was made Guard General in the eighth month of 424. He dates the five-word poem in the spring of 424 and the four-word in the winter of that year. But P'ang could not have gone from Hsün-yang to Chiang-ling to take service with Hsieh Hui in the spring of 424. This difficulty is surmounted by Young Yong (*Chiao-chien*, pp. 462–63) by moving the two poems to 425, for he approves of Lu's argument for identifying the Guard General as Hsieh Hui. Nothing, however, can be brought forward to show any other possible link between Aide P'ang and Hsieh Hui, whereas a continuing connection between P'ang Tsun (T'ung-chih) and Wang Hung, first as Aide and General and then as Registrar and Prime Minister would seem to merit being called probable and can also be seen to be further supported by T'ao's own good relations with Wang Hung. T'ao Shu's date of 423 for the two poems to Aide P'ang and his suggestion that the journeys between Hsün-yang, Chiang-ling and the capital concerned the manoeuvres to seat the Prince of I-tu on the throne are plausible and I have put them forward in the Commentary (see vol. 1, p. 23).

Finally, T'ao Shu's own objections to identifying Aide P'ang with Registrar P'ang may be reconsidered. The first has in fact been disposed of in the foregoing. The second that the *Resentful Poem*, because it catalogues the misfortunes of the poet's whole life, requires that Registrar P'ang should have been a friend of long standing is not in itself compelling. In any case the impression which T'ao Shu derived from the biographies that P'ang Tsun (T'ung-chih) *was* a very old friend need not be a correct one.

Additional Notes

I, 1. This is the opening line of *Song* 138, which continues 可以棲遲 'one may find rest'. This is one of the most frequent allusions in the literature of hermitage.

I, 2. The conception of the first stanza and the wording of this line and of line 7 are derived from the story of the wife of Wu-ling Tzu-chung (= Ch'en Chung-tzu of *Meng-tzu* 3B, 10 and 7A, 34: *Chan-kuo ts'e* 4, 65b also reads Tzu-chung). This story appears in *Lieh-nü chuan* 2, 24a–b and in *Kao-shih chuan* B, 5b. In another version in *Han-shih wai-chuan* 9, 12a Wu-ling Tzu-chung appears as Pei-kuo hsien-sheng 北郭先生; this version, at least in its current form, lacks both of the phrases which T'ao uses in his poem, so that it may probably be ruled out as his source. Between the other two there is no means of deciding; either is possible. The story (*Lieh-nü* version) reads: 'The King of Ch'u heard that Wu-ling Tzu-chung was a worthy man and wished to make him prime minister. So he sent an emissary with a hundred *i* of gold to invite him. Wu-ling Tzu-chung said: "I have a 'dustpan and brush handmaid'. Pray let me go in and discuss it with her." When he had gone in, he said to his wife: "The King of Ch'u wishes me to be his prime minister and has sent an emissary with gold. If today I become prime minister, tomorrow they will harness a four-horse carriage for me and draw up horsemen and set out food for me on a table ten feet square. May I do it?" His wife replied: "You make your living by weaving sandals [here there must be a lacuna in the present text, cf. *Han-shih wai-chuan* version] (?) Is it not because you are not concerned with government? *To the left is a lute, to the right books* and happiness indeed lies in their midst. As for the harnessing of a four-horse carriage and the drawing up of horsemen, what gives content is no more than 'room for one's knees'. As for the setting out of food on a table ten feet square, delight [in food] does not require more than one piece of meat. Now when you have the content of 'room for your knees' and the flavour of one piece of meat, should you yet embrace the cares of the state of Ch'u? In a disorderly age there are many dangers. I fear that you will not preserve your life." Thereupon Tzu-chung went out and thanked the emissary but did not accept. So he fled with his wife and *watered another man's garden*.'

I, 4. This line has a *Songs* form, cf. *Song* 113, 1: 爰得我所 'Then we shall find our place.'

III, 3. From *Song* 161, 3: 'I have a good wine,/With it I feast and make glad the heart of my guest.'

III, 7–8. A combination of lines from *Song* 72, 1: 'If for one day I do not see him,/It is like three months.' and *Song* 66, 1. 'My lord has gone on service,/How should I not think of him?'

IV, 1. With *wei-i*, cf. 無敖 *Song* 2, 2 *et passim*.

IV, 2. *Shih-chiang* = 逝將 of *Song* 113, 1.

IV, 7. From *Song* 229, 1&8.

V, 2. 'Then the oriole sang' is a reference to *Song* 154, 2: 'In the spring days there is warmth;/There is the singing oriole.' The first half of this stanza shows some influence from *Song* 167, 6: 'Before when we went out,/The willows were in full leaf;/Now when we come back,/The falling snow is thick.'

V, 8. This is based on a line which occurs in five *Songs* (121, 162, 167, 169 and 205) 王事靡盬 'The royal service may not be scamped.' T'ao perhaps had in mind the quotation of the line (from *Song* 162 or 167) in *Tso-chuan*, Hsiang twenty-ninth year: 'The Song says: "The royal service may not be scamped; we have no leisure to kneel or sit." We go to the east, to the west, to the south, to the north. Who dares to rest quiet?'

VI, 1–2. These lines are reminiscent of Wang Ts'an's *To Ts'ai Tzu-tu* 贈蔡子篤詩 (*Wen-hsüan* 23, 35a): 烈烈冬日，蕭蕭淒風 'Bitter are the winter days;/Mournful is the chill wind.' The same poem (loc. cit., 34b) contains the lines: 舫舟翩翩，以泝大江 'The double boat rises and falls,/As it goes up the Great River [i.e. the Yangtze].'

VI, 5. *Hsü tsai* is from *Shu, Mu-shih* (6, 7b.): 勖哉夫子 'Masters, exert yourselves!'

VI, 6. Here T'ao was probably recalling the words of Shu-hsiang, who was himself on a mission, in *Tso-chuan*, Chao fifth year: 敬始而思終 'Respect the beginning and think of the end.'

7 TO ENCOURAGE FARMING

勸　農

I

悠悠上古　　　　　　　　智巧既萌
厥初生民　　　　　　　　資待靡因
傲然自足　　　　　　　　誰其贍之
抱樸含眞　　　　　　　　實賴哲人

II

哲人伊何　　　　　　　　舜既躬耕
時惟后稷　　　　　　　　禹亦稼穡
贍之伊何　　　　　　　　遠若周典
實曰播植　　　　　　　　八政始食

III

熙熙令德　　　　　　　　紛紛士女
猗猗原陸　　　　　　　　趨時競逐
卉木繁榮　　　　　　　　桑婦宵興
和風清穆　　　　　　　　農夫野宿

IV

氣節易過　　　　　　　　相彼賢達
和澤難久　　　　　　　　猶勤壟畝
冀缺攜儷　　　　　　　　矧伊眾庶
沮溺結耦　　　　　　　　曳裾拱手

V

民生在勤　　　　　　　儋石不儲
勤則不匱　　　　　　　飢寒交至
宴安自逸　　　　　　　顧余儔列 *
4　歲暮奚冀　　　　　　能不懷愧　　8

* 余，湯本作余，註云一作爾，陶注本從之。

VI

孔耽道德　　　　　　　若能超然
樊須是鄙　　　　　　　投迹高軌
董樂琴書　　　　　　　敢不斂衽
4　田園不履　　　　　　敬贊德美　　8

Additional Notes

I, 1–2. T'ao certainly had *Song* 245 immediately in mind, since he quotes the opening line of the *Song* as his line 2 and also derives II, 2 from the same source. There is also, however, a possible reminiscence of Ying Chen's *Chin Wu-ti Hua-lin yüan chi shih* ('The Gathering in Chin Wu-ti's Park of Flowering Groves', *Wen-hsüan* 20, 23a): 悠悠太上，民之厥初 'Far off in highest antiquity/Was the people's beginning.'

I, 4–5. The thought and in part the wording of these lines have their origin in *Lao-tzu* 19: 絕聖棄智 ... 絕巧棄利 ... 見素抱樸 'Put an end to wisdom, banish knowledge ... Put an end to cleverness, banish acuteness ... let them look at simplicity and cherish substance.' The Ho-shang kung commentary reads: 見素者當抱素守眞，不尚文飾 'He who looks at simplicity must cherish simplicity and preserve truth and will not esteem ornament.'

II, 5. Shun is said to have ploughed on Li-shan 歷山 (*Shih-chi* 1, Annals of the Five Emperors, I, p. 46), which has been located in widely separated places, see *Cheng-i*, loc. cit.

II, 6. Yü is mentioned, together with Hou Chi, as sowing with his own hand in *Lun-yü* 14, 6.

II, 8. The 'eight rules of government' form the third of the nine sections of *Hung-fan* (*The Great Plan*) and food is the first rule.

IV, 8. The source of the expression *i-chü* (trail one's gown) in the sense of 'be a hanger-on at court' seems to be in *Han shu* 51 (Biography of Tsou Yang), 8b; 飾固陋之心，則何王之門不可曳長裾乎 'If one puts a gloss over one's boorish mind, at what king's gate can one not trail one's long gown?' Tzu-lu 'folded his hands' in his encounter with 'the old man who planted his staff', see *At the Beginning of Spring in the Year Kuei-mao*, I, p. 73.

V, 1–2. Quotation from *Tso-chuan*, Huan twelfth year. The same proverb appears in what is described as a 'constant saying' of T'ao K'an in a fragment of the latter's biography in Sun Sheng's *Chin yang-ch'iu*, preserved in Liu Hsiao-piao's commentary to *Shih-shuo hsin-yü*, A/B, 6a: 又好督勤於人，常云，民生在勤，大禹聖人，猶惜寸陰，至於凡俗，當惜分陰，豈可遊逸，生無益於時，死無聞於後，是自棄也 'He also liked to admonish others, constantly saying: "The people's life rests on carefulness. The great Yü, sage though he was, was still careful of an inch of shadow. Ordinary men then ought to be careful of a tenth of an inch; surely they cannot take their ease. Alive to be of no profit to one's time, dying to have no reputation among posterity, this is to cast oneself away."' The preceding sentences in this fragment of K'an's biography refer to his carefulness over farming and to his urging it even upon soldiers. T'ao Yüan-ming would certainly have known this biography of K'an (he mentions Sun Sheng in his biography of his maternal grandfather Meng Chia, see p. 144) and he could have had this passage in mind, when he was writing this stanza of the poem. To see T'ao Yüan-ming's intention in writing the whole poem as being based on this passage, as Young Yong (*Chiao-chien*, p. 26) does, seems to me, however, mistaken. If the interpretation which I have suggested in the Commentary is accepted, T'ao is not to be seen as writing a tract for the encouragement of farming.

V, 5. T'ao may well have derived the phrasing of this line from *Han shu* 87A (Biography of Yang Hsiung), 2a, since there is evidence of his familiarity with this chapter in *Drinking Wine*, XVIII, see p. 95.

VI, 3–4. The story of Tung Chung-shu not inspecting his garden for three years appears in *Shih-chi* 121 (Biographies of Confucian Scholars), p. 26 and in his biography in *Han shu* 56, 1a.

VI, 5–6. These lines were perhaps expanded from *Ch'u-tz'u, Pu-chü* (6, 2a): 寧超然高舉 'I would rather, transcending, soar high . . .'

VI, 7. *Lien jen* 'adjust the lapel of one's robe', i.e. adopt a respectful attitude, seems to occur for the first time in *Chan-kuo ts'e* 14 (*Ch'u-ts'e* 1), 5, 4b.

8 CHARGE TO MY SON

命子

I

悠悠我祖
爰自陶唐
邈焉虞賓
歷世重光

御龍勤夏
豕韋翼商
穆穆司徒
厥族以昌

II

紛紛戰國 *
漠漠衰周
鳳隱於林
幽人在丘

逸虯遶雲
奔鯨駭流
天集有漢
眷余愍侯

* 紛紛，曾集本作紛紜，註云一作紛紛。今從之。

III

於赫愍侯
運當攀龍
撫劍風邁
顯茲武功

書誓山河
啓土開封
亹亹丞相
允迪前蹤

IV

渾渾長源
蔚蔚洪柯
羣川載導
眾條載羅

時有語默
運因隆窊
在我中晉
業融長沙

V

桓桓長沙
伊勳伊德
天子疇我
專征南國

功遂辭歸
臨寵不忒
孰謂斯心
而近可得

VI

肅 矣 我 祖
慎 終 如 始
直 方 三 臺 *
惠 和 千 里 (4)

於 皇 仁 考 +
淡 焉 虛 止
寄 迹 風 雲
眞 茲 慍 喜 # (8)

* 三，曾集本作二，註云一作三，今從之。
+ 皇，曾集本作穆，註云一作皇，今從之。
# 眞，陶注云各本作眞；湯本云眞，一作冥，今從之。

VII

嗟 余 寡 陋
瞻 望 弗 及
顧 慚 華 鬢
負 影 隻 立 (4)

三 千 之 罪
無 後 爲 急
我 誠 念 哉
呱 聞 爾 泣 (8)

VIII

卜 云 嘉 日
占 亦 良 時
名 汝 曰 儼
字 汝 求 思 (4)

溫 恭 朝 夕
念 茲 在 茲
尚 想 孔 伋
庶 其 企 而 (8)

IX

厲 夜 生 子
遽 而 求 火
凡 百 有 心
奚 特 于 我 (4)

既 見 其 生
實 欲 其 可
人 亦 有 言
斯 情 無 假 (8)

X

日 居 月 諸
漸 免 于 孩
福 不 虛 至
禍 亦 易 來 (4)

夙 興 夜 寐
願 爾 斯 才
爾 之 不 才
亦 已 焉 哉 (8)

Additional Commentary

The cautionary *To My Sons, Yen and the Others* (p. 153) has the words: 'although you are not of one mother', and from this it has been concluded that T'ao married twice (see Wu Jen-chieh, *nien-p'u*, sub T'ai-yüan 19). It could of course be objected that some of his sons were borne by a concubine. Ho Meng-ch'un, commentary to *To My Sons*, in fact suggested that this might be so and that his third and fourth sons, who appear with the same age in *Reproving My Sons* (p. 105), might be the children of different mothers. There is, however, other evidence to be considered. In the *Resentful Poem in the Ch'u Mode* (p. 47) T'ao says that he lost his wife and by an allusion to *Li-chi* marks this event as happening in his thirtieth year (394). Now, there is a reference to 'my wife' in *In Return for a Poem by Liu Ch'ai-sang* (p. 55), which dates from about 403 at the earliest. Thus the hypothesis that he married twice seems fairly certain.

The matter can be taken further. From *Reproving My Sons* the relative ages of T'ao's five sons are known: eight years separated the birth of his eldest son Yen and that of his youngest T'ung. If T'ao's first wife bore him at least one son before she died in 394, then his youngest son would have been born at the latest in 402. Since in *Answering a Poem by Registrar Kuo* (p. 56) there are the lines: 'My young son plays at my side;/Learning to talk, not yet perfect in his sounds', and this poem might on other grounds be dated 402–404 or shortly after 405, T'ao's youngest son could not have been born much earlier than 402. Conversely, his eldest son could not have been born much earlier than 394. Chang Chih's dating of this poem in T'ao's twenty-second or twenty-third year, i.e. 386 or 387 (op. cit., p. 30) seems definitely to be too early, and probably Young Yong's 391 (*Chiao-chien*, pp. 413–14) is also. Wang Yao's 393 (p. 9) might be possible. One more known fact may, however, be brought into the argument.

If one sets aside the interval between the births of T'ao's fourth and fifth sons as falling after his first wife's death, then the only point at which one might place T'ao's remarriage is between the births of his first and second sons, where there is an interval of two years. Thus T'ao Shu's suggestion that Yüan-ming's first wife was the mother of his first son only (*nien-p'u k'ao-i*, sub T'ai-yüan 19) seems to be correct. If one further considers that two years only separated the births of his first and second sons (in actual fact the two years is a round figure, the real interval could be much less than twenty-four months, though on the other hand it could be greater) and that these two years (more or less) would have had to cover the period of mourning for his first wife (probably at least nine months), his remarriage and the begetting of his second son, then it would seem very likely that his first son was born in the year in which his first wife died. One might even speculate that she died in childbirth.

Additional Notes

I, 1–2. In framing his genealogy T'ao had especially in mind the model of Wei Meng in his *Feng-chien shih* (*Han shu* 73, 1a): 蕭蕭我祖，國自豕韋 'Grave were my ancestors;/Their state began with the Shih-wei', but he starts further back with the emperor Yao. In doing this he follows closely the genealogy given by Fan Hsüan-tzu for his family in *Tso-chuan*, Hsiang twenty-fourth year: 昔匄之祖，自虞以上，爲陶唐氏，在夏爲御龍氏，在商爲豕韋氏 'As for my ancestors of old, in the time before Yü [i.e. Shun] they were the T'ao and T'ang family. Under the Hsia they were the Yü-lung and under the Shang, the Shih-wei.' An explanation of these links is offered in *Tso-chuan*, Chao twenty-ninth year: 有陶唐氏旣衰，其後有劉累學擾龍於豢龍氏，以事孔甲，能飲食之，夏后嘉之，賜氏曰御龍以更豕韋之後 'When the family of the Lord of T'ao and T'ang had declined, there was among his descendants Liu Lei, who had studied the training of dragons under the Huan-lung. With his skill he served K'ung-chia, being able to make the dragons eat and drink. The ruler of Hsia [K'ung-chia] was pleased with him and gave him the name Yü-lung and set him in the place of the descendants of Shih-wei.' Tu Yü, commenting on this passage, concludes (on account of the Hsiang twenty-fourth year statement) that the Shih-wei recovered their territory under the Shang. It may also be noted that Fan Hsüan-tzu's genealogy was made use of in compiling a genealogy for Han Kao-tsu and the house of Liu (see *Han shu* 1B, *tsan*).

I, 3. The expression 'the guest of Yü' is used in *Shu*, *I-chi* (2, 12b), where the pseudo K'ung An-kuo commentary defines as Chu of Tan 丹朱, son of Yao.

I, 7. For T'ao Shu see *Tso-chuan*, Ting fourth year: 周公相王室以尹天下 . . . 分康叔 . . . 殷民七族，陶氏 . . . 聃季授土，陶叔授民 'The Duke of Chou aided the royal house to regulate the empire . . . he allotted to K'ang Shu . . . seven clans of the Yin, the T'ao . . . Tan Chi presented to him the land, T'ao Shu, the people.' That T'ao Shu was *ssu-t'u* (Minister of Instruction) is specifically stated only by Tu Yü in his commentary.

II, 7. For the use of *chi*, the 'settling' of the mandate of Heaven, see *Song* 236, 4.

II, 8. For the enfeoffment of T'ao She 舍 as Marquis of K'ai-feng, see *Han shu* 16, 49a.

III, 1. Cf. again *Feng-chien shih* (loc. cit., 1b): 於赫有漢.

III, 2. *P'an-lung* is an abbreviation of the expression 攀龍鱗附鳳翼 'to grasp the dragon's scales and depend on the phoenix' wings', of which the oldest extant source is Yang Hsiung's *Fa-yen* 11, 1a.

III, 5. For the form of oath sworn by Han Kao-tsu at the enfeoffment of nobles, see *Han shu* 16, 1a–b: 誓曰使黄河如帶泰山若厲，國以永存爰及苗裔，於是申以丹書之信，重以白馬之盟 'He swore an oath: "Though the Yellow River become like a girdle and T'ai-shan like a whetstone, may your state last for ever and pass to your remote descendants." Then he added to it a pledge in red writing and made besides a covenant with a white horse.'

III, 6. The expression *ch'i-t'u* perhaps derived from *Shu, Wu-ch'eng* (a forged book) 6, 8b: 惟先王建邦啟土.

III, 7. For T'ao Ch'ing 青 see *Han shu* 19B, 10a. *Han shu* 5, 2b gives his name as Ch'ing-ti 青翟; see discussion in Dubs, *The History of the Former Han Dynasty*, I, p. 310. For *wei-wei*, cf. *Songs* 235, 2; 259, 2.

III, 8. *Yün-ti* is a *Shu* expression, cf. *Kao Yao mo* (2, 6b): 允迪厥德, 'if he faithfully follows his virtue'.

IV, 5. *Yü-mo* is from Confucius' saying in *I, Hsi-tz'u* A, 6: 君子之道或出或處，或默或語 'The Way of the gentleman is sometimes to go out and other times to stay at home, sometimes to speak and other times to keep silent.'

IV, 8. For T'ao K'an's appointment as Grand Commandant (*t'ai-wei*) and being given the title of Duke of Ch'ang-sha, see *Chin shu* 7, 3b.

V, 1. *Huan-huan* is derived from *Song* 294 but there is also a play on T'ao K'an's posthumous name which is written with the same character 桓.

V, 3. The suggestion that *ch'ou* derives from *Shu, Yao-tien* (1, 3a): 疇咨若時登庸 'Who can conform to these things? I will raise him up and employ him.' made by Ch'eng Mu-heng (see ap. Ting Fu-pao) has been adopted by many recent writers. Thus Wang Yao, for example, glosses 訪察. No one, however, has produced a parallel for this rather strange usage, whereas it is possible to find a close parallel for this line with a normal usage of *ch'ou* in Lu Chi's *Han Kao-tsu kung-ch'en sung* 漢高祖功臣頌 (*Wen-hsüan* 47, 26b): 帝疇爾庸. I accordingly understand *ch'ou* as 'requite'.

V, 5. This line is probably an adaptation of *Lao-tzu* 9: 功遂身退 'When one's work is done, one's person should be withdrawn' (following the Wang Pi reading, which T'ao's line seems to support, see the discussion in *Lao-tzu chiao-ku*, p. 63).

VI, 2. is from *Lao-tzu* 64.

VI, 3. The expression *chih-fang* is derived from *I*, hexagram 2. Though on the principle of *lectio difficilior* the reading *erh t'ai* might seem preferable, no one has offered a very satisfactory explanation for the present context, whereas the variant *san t'ai* as a term for the central government authorities does provide a reasonable balance for the 'thousand *li*' signifying his grandfather's provincial post in the following line.

VI, 6. The qualities which T'ao ascribes to his father are Taoist, cf. *Chuang-tzu* 15 (6A, 4b–5a): 聖人 ... 虛無恬惔乃合天德 ... 無所於忤, 虛之至也，不與物交，惔之至也 'The saint ... is empty and dispassionate, so he conforms with the virtue of Heaven ... There is nothing with which he is at odds, this is the height of emptiness; he has no contact with things, this is the height of dispassionateness.'

VII, 1. Cf. *The Tree in Blossom*, III, 1–2.

VII, 2. This line is a quotation of *Song* 28.

VII, 4. There is a possible reminiscence here of the *Ta chih* 達旨 ('Achieving One's Will') of Ts'ui Yin, preserved in his biography in *Hou-Han shu* 82, 4b: 抱景特立，與士不羣 'Cherishing your shadow, you stand alone; you do not join in the company of scholars.'

VII, 5–6. This saying seems to have been formed out of the combination of two texts from the classics, viz. *Hsiao-ching* 11 (11b): 五刑之屬三千而罪莫大於 不孝 'In the Five Punishments there are three thousand categories, but of crimes there is none greater than unfilialness' and *Meng-tzu* 4A, 26: 不孝有三，無後爲大 'There are three things which are unfilial, and to have no heir is the worst.' It is not, however, T'ao's doing. A very similar and earlier statement was made by Hsieh Shang (308–357): 夫無後之罪三千所不過 'Than the crime of having no heir none of the three thousand is greater.' (*Chin shu* 79, 1b.)

VII, 8. This is probably adapted from *Shu, I-chi* (2, 11b–12a): 啓呱呱而泣 'When Ch'i [the infant son of the emperor Yü] cried and wept...'

VIII, 1–4. This half-stanza is perhaps influenced by *Li-sao*, stanza 2 (*Ch'u-tz'u* 1, 3b): 皇覽揆余初度兮，肇錫余以嘉名．名余曰正則兮，字余曰靈均 'When my august father examined my first measures [i.e. the time of my birth],/He devised and conferred on me an auspicious name./He named me Cheng-tse [Correct Pattern];/He styled me Ling-chün [Holy Levelness].

VIII, 5. The complete *Li-chi* sentence from which T'ao took his son's name reads: 毋不敬儼若思 so that probably this line, taken from *Song* 301, develops the first half ('Never fail to be respectful').

VIII, 6. This saying is quoted in *Tso-chuan*, Hsiang twenty-first year as coming from the *Hsia-shu* ('The Documents of Hsia'). It has been collected into one of the forged books of the *Shu*, *Ta Yü mo* (2, 3a). It develops the second half of the *Li-chi* sentence from which the name is taken.

VIII, 7–8. These lines expand the reference to K'ung Chi (Tzu-ssu) in the courtesy-name ('Seeking Ssu').

IX, 1–2. This saying derives from *Chuang-tzu* 12 (5A, 24b): 厲之人夜半生其子，遽取火而視之，汲汲然唯恐其似己也 'An ugly man, when his son is born in the middle of the night, immediately takes a light and looks at him, anxious lest he be like himself.' Liu Wen-tien notes that in the *Shih san-p' o lun* 釋三破論 of Seng-shun 僧順 (*Hung-ming chi* 8, 8b) the saying appears with the reading 厲婦 'an ugly woman'. Since the quotation in *T'ai-p'ing yü-lan* 382, 4a reads: 厲人夜半生子，其父取火視之, he concludes that the text is to be understood: 'When an ugly woman bears a son in the middle of the night, the father immediately takes a light and looks at him, anxious lest he be like her.' This is certainly not T'ao's understanding of the passage. Kuo Hsiang in his commentary remarks that 'everyone in the world wishes not to be ugly'. This perhaps influenced T'ao's next lines.

IX, 3. *Fan-pai* is a *Songs* expression, see *Songs* 194, 3&4; 200, 7.

IX, 7. See Additional Note to *Hanging Clouds*, III, 5, p. 2.

X, 1. This line occurs in *Songs* 26, 5; 29 (four times).

X, 3–4. These lines may be a reminiscence of *Huai-nan-tzu* 10, 12a: 禍福不虛至矣 'Misfortune and good fortune do not come without reason.'

X, 5. This line is to be found three times in the *Songs*, in *Songs* 58, 5; 196, 4; 256, 4. It is probably 196 which T'ao had in mind: 夙興夜寐，無忝爾所生 'Early rise and late sleep;/Do not disgrace those who gave you life.'

X, 8. This is the last line of *Song* 58.

9 THE BIRD WHICH HAS COME HOME

歸 鳥

I

翼翼歸鳥	和風弗洽
晨去于林	翻翮求心
遠之八表	顧儔相鳴
近憩雲岑	景庇清陰

4   8

II

翼翼歸鳥　　　　　遇雲頡頏
載翔載飛　　　　　相鳴而歸
雖不懷游　　　　　遐路誠悠
4　見林情依　　　　性愛無遺　　8

III

翼翼歸鳥　　　　　雖無昔侶
相林徘佪 *　　　　眾聲每諧
豈思天路　　　　　日夕氣清
4　欣反舊棲　　　　悠然其懷　　8

* 相，陶注云，各本作馴，湯本云一作相，何校宣和本作相，今從之。

IV

翼翼歸鳥　　　　　晨風清興
戢羽寒條　　　　　好音時交
遊不曠林　　　　　矰繳奚施 *
4　宿則森標　　　　已卷安勞　　8

* 施，陶注云，湯本作功，非。

Additional Notes

I, 1. The compound *i-i* occurs nine times in the *Songs* and has been given a variety of definitions by the commentators (Karlgren, Gloss 433 has considered the problem at length). None of the glosses of the Mao or Cheng Hsüan commentaries appears to give a satisfactory sense for T'ao's use here, which is probably descriptive of the bird's flight as in the Wang Ts'an poem, cited in II, 1 below. I have accordingly rendered it 'fluttering'.

I, 3. 'Beyond the Eight Directions', cf. *Hanging Clouds*, I, 3.

I, 8. Cf. *Drinking Wine*, IV, 10–12.

II, 1–2. There is a close similarity with the opening lines of Wang Ts'an's *To Ts'ai Tzu-tu* 贈蔡子篤詩 (*Wen-hsüan* 23, 34b): 翼翼飛鸞，載飛載東 'Fluttering was the flying phoenix;/It flew; it went eastward.'

IV, 2. Cf. *Drinking Wine*, IV, 1.8.

IV, 7. This line might well be derived from Han Kao-tsu's song to his favourite concubine (found in *Shih-chi* 55, p. 27 and *Han shu* 40, 9a), since the Four White-heads, to whom T'ao refers on several occasions, appear in the context. In 195 BC Kao-tsu sought, before he died, to set aside the Empress Lü's son Ying and to appoint the Lady Ch'i's son Ju-i heir-apparent in his place. The empress, on the advice of Chang Liang, countered this by sending to Kao-tsu the Four White-heads to support her son. Kao-tsu was thus dissuaded from his intention. *Shih-chi* describes the scene in which he informed the Lady Ch'i: 'He summoned the Lady Ch'i and showed her the four men, saying: "I wished to replace him, but these four men supported him. His wings [i.e. his supporters] were ready and hard to move. The Empress Lü truly is your mistress." The Lady Ch'i wept. The emperor said: "If you will dance a Ch'u dance for me, I shall sing you a Ch'u song." The words of the song were:

> The wild swan flies high,
> In one soaring a thousand *li*.
> Its wings are perfect;
> It has crossed the Four Seas.
> It has crossed the Four Seas;
> Then what can be done?
> Though one has a stringed arrow,
> Yet where shall one shoot it?'

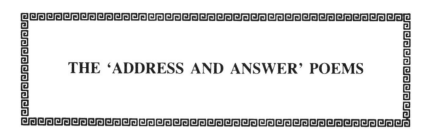

THE 'ADDRESS AND ANSWER' POEMS

10 BODY, SHADOW AND SOUL

形 影 神

序 貴賤賢愚，莫不營營以惜生，斯甚惑焉。故極陳形影之苦，言神辨自然以釋之。好事君子，共取其心焉。

I
形贈影

天地長不沒　　　　奚覺無一人
山川無改時　　　　親識豈相思
草木得常理　　　　但餘平生物
霜露榮悴之　（4）　舉目情悽洏　（12）
謂人最靈智　　　　我無騰化術
獨復不如茲　　　　必爾不復疑
適見在世中　　　　願君取吾言
奄去靡歸期　（8）　得酒莫苟辭　（16）

II
影答形

存生不可言　　　　此同既難常
衛生每苦拙　　　　黯爾俱時滅
誠願遊崑華　　　　身沒名亦盡
邈然茲道絕　（4）　念之五情熱　（12）
與子相遇來　　　　立善有遺愛
未嘗異悲悅　　　　胡為不自竭
憩蔭若暫乖　　　　酒云能消憂
止日終不別　（8）　方此詎不劣　（16）

III

神釋

大鈞無私力	老少同一死
萬理自森著	賢愚無復數
人爲三才中	日醉或能忘
4 豈不以我故	將非促齡具 16
與君雖異物	立善常所欣
生而相依附	誰當爲汝譽
結託既喜同*	甚念傷吾生
8 安得不相語	正宜委運去 20
三皇大聖人	縱浪大化中
今復在何處	不喜亦不懼
彭祖愛永年+	應盡便須盡
12 欲留不得住	無復獨多慮 24

* 既喜，陶注云，各本作善惡同，湯本云善惡一作既喜，今從之。
+ 愛，陶注云，各本作壽，湯本云一作愛，焦本作愛。

Additional Notes

PREFACE. T'ao's opening words seem clearly to have been influenced by the discussion of life and death between Confucius' disciple Tzu-kung and the aged Lin Lei in *Lieh-tzu* 1, pp. 14–15, especially Lin Lei's remark: 吾又安知營營而求生〈之 rest. Wang Shu-min〉非惑乎 'How too do I know that being busy in seeking life is not a delusion?'

I, 5. The reference might be to *Shu, T'ai-shih* (a forged book; 6, 1a): 'Heaven and Earth are the parents of the Ten Thousand Things. Man is the most divine of the Ten Thousand Things.' But the whole context of T'ao's comparison of man with other of the Ten Thousand Things has general parallels which show it to have been a familiar formulation but one which might be turned in a variety of directions. As Ku Chih noted, T'ao's formulation reverses the sense of Hsiang Hsiu's words in his *Criticism of (Hsi K'ang's) Yang-sheng lun* 難養生論, *Hsi K'ang chi* 4, 1a: 'Now man receives form from the Creator and exists together with the Ten Thousand Things. He is the most divine of living things. He differs from plants and trees which cannot avoid wind and rain or get away from axes; he differs from birds and beasts which cannot keep away from nets and escape cold and heat.' There is no need to suggest that T'ao is deliberately taking an opposite position to

Hsiang Hsiu, though he may have known his work directly or indirectly. We can be certain that he would have known *Lieh-tzu* 7, which offers another version of the comparison (p. 149): 'Man is like in kind to Heaven and Earth, he embraces the nature of the Five Constants [the Five Elements], he is the most divine of living things. Man's claws and teeth are insufficient to furnish him protection; his flesh and skin are insufficient to shield him; his speed of foot is insufficient for him to escape injury; he is without hair or feathers to withstand cold or heat. He must rely on other things to support his nature, depend on knowledge and not trust to his strength.'

I, 8. For this manner of reference to death the Han burial song *The Dew on the Garlic* (*Hsieh-lu*): 'When a man dies, once gone, when will he return?' (cf. vol. 1 p. 166) and T'ao's own *In Imitation of Burial Songs*, II, 11–12: 'One morning I went out of the gate,/But a return there can truly never be' may be compared.

I, 16. Cf. *In Imitation of Burial Songs*, I, 14, p. 130.

II, 1. The term *ts'un sheng* occurs in *Chuang-tzu* 19 (7A, 1b): 'One cannot reject the coming of life, one cannot stop its going. Alas! the men of the world think that the nourishment of the body can preserve life, but the nourishment of the body truly cannot preserve life.' T'ao who is concerned in the first four lines of the shadow's reply to dismiss the pursuit of 'immortality' could well have this context in mind. *Wei sheng* in line 2 is also a term which derives ultimately from *Chuang-tzu* (23; 8A, 9a), but T'ao uses this term also to describe the prolongation of life by artificial means. His attitude is that of *Old Poem*, XIII, 15–16: 'Taking preparations to seek to become immortals,/ Many have been deluded by drugs.'

II, 7–8. Cf. *Quieting the Affections*, 59–62, p. 136.

II, 11. Underlying this line is *Lun-yü* 15, 19: 'The gentleman is distressed that when he is dead, his name may not be praised', which provided a life-aim for the orthodox Confucian; cf. Yang Ch'üan's 'Their bodies have died, but their names survive' (*Tsan shan fu*, quoted in the Commentary; see vol. 1, p. 39).

II, 13. For the expression *i-ai*, cf. *Tso-chuan*, Chao twentieth year: 'When Tzu-ch'an [the statesman of Cheng] died, Chung-ni [Confucius] shed tears, saying: "[His was a case like] the ancients' leaving behind affection."'

II, 15. An early example of this saying is found in *Han shu* 65 (Biography of Tung-fang Shuo), 7b: 'To dispel grief nothing equals wine.'

III, 1. *Ta-chün* has generally been referred to the *Fu-niao fu* 鵩鳥賦 of Chia I,

which in the version in *Han shu* 48, 4a (followed by *Wen-hsüan* 13, 23a)
contains the line: 大鈞播物; *Shih-chi* 84, p. 31, however, reads: 大專槃物.
The *Shih-chi* commentators P'ei Yin and Chang Shou-chieh accepted the *Han
shu* 大鈞 version in the sense of 'Great Potter' (i.e. Creator), proposed by the
commentator Ju Ch'un, and forced the *Shih-chi* text into agreement with it
(see *Shih-chi*, loc. cit.). I believe, however, that they lost the correct sense by
thus reducing the more difficult to the simpler reading. Chia I's *fu* is a
patchwork of citations from *Chuang-tzu* and *Lao-tzu*, and *Chuang-tzu* can aid
in providing a solution to the problem. The expressions 天鈞, 天均 and 大均
are found in the current text of *Chuang-tzu* and in these 鈞 and 均 are
obviously interchangeable variants. It is merely fortuitous that 大鈞 does not
occur. 大均 with similar terms such as 大一 (the Great Unifier) is found in
chapter 24 as a description of *t'ien* (Nature): 大均緣之 (8B, 26a), which I
would suggest is to be rendered: 'as the Great Circler it borders', i.e. *t'ien*
enfolds all things within itself. Chapter 27 (9A, 16b) has 萬物皆種也,
以不同形相禪. 始卒若環, 莫得其倫, 是謂天均, 天均者天倪也 which I would
translate: 'The Ten Thousand Things all are [separate] kinds, and with
dissimilar forms they take each other's places. Their beginning and end are
like a ring; none can understand the principle. This is called the cycle
[circling] of Nature. The cycle of Nature is the boundary of Nature.' In
chapter 2 (1B, 17a) the current text has 天鈞 apparently in the same sense.

If 大/天均/鈞 embraces the idea of *t'ien* both as a circle and a cycle
(encircling and circling), it can explain how the different *Shih-chi* and *Han
shu* readings arose. 專 (= 圓) can have the sense of 'round', as some *Shih-chi*
commentators (loc. cit.) have suggested, and thus can be a synonym for 均/鈞
in the meaning for which I have argued above. Chia I's line, therefore, in
either version may be understood: 'The Great Cycle makes things revolve.'
Can this interpretation be applied to T'ao's line? The answer cannot be
assured. There are at least three possibilities. He might have understood the
term according to the interpretation of the *Han shu* commentators, i.e. as
'Great Potter'. Or he might have understood it in what I believe to be the
correct sense of 'Great Cycle'. Or he might, going back to *Chuang-tzu* rather
than Chia I, have followed the interpretation of the commentator Kuo Hsiang
of 大均 as 'Great Impartiality' (see chapter 24, loc. cit.; Kuo Hsiang adopts
the sense of 'impartial', i.e. 均 in explaining all the variant forms discussed
above). While I think that we may reject 'Great Potter' with some confidence,
it is difficult to decide between the other two alternatives. A further example
of 大鈞 in a poem of Lu Ch'en (*To Liu K'un* 贈劉琨, *Wen-hsüan* 25, 19b):
大鈞載運, 良辰遞往, 瞻彼日月, 迅過俯仰 seems to admit of the translation
'Great Cycle' ('The great Cycle revolves;/Fair mornings successively pass./As
one watches the days and months,/They pass away swiftly in a moment.').

III, 3. The expression *san ts'ai* 'Three Powers' derives from *I, Hsi-tz'u chuan*
II, 8.

III, 9–14. These words of the soul show a general similarity of expression with the passage on death as common to all in *Lieh-tzu* 7, p. 139: 'Yang Chu said: "That in which the Ten Thousand Things differ is life; that in which they are alike is death. In life there are wise and foolish, noble and base; this is wherein they differ. In death they decay and stink, are dissolved and destroyed; this is wherein they are alike. Yet neither wisdom, folly, nobility and baseness nor decay, stinking, dissolution and destruction is within their own capacity. . . . The ten-year-old dies; the centenarian dies; the good and the sage die; the evil and the foolish die. In life a Yao or Shun, in death rotting bones; in life a Chieh or Chou, in death rotting bones. The rotting bones are one; who can tell the difference?"'

11　LIVING IN RETIREMENT ON THE NINTH DAY

九日閒居

序　余閒居，愛重九之名。秋菊盈園，而持醪靡由。空服九
華，寄懷於言。

I

世短意常多	菊爲制頹齡 *
斯人樂久生	如何蓬廬士
日月依辰至	空視時運傾　12
4　舉俗愛其名	塵爵恥虛罍
露淒暄風息	寒華徒自榮
氣澈天象明	歛襟獨閒謠
往燕無遺影	緬焉起深情　16
8　來雁有餘聲	棲遲固多娛
酒能祛百慮	淹留豈無成

* 爲，曾集本作爲，註云宋本作解，陶注本作解。

Additional Commentary

Wang Chih, though he connected this poem with the Wang Hung episode in the biographies, did not assign it to a particular year of Wang's governorship of Chiang-chou. The modern critics, however, with their desire for precision have attempted to go further. Thus Wang Yao (p. 80) provisionally placed the poem in the second year of Wang's governorship (419) without offering a reason (he was followed by Ōyane Bunjirō, p. 670). Li Ch'en-tung, on the other hand, placed it in the last year (425), and Young Yong in 424. Young Yong makes his choice on the remarkably weak ground, when one considers the generally poor chronological arrangement of the biographies, that the Double Ninth anecdote in the *Sung shu* biography comes after the mention of Yen Yen-chih's appointment as Prefect of Shih-an, which is usually dated 424, but in fact probably was in 422 (see pp. 183–84). It should also be mentioned that T'ang Han with his usual propensity discovered a reference to the change of dynasty in the *shih yün ch'ing* of line 12 of the poem, but this will be completely negatived if my view of the date is accepted.

Additional Notes

LINE 13. In this line T'ao adapts *Song* 202, 3: 餅之罄矣，維罍之恥 'The emptiness of the jug is the shame of the jar.'

LINE 14. The expression *han-hua* 'cold flowers' as a substitute for 'autumn chrysanthemums' had already been used by Chang Hsieh, *Tsa-shih*, III (*Wen-hsüan* 29, 36b): 寒花發黄采 'The cold flowers display their yellow colours.'

LINE 17. *Hsi-ch'ih* evokes *Song* 138, 1: 衡門之下，可以棲遲 'Under a cross-beam door/It is possible to rest', which is one of the very common references in the vocabulary of hermitage; cf. *Written in the Twelfth Month of the Year Kuei-mao for My Cousin Ching-yüan*, 1.1 (p. 74).

LINE 18. This line is borrowed from *Chiu-pien*, I (*Ch'u-tz'u* 8, 3a): 時亹亹而過中兮，蹇淹留而無成 'His time is hurrying on and has passed its noon;/Yet he has lingered without achievement.' Elsewhere T'ao uses the line in its original form, cf. *Drinking Wine*, XVI (p. 88), but here he turns it into the opposite sense.

12   RETURNING TO LIVE IN THE COUNTRY

歸園田居五首

I

少無適俗韻　　　　　　誤落塵網中
性本愛丘山　　　　　　一去已十年*　　　　4

* 已，各本作三，陶澍案三當作已，今從之。

羇鳥戀舊林
池魚思故淵
開荒南野際
8　守拙歸園田
方宅十餘畝
草屋八九間
榆柳蔭後簷
12　桃李羅堂前

曖曖遠人村
依依墟里煙
狗吠深巷中
雞鳴桑樹巔　16
戶庭無塵雜
虛室有餘閒
久在樊籠裏
復得返自然　20

II

野外罕人事
窮巷寡輪鞅
白日掩荊扉
4　虛室絕塵想
時復墟曲中
披草共來往

相見無雜言
但道桑麻長　8
桑麻日已長
我土日已廣
常恐霜霰至
零落同草莽　12

III

種豆南山下
草盛豆苗稀
晨興理荒穢
4　帶月荷鋤歸

道狹草木長
夕露霑我衣
衣霑不足惜
但使願無違　8

IV

久去山澤游
浪莽林野娛
試攜子姪輩
4　披榛步荒墟
徘徊丘壟間
依依昔人居
井竈有遺處
8　桑竹殘朽株

借問採薪者
此人皆焉如
薪者向我言
死沒無復餘　12
一世異朝市
此語眞不虛
人生似幻化
終當歸空無　16

V

悵恨獨策還	隻鷄招近局
崎嶇歷榛曲	日入室中闇
山澗清且淺	荆薪代明燭
4 　可以濯吾足	歡來苦夕短
漉我新熟酒	已復至天旭

8

Additional Commentary

The considerable controversy between the commentators over the fourth line of Poem I essentially divides according to their individual understanding of *san-shih nien* 三十年, which is the earliest known reading, as either a period of years of service (of being 'caught in the Dusty Net') or as an expression of age. The Southern Sung chronologists Wang Chih and Wu Jen-chieh already represent these differing positions. Wang Chih, taking 'thirty years' to be the poet's age, placed these poems in 394 (T'ao's thirtieth year by the traditional dating). He would seem to have read the line: 'When once I got out (of the Dusty Net), I was thirty.' Wu Jen-chieh (sub I-hsi 2 = 406), on the other hand, referring it to years of service, struck an impossibility and proposed an emendation of *san-shih* (thirty) to *shih-san* (thirteen), for he regarded thirteen years as covering the period between T'ao's first appointment as Provincial Libationer, which he dated 393, and his last as Magistrate of P'eng-tse in 405. Wu dated the poems in 406 and this dating has been very commonly followed. Wu's emendation has also been quite widely accepted, although Liu Li (*Hsüan-shih pu chu* 5, 6a) offered the alternative suggestion of *yü* 踰 for *san* 三, i.e. 'more than ten years' (such a suggestion is not easy to justify on grounds of graphic corruption), while T'ao Shu proposed *i* 巳 for *san*. It is T'ao Shu's proposal, which involves an easily imagined graphic confusion, that I have adopted, since I date the poems no later than 402.

Wang Chih's reference of *san-shih nien* to the poet's age found few if any supporters until modern times, when departure from the traditional date for the poet's birth became more common. For Ku Chih who dated T'ao's birth 376 it was possible to accept Wu Jen-chieh's dating for the poems, while rejecting the rest of his argument. He was, however, forced to understand line 3 as a periphrasis for 'being born', which in the whole context is not at all satisfactory. For Liang Ch'i-ch'ao (p. 49), who decided on 372 as the date of T'ao's birth, to date these poems 406 was not so satisfactory and this perhaps turned his attention to the objections to such a dating, which I have raised in the Commentary (see vol. 1, p. 48). He therefore proposed a date of 403.

Chang Chih (pp. 33 and 60–61), who follows the traditional date of birth and dates the poems 406, exceptionally believes that this line refers to T'ao's thirtieth year. His view would seem to require reading line 4: 'my going out [to public life] was in my thirtieth year'. Although such a reading is consistent with the apparent fact, established by other references and would possess the very great advantage of requiring no emendation of the text, it does not seem to me very happy linguistically. Also from a comparison of the various contexts where the poet refers to his age, the evidence points to *san-shih nien* being more likely to mean 'thirty years' rather than 'thirtieth year.'

Additional Notes

I, 3. There seems to be only one example of the expression *ch'en-wang* that could be earlier than T'ao's use and this occurs in the *rifacimento* of the collected works of Tung-fang Shuo in a piece entitled *Letter to a Friend*. Yen K'o-chün (*Ch'üan Han-wen* 25, 7b) has discovered no early source for this piece and it must be considered suspect. Though the expression is later used by Buddhists, there seems no reason to think that it is essentially Buddhist in conception. It is not impossible for T'ao to have been its originator. The use of 'dust' represent the world is common in *Chuang-tzu*; cf. also *ch'en-hsiang* in Poem II of this series.

I, 5-6. The image here first appears in a simple form in *Old Poem*, I: 胡馬依北風，越鳥巢南枝 'The Tartar horse relies on the northern air;/The Yüeh bird nests on the southern branch.' Among the Western Chin poets it appears in a considerable number of variations, e.g. P'an Yüeh's *Ch'iu-hsing fu* 秋興賦 preface (*Wen-hsüan* 13, 5b): 譬猶池魚籠鳥，有江湖山藪之思 'Like the fish in the pool, the bird in the cage, I had thoughts of rivers and lakes, hills and marshes'; Lu Chi's *Tseng ts'ung-hsiung Ch'e-ch'i* 贈從兄車騎 (*Wen-hsüan* 24, 28b): 孤獸思故藪，離鳥悲舊林 'The solitary beast thinks of its former preserve;/The lone bird grieves for its old forest'; Chang Hsieh, *Tsa-shih*, VIII (*Wen-hsüan* 29, 40b): 流波戀舊浦，行雲思故山 'The drifting wave longs for its former bank;/The drifting cloud thinks of its old mountain.' In T'ao's fifth line it seems to me that *chi* is better understood as 'confined' rather than 'wandering', cf. *Ch'iu-hsing fu* parallel.

I, 8. Cf. the final line of P'an Yüeh's *Hsien-chü fu* 閒居賦 (*Wen-hsüan* 16, 10a): 終優遊以養拙 'I shall put an end to wandering and cultivate rusticity.'

I, 14. *I-i* here is 'thick' as in *Song* 167, 6.

I, 15-16. These lines imitate the opening lines of the song *Chi-ming* 雞鳴 (*Sung shu* 21, 3a) and are possibly intended to make an ironic comparison of the poet's circumstances with those there described: 'Cocks crow at the tops of the tall trees;/Dogs bark in the depths of the palace.'

II, 1. 'I take little part in men's affairs': T'ao used the same expression in *Drinking Wine*, XVI, p. 88.

II, 2. For *ch'iung-hsiang* 'narrow lane', cf. *Suffering a Fire in the Sixth Month of the Year Wu-wu*, 1.1, p. 80 and *Reading the Shan-hai-ching* I, 7, p. 126. An early example of this expression which is a favourite with T'ao is to be found in *Shih-chi* 56 (Biography of Ch'en P'ing), p. 3: 'P'ing ... lived in a humble lane, backing on to the outer wall of the city. He had a worn-out mat for a gate. Yet outside the gate there were many tracks of important men's carriages.'

II, 3. 'The bright sun', in addition to having an immediate meaning of 'daylight', will probably be a symbol of the official world which the poet has left; cf. the equation of *pai-jih* with 'the ruler' in the political interpretation of the *Ch'u-tz'u*.

III, 1–2. The opening lines and to some degree the whole poem are influenced by the song of Yang Yün (*Han shu* 66, 11b): 'I ploughed that southern hill,/But the weeds were not controlled./I planted a *ch'ing* of beans,/But they withered and became dry stalks./Man's life is simply to walk in joy./What time is there to wait for riches and honour?'

IV, 13. The earliest example of the form of expression of this line, which occurs again in *At the End of the Year Answering a Poem by Attendant Chang*, 1.1, p. 63 is found in a quotation of a Han song, entitled *Ch'u Hsia-men hsing* 出夏門行 in Li Shan's commentary to Lu Chi's *yüeh-fu*, *Men yu ch'e-ma k'o hsing* 門有車馬客行 (*Wen-hsüan* 28, 7b): 市朝人易，千歲墓平 'In markets and courts men change;/In a thousand years the grave-mounds are levelled.' These two lines do not occur in the surviving version of this song; see Huang Chieh, *Han-Wei yüeh-fu feng chien* 4, 4b–5a.

V, 2. The expression *ch'i-chü* also occurs in *Return Home!*, 1.44, p. 138.

V, 3–4. T'ao here adapts the song which concludes the piece *Yü-fu* ('The Fisherman') in *Ch'u-tz'u* 7, 2b: 'When the water of Ts'ang-lang is clear, it serves for washing my cap-strings. When the water of Ts'ang-lang is muddy, it serves for washing my feet.' Wang I's interpretation is that in the first case, when the age is bright, it is appropriate to take office; in the second case, when the age is murky, it is appropriate to retire. If T'ao was conscious of this interpretation, and there seems good reason to assume that he was (see Additional Notes to *Drinking Wine*, IX, p. 93), his meaning must be that although it would be appropriate for him to accept office, he did not want to do so. If this argumentation is correct, he is alleging a personal disinclination towards public life, as he does in the preface to *Return Home!*, p. 137.

V, 7–8. There is an oblique reference here to *Old Poem*, XV, ll. 3–4 quoted in the Additional Note to *Drinking Wine*, XIII, p. 94.

13   AN EXCURSION TO HSIEH-CH'UAN

遊　斜　川

序　辛丑* 正月五日，天氣澄和，風物閒美。與二三鄰曲，
同遊斜川。臨長流，望曾城。魴鯉躍鱗於將夕，水鷗乘
和以翻飛。彼南阜者，名實舊矣，不復乃爲嗟歎。若夫曾
城，傍無依接，獨秀中皋。遙想靈山，有愛嘉名。欣對
不足，率爾賦詩。悲日月之遂往，悼吾年之不留。各疏
年紀鄉里，以記其時日†。

開歲倏五日	雖微九重秀	
吾生行歸休	顧瞻無匹儔	12
念之動中懷	提壺接賓侶	
4　及辰爲茲遊	引滿更獻酬	
氣和天惟澄	未知從今去	
班坐依遠流	當復如此不	16
弱湍馳文魴	中觴縱遙情	
8　閒谷矯鳴鷗	忘彼千載憂	
迴澤散游目	且極今朝樂	
緬然睇曾丘	明日非所求	20

* 丑，曾集本云一作酉。
† 日，曾集本作十，註云一作日，湯注本作日。

Additional Commentary

If one accepts the hypothesis that one of the four variants here is the result of a chance error and another is the result of emendation, we may examine them to see which combination or combinations would have made some emendation necessary. We are, I think, entitled to assume that our hypothetical editor would have believed that T'ao was born in 365 and was thus in 401 in his thirty-seventh year and in 421 in his fifty-seventh year.

It will be found that there is only one combination which would have required emendation, viz. *hsin-ch'ou — wu-shih* (401 — fifty years old). We may then reconstruct the course of the textual changes in the following two possible ways:

	(i)	(ii)
Stage A (original)	*hsin-ch'ou — wu-jih*	*hsin-yu — wu-shih*
Stage B (corrupted)	*hsin-ch'ou — wu-shih*	*hsin-ch'ou — wu-shih*
Stage C (emended)	*hsin-yu — wu-shih*	*hsin-ch'ou — wu-jih*

Either (i) or (ii) would thus account for the appearance of all the variants, and I believe that one of them must represent the actual course of events. When we consider whether (i) or (ii) possesses the greater probability, there are two arguments in favour of (i). Firstly, the graphic corruption of *jih* 日 into *shih* 十 is more probable than *yu* 酉 into *ch'ou* 丑; secondly, the emendation by an editor of *hsin-ch'ou* (to his mind an impossible date) would be likely to seem more obvious than changing *wu-shih* to *wu-jih*. We have thus a logical case for preferring *hsin-ch'ou* and *wu-jih* as the original readings, though we should be careful to realize that the case cannot be absolutely proven. At least such an attempt must be methodologically preferable to a purely subjective choice among the variants, such as Chang Chih's. He (pp. 84–85) chooses *hsin-yu* on the ground that *hsin-ch'ou* would be incompatible with line 2 of the poem ('My life goes onward to its rest') and *wu-jih* because *wu-shih* would create too many problems in dating. But he has failed to notice that an almost identical expression ('I am moved by my life's moving to its rest') occurs in *Return Home!* (405). Even worse is Ku Chih's approach, for having decided that *wu-shih* is correct, he proceeded to add to the total of variants by proposing to emend *hsin-ch'ou* to *i-ch'ou* 乙丑 (425), since he believed T'ao was born in 376.

One further approach to the problem deserves comment. This is the suggestion of Lu Ch'in-li that *hsin-yu*, which he accepts as the correct reading, is the cyclical sign for the day, displaced from its appropriate position, and not the sign for the year. He accepts *wu-shih* in the first line of the poem and since the cyclical sign for the fifth day of the first month of 425 was *hsin-yu*, he thus feels that this poem provides important evidence for the view which he shares with Ku Chih that T'ao was born in 376. He gives a number of reasons for taking *hsin-yu* as the sign for the day. Firstly, all the dated poems are in the third chüan of the collected works and so if this poem had a year date, it should have been placed there. This reasoning is not completely valid, since all the dated poems to which Lu refers have a date in the title, whereas in this poem the date is in the preface. Secondly, all the year dates are accompanied by the word *sui* 歲: this is the only exception. Here again Lu is not entirely correct. The Fang-Su hsieh text of this poem has *sui*, and in the case of the second of the *Kuei-mao* poems in the third chüan both the T'ang Han and Li Kung-huan texts lack *sui*. Thus the argument is clearly not strong. In his third reason Lu is strongly influenced by the deep-rooted idea of the poet's loyalty to the fallen Chin dynasty. According to the preface to a *Tsu fu* 祖賦 by Hsi Han 嵇含, nephew of Hsi K'ang's son Shao 紹 (preserved in *Sung shu* 12, 28b), Chin performed the sacrifice to the Spirit of the Roads (Tsu-shen 祖神) on a *yu* 酉 day in the first month of the year. Thus Lu thinks that T'ao was secretly maintaining a Chin practice. Unfortunately there seems to be nothing in the poem to support this idea; it is solely a matter of the correspondence of the cyclical signs. If Lu's view that *hsin-yu* is the sign for the day could be supported by other evidence, then his idea would require serious consideration. Finally, his view depends very largely on the correctness of his dating T'ao's birth in 376 and such evidence as we have does not favour this.

Additional Notes

PREFACE. The expression *yüeh lin* 'danced their scales' occurs in P'an Yüeh's *Hsi-cheng fu* 西征賦 (*Wen-hsüan* 10, 38a): 華魴躍鱗 and may be a reminiscence from there. The 'Divine Mountain' is the K'un-lun. *Ch'u-tz'u*, *T'ien-wen* (3, 6b) has: 崑崙縣圃其尻安在，增城九重其高幾里 'Where is the site of the K'un-lun's Hanging Gardens? How many *li* high are the nine stages of the Tiered Walls?' According to a *K'un-lun shuo*, quoted in *Shui-ching chu*, chapter 1, p. 1, Ts'eng-ch'eng (also called the Court of Heaven 天庭) was the highest of the three levels of the K'un-lun (Hsüan-p'u, the Hanging Gardens, was the middle level); cf. also *Huai-nan-tzu*, 4, 2a–b, where the height of the nine stages of Ts'eng-ch'eng is given as 11,000 *li*. The Ts'eng of Ts'eng-ch'eng is variously written 曾, 增, 層; the last would seem to be orthographically correct.

LINE 2. There is probably no need to refer the term *kuei-hsiu* back to *Chuang-tzu* 21 (歸) and 15 (休) as most recent commentators following Ku Chih have done, since T'ao seems to use it as a straightforward euphemism for death without philosophical overtones.

LINE 18. 'Thousand years' sorrows' comes from *Old Poem*, XV: 'Life's years do not fill a hundred,/But always they embrace a thousand years' sorrows.'

LINES 19–20. These last lines continue in the vein of *Old Poem*, XV.

14   TO SECRETARY CHOU, TSU AND HSIEH

示周掾祖謝*

負疴頹簷下	道喪向千載	
終日無一欣	今朝復斯聞	
藥石有時閒	馬隊非講肆	
4　念我意中人	校書亦已勤	12
相去不尋常	老夫有所愛	
道路邈何因	思與爾為鄰	
周生述孔業	願言誨諸子	
8　祖謝響然臻	從我潁水濱	16

* 詩題李箋注本作示周續之祖企謝景夷三郎。

† 曾集本註云一作客，一作勉諸生，一作但願還渚中。

Additional Commentary

Chang Chih (p. 75) has gone further than other modern critics who date this poem 416. He states that the episode which connects Chou Hsü-chih with T'an Shao must fall in the sixth to seventh months of 416 and that T'ao's poem must belong to the same time. For he assumes that Chou's teaching at Chiang-chou was undertaken between the death of the previous governor, Liu Liu, in the sixth month (he is assuming also that T'an Shao took up the post immediately) and the start of Liu Yü's northern expedition in the eighth month. During Liu Yü's northern expedition, Chou Hsü-chih, according to his biography in *Sung shu* 93, 3b, was received by Liu Yü's son, who had been left in charge of the capital Chien-k'ang, and lodged in the An-lo monastery. According to the same source, he stayed for something over a month and then returned again to the mountains (i.e. Lu-shan, for Shen Yüeh follows this immediately with an account, which is of course out of chronological order, of Liu Liu recommending Chou to Liu Yü). Chang Chih's assumption is in fact quite unjustified, since there is nothing in the *Sung shu*, which specifies at what time within Liu Yü's absence from Chien-k'ang (eighth month, 416 to twelfth month, 417) Chou made his visit.

Additional Notes

TITLE. Li Kung-huan's text reads the title as　示周續之祖企謝景夷三郎　'To the Three Gentlemen, Chou Hsü-chih, Tsu Ch'i and Hsieh Ching-i'. This version is noted as a variant in the Tseng Chi text and in T'ang Han's edition (which omits the 掾 of the Tseng Chi title). I should regard it as secondary and probably derived from Hsiao T'ung's biography of T'ao. Li Kung-huan follows the title with the words 時三人皆 (the *Ssu-pu ts'ung-k'an* text has 比) 講禮校書. This differs slightly from the 時三人共在城北講禮校書 which the Tseng Chi text notes with its variant reading and is also probably added from Hsiao T'ung's biography. The word 掾 in the Tseng Chi title, which I have translated 'Secretary' is very interesting, since Shen Yüeh in his biography of Chou Hsü-chih follows his unchronological recording of the recommendation of him to Liu Yü by Liu Liu with the statement that he was immediately appointed 太尉掾 but did not accept the appointment, i.e. to the personal staff of Liu Yü whose chief title at this time (415–16, the period of Liu Liu's governorship in Chiang-chou) was Grand Commandant. *Yüan* might of course be a later insertion, though it is hard to imagine what might have prompted it. It seems preferable to regard it as original and consider its significance. Since the word is common in the titles of minor posts in this period, one might argue that it refers to some other post which Chou Hsü-chih actually held but is otherwise unrecorded. But as there is the statement by Shen Yüeh, it may be unreasonable to ignore it. If we do not, are we to conclude that T'ao called Chou by a title which he had refused and even did so with ironic intent? Such a conclusion, however much one might believe in T'ao's capacity for political criticism and innuendo, seems to me utterly unlikely. I would more easily believe that Shen Yüeh was in error about Chou's non-acceptance. Certainly Shen himself provides a good deal of evidence for Chou Hsü-chih being willing to accept hospitality and favour from Liu Yü both before and after the latter became the first emperor of Sung.

LINE 5. *Pu hsün-ch'ang: hsün* is a measure of eight (Chinese) feet and *ch'ang* of sixteen feet. The phrase is usually understood as meaning 'not near', 'far', but I believe that T'ao meant rather 'not [a matter of] feet', 'not measurable'. For the separation to which he refers in this poem is surely not simply a physical one.

LINE 8. *Hsiang-jan chen* 'come like an echo' may derive from K'ung Jung's *Memorial to Recommend Mi Heng* 薦禰衡表 (*Wen-hsüan* 37, 1b): 羣士響臻 'The host of scholars come like an echo.'

LINE 9. Cf. *Drinking Wine*, III, 1, p. 85.

LINE 10. Refers obliquely to *Lun-yü* 4, 8: 'The Master said: "To hear of the Way in the morning and to die in the evening is tolerable."'

LINES 11–12. See Hsiao T'ung biography, p. 173.

LINES 13–14. Since Chou and the others are setting forth the 'true Way', T'ao as a good father should bring his sons into contact with them. The poet seems to be maintaining the irony of the preceding lines.

LINE 15. The ambiguity of *chu-tzu*, which I, like Suzuki, have taken to refer to T'ao's sons, is probably the cause of the many variant readings for this line: they appear to be the result of editorial emendations. I regard the reading of the Tseng Chi and Li Kung-huan texts as most probably correct.

LINE 16. The story of Hsü Yü's withdrawal to the north side of the Ying appears in Hsi K'ang's *Sheng-hsien kao-shih chuan* (fragment ap. *I-wen lei-chü* 36, 2b), a work for which Chou Hsü-chih wrote a commentary.

15   BEGGING FOR FOOD

乞　食

飢來驅我去	觴至輒傾盃	8
不知竟何之	情欣新知歡 *	
行行至斯里	言詠遂賦詩	
叩門拙言辭　(4)	感子漂母惠	
主人解余意	愧我非韓才	12
遺贈豈虛來	銜戢知何謝	
談諧終日夕	冥報以相貽	

* 歡，曾集本作勸，註云一作歡，陶注本作歡。

Additional Notes

LINES 11–12. The story of Han Hsin and the fuller-woman may be found in *Shih-chi* 92, p. 2 and *Han shu* 34, 9b.

LINE 14. *Ming-pao* 'a requital in the shades' has a classical source in *Tso-chuan*, Hsüan fifteenth year, where there is a story of the ghost of an old man helping Wei Ko in battle in return for the sparing of the life of his daughter whom Wei Ko's father (the girl had been his concubine) had ordered to be buried with him.

16 WE ALL ENJOY OURSELVES TOGETHER BENEATH THE CYPRESSES AT THE TOMBS OF THE CHOU FAMILY

諸人共游周家墓柏下

	今日天氣佳	清歌散新聲
	清吹與鳴彈	綠酒開芳顏
	感彼柏下人	未知明日事
4	安得不爲歡	余襟良已殫	8

Additional Commentary

There are two other quotations in *T'ai-p'ing yü-lan* with the heading *Chih-k'uai chi* 志怪集 besides the one in chapter 559 which contains the story about T'ao K'an burying his father. No work with this title appears in the *Sui shu ching-chi chih*. There is, however, another quotation of the T'ao K'an story, although without the reference to Chou Fang, in *T'ai-p'ing yü-lan* 900, 4b. In this case the source is given as the *Chih-k'uai* of Tsu T'ai-chih 祖台之 志怪. This work is listed in *Sui shu ching-chi chih* (p. 60) in 2 chüan, and is regarded as a work of the Chin period. Lu Hsün collected the fragments of this work in his *Ku hsiao-shuo kou-ch'en*, vol. I, pp. 207–11.

17 RESENTFUL POEM IN THE CH'U MODE TO REGISTRAR P'ANG AND SECRETARY TENG

怨詩楚調示龐主簿鄧治中

	天道幽且遠	夏日長抱飢	
	鬼神茫昧然	寒夜無被眠	12
	結髮念善事	造夕思鷄鳴	
4	僶俛六九年	及晨願烏遷	
	弱冠逢世阻	在己何怨天	
	始室喪其偏	離憂悽目前	16
	炎火屢焚如	吁嗟身後名	
8	螟蜮恣中田	於我若浮煙	
	風雨縱橫至	慷慨獨悲歌	
	收斂不盈廛	鍾期信爲賢	20

Additional Notes

TITLE. *Ch'u tiao* is one of the five modes according to which the *hsiang-ho* group of *yüeh-fu* was later classified (see introduction to *hsiang-ho* section in *Yüeh-fu shih chi* 26, 1a). *Chih-chung* (Secretary) was an assistant to a provincial governor.

LINE 1. T'ao possibly had in mind the saying of the statesman Tzu-ch'an in *Tso-chuan*, Chao eighteenth year: 天道遠，人事邇 'The Way of Heaven is remote; the affairs of men are near at hand.'

LINE 3. *Chieh-fa*, cf. *tsung-fa* 總髮 in *Suffering a Fire in the Sixth Month of the Year Wu-wu*, 1.13 (p. 81).

LINE 4. *Min-mien* 僶俛 in *Songs* written 黽勉; T'ao might have had *Song* 193, 7 especially in mind: 黽勉從事 ... 下民之孽匪降自天 'I strive to carry out my duties ... the misfortunes of the people below do not come down from Heaven.'

LINES 5–6. See *Li-chi* 1 (1, 3a): 二十曰弱，冠，三十曰壯，有室 'When he is twenty, he is called a youth and capped; when he is thirty, he is called mature and has a house [i.e. is married].'

LINE 8. *Ming-yü* according to Li Kung-huan should read *ming-te* 螟貣. The combination *ming-yü* is, however, found also in *Lü-shih ch'un-ch'iu* 26, 7b (Kao Yu notes variant 螣 *te*) and *Hou-Han shu* 2, 7a (Ch'ien Ta-hsin proposed correction to 蟘, same word as 螣) and it should probably be regarded as an established use and not requiring emendation here. Cf. *Song* 212, 2: 去其螟螣 (variant ap. *Shuo-wen* 蟘) 及其蟊賊 'We remove the insects from the ears and leaves and from the roots and stems' (following the definition of *Erh-ya* 15: 食苗心螟，食葉螣，食節賊，食根蟊).

LINE 15. In framing this line, although he is expressing his own feeling, T'ao was perhaps consciously providing an echo of *Lun-yü* 14, 37: 不怨天，不尤人 'I do not blame Heaven; I do not find fault with others.'

LINE 17. For *shen-hou ming*, see Additional Note to *Drinking Wine*, XI, 5, p. 93.

LINE 18. Cf. *Lun-yü* 7, 15: 不義而富且貴，於我如浮雲 'The Master said: "... Riches and honour without righteousness, to me are like floating clouds.'

LINE 20. The story of Po-ya and Chung Tzu-ch'i occurs in a number of late Chou and Han texts: *Lü-shih ch'un-ch'iu* 14, 4b–5a; *Lieh-tzu* 5, p. 111;

Han-shih wai-chuan 9, 3a; Shuo-yüan 8, 9b–10a; Feng-su t'ung-i 6, p. 47. The last three all appear to derive from the *Lü-shih ch'un-ch'iu* version, whereas the latter and the *Lieh-tzu* show a considerable degree of independence, though they are still close enough to have had a common source. T'ao's line seems a little more likely to have been framed with the *Lü-shih ch'un-ch'iu* in mind, so I have translated this version:

> Po-ya was playing the lute and Chung Tzu-ch'i was listening to him. Just as he was playing, his thoughts rested on T'ai-shan. Chung Tzu-ch'i said: 'Excellent is your playing, towering like T'ai-shan.' After a little while his thoughts rested on flowing water. Chung Tzu-ch'i again said: 'Excellent is your playing, rolling like flowing water.'
> When Chung Tzu-ch'i died, Po-ya smashed his lute and broke its strings; till the end of his life he did not play again, because he thought that there was no one in the world worth playing for. It is not only lute-playing that is like this; with the wise man it is the same case. Although there is a wise man, if men attach themselves to him without propriety, how can the wise man give all his loyalty? It is just as the horse Chi cannot of himself go a thousand *li*, if his driver is not skilled.

T'ao probably intended an elegant compliment to his friends in this last line, which I have tried to suggest in the translation.

18   IN REPLY TO AIDE P'ANG

答龐參軍

序　三復來貺，欲罷不能。自爾鄰曲，冬春再交。欵然良對，
忽成舊游。俗諺云，數面成親舊。況情過此者乎。人事
好乖，便當語離。楊公所歎，豈惟常悲。吾抱疾多年，
不復爲文。本既不豐，復老病繼之。輒依周禮＊往復之
義，且爲別後相思之資。

相知何必舊　　　談諧無俗調
傾蓋定前言　　　所說聖人篇
有客賞我趣　　　或有數斗酒
4　　每每顧林園　　　閒飲自歡然　　8

＊ 周禮，各本作周孔，曾集本註云一作禮，今從之。

我實幽居士　　　　　　　情通萬里外
無復東西緣　　　　　　　形跡滯江山
物新人唯舊　　　　　　　君其愛體素
12　弱毫多所宣⁺　　　　　來會在何年　　16

⁺多，曾集本作夕，湯注本作多。今從之。

Additional Notes

PREFACE. *San fu* (literally, 'three times repeat') has a *locus classicus* in
Lun-yü 11, 5 where Confucius is said to have given his elder brother's
daughter in marriage to Nan Jung because he three times repeated the 'white
jade sceptre' 白圭 (i.e. verse 5 of *Song* 256, which counsels discretion: 'A flaw
in a white jade sceptre/Still may be ground out;/For a flaw in these
words/Nothing can be done.') *Yü pa pu neng* is equally a reminiscence of
Lun-yü: from the famous passage in 9, 10 where Yen Hui complains of the
difficulty of the Master's teaching. The reference to Yang Chu probably may
be traced to *Huai-nan-tzu* 17, 14b: 楊子見逵路而哭之，爲其可以南可以北.
'Master Yang wept when he saw a crossroads, because he could go south or
go north.' Kao Yu's comment is that Yang Chu 'grieved at the parting'. The
reference of 'Chou rites' is to *Li-chi* 1 (1, 2b): 禮尚往來，往而不來，非禮也，
來而不往，亦非禮也 'The rites set value on going and coming [i.e. giving and
receiving presents]. If one gives and receives no return, it is contrary to the
rites. If one is given a gift and makes no return, it is also contrary to the rites.'

LINES 1–2. T'ao probably had in mind the saying quoted in the biography of
Tsou Yang (*Shih-chi* 83, p. 21; *Han shu* 51, 11a): 有白頭如新，傾蓋如故.
何則知與不知也 'There are white-headed men who are like new [friends] and
men for whom one inclines one's canopy who are like old. What is it that
produces intimacy or not?' This means that there are some persons whom one
may know all one's life without their becoming more than newly-met
acquaintances, while there are others who at a chance meeting immediately
become old friends. The expression *ch'ing-kai* (to incline the canopy of one's
carriage), used with this sense, seems to originate in a story of Confucius,
which is extant in three versions: *K'ung-tzu chia-yü* 2, 8b; *Han-shih wai-chuan*
2, 10a and *Shuo-yüan* 8, 20b: 孔子之郯，遭程子於塗，傾蓋而語終日，甚相親
(*Chia-yü* reading) 'When Confucius was on his way to Tan, he met Master
Ch'eng in the road. They inclined their canopies and talked the whole day and
were very intimate.'

LINE 11. T'ao adapts the saying in *Shu, P'an Keng* (5, 3b): 人惟求舊，器非求
舊，惟新 'In men one seeks the old [i.e. those that are known]; in utensils one
does not seek the old but the new.'

19 WRITTEN ON THE FIRST DAY OF THE FIFTH MONTH TO ANSWER A POEM BY REGISTRAR TAI

五月旦作和戴主簿

虛舟縱逸棹	既來孰不去
回復遂無窮	人理固有終
發歲始俛仰	居常待其盡
星紀奄將中 (4)	曲肱豈傷沖 (12)
南窗罕悴物	遷化或夷險
北林榮且豐	肆志無窊隆
神淵寫時雨	即事如已高
晨色奏景風 (8)	何必升華嵩 (16)

Additional Notes

LINES 1–2. T'ao perhaps borrowed his image of the empty, undirected boat from *Chuang-tzu* 20 (7A, 23a) and 32 (10A, 14b) and used it to a different end. In *Chuang-tzu* it illustrates the way of life of the Taoist sage.

LINE 5. Two fairly different readings, which may have originated in graphic confusion, occur in this line. I have preferred the reading *nan ch'uang han ts'ui wu*, because *nan ch'uang* provides for *pei lin* in the next line a type of parallelism of which T'ao was particularly fond. In the alternative reading *ming liang ts'ui shih-wu* 'the brightness is doubled, making the seasonal things luxuriant', *ming liang* would presumably derive from *I*, hexagram 30 and refer to the summer heat.

LINE 7. *Shen-yüan* 'the divine abyss' is the abode of the rain-dragons; cf. Ts'ao Chih, *Ch'i-ch'i* 七啓 (*Wen-hsüan* 34, 32a).

LINE 8. *Ching-feng* 'the fortunate wind' is defined as the south wind in *Shuo-wen* (sub *feng*, p. 284). Cf. the *I-wei*, *T'ung-kua-yen* 通卦驗 fragment quoted in Li Shan's commentary to *Wen-hsüan* 42, 11b (Wei Wen-ti, *Letter to Wu Chih, Magistrate of Chao-ko*).

LINE 10. This line may have been written with *Lieh-tzu* 1, p. 12 in mind: 生者理之必終者也 ，終者不得不終，亦如生者之不得不生 'Life is an activity which must end. The end cannot not be made, just as life cannot not be lived.' See also next.

LINE 11. There are several possible sources from which T'ao might have
known the story of Jung Ch'i-ch'i, but in view of the fact that in *Lieh-tzu* the
story occurs in chapter 1 (pp. 13–14), following closely on the passage which
could have inspired T'ao's preceding line, it seems reasonable to assume that
the *Lieh-tzu* version was his source. I have given a complete translation of the
passage in the Additional Note to *Drinking Wine*, II, 5 (p. 90). The current
text of *Lieh-tzu* reads 處常得終 , but there are a number of quotations as well
as the parallel texts with the reading 居常以待終 (see Wang Shu-min,
Lieh-tzu pu-cheng 1, 13b) and this is the reading which T'ao must have seen.

LINE 12. The word *ch'ung* (translated 'quiet') is difficult to render with
certainty. It occurs in *Lao-tzu* 4 in the meaning of 'empty' as an attribute of
the Way, and it is perhaps an extension of this meaning to describe a personal
'impassivity' that is in question here.

LINE 13. *Ch'ien-hua*: in *At the End of the Year Answering a Poem* by
Attendant Chang, l.18 (p.63) and *Written when Passing through Ch'ü-o*, l.19
(p.67) written *hua-ch'ien*.

20   DRINKING ALONE DURING CONTINUOUS RAINS

連雨獨飲

運生會歸盡		天豈去此哉
終古謂之然		任眞無所先
世間有松喬		雲鶴有奇翼
4　於今定何閒		八表須臾還　12
故老贈余酒		自我抱茲獨
乃言飲得仙		僶俛四十年
試酌百情遠		形骸久已化
8　重觴忽忘天		心在復何言　16

Additional Notes

LINE 1. Cf. *Written on the First Day of the Fifth Month*, Additional Note to
1.10, p. 51.

LINE 4. The variant 閑 which is noted in the Tseng Chi and other texts is
obviously an attempt to simplify the apparently difficult 閒, but as Wang

Shu-min has suggested, this may be understood in the sense of 瞯 'to observe' and there is no need to follow Ku Chih in adopting 閒.

LINE 8. *Wang t'ien* derives from *Chuang-tzu* 12 (5A, 13b): 忘乎物, 忘乎天, 其名爲忘己, 忘己之人是之謂入於天 'To forget things, to forget Heaven is called forgetting self. A man who has forgotten self is said to have entered into Heaven.'

LINE 10. *Jen chen* 'trust in the True [the Way, Nature]' is applied to T'ao by Hsiao T'ung, see Biography, p. 170. *Hsien* seems to be in the sense of 'To be first', 'to initiate', as in *Chuang-tzu* 15 (6A, 3b):聖人 ... 不爲福先, 不爲禍始 'The sage ... is not the initiator of good fortune, is not the originator of misfortune' or *Lao-tzu* 67: 不敢爲天下先 'Not dare to be first in the world' or *Lieh-tzu* 1, p. 13: 物莫先焉 'There are no things which he sets himself in front of'.

LINES 13–16. Cf. *Suffering a Fire in the Sixth Month of the Year Wu-wu*, ll. 13–16, p. 81.

21 MOVING HOUSE

移居二首

I

昔欲居南村　　敝廬何必廣
非爲卜其宅　　取足蔽牀席　8
聞多素心人　　鄰曲時時來
4　樂與數晨夕　　抗言談在昔
懷此頗有年　　奇文共欣賞
今日從茲役　　疑義相與析　12

II

春秋多佳日　　相思則披衣
登高賦新詩　　言笑無厭時　8
過門更相呼　　此理將不勝
4　有酒斟酌之　　無爲忽去茲
農務各自歸　　衣食當須紀
閒暇輒相思　　力耕不吾欺　12

Additional Notes

I, 4. I have preferred to read 數 as a verb (*shu*), as Wu Chan-t'ai did, rather than as 'frequent' (*shuo*). The use of 'mornings and evenings' may by itself indicate frequent meetings, see *Li-chi* 17 (10, 13a).

I, 10. *K'ang-yen*, literally, 'opposed words', would seem here to describe the frank speech of equals who need not show ceremonious deference to each other.

22 ANSWERING A POEM BY LIU CH'AI-SANG

和劉柴桑

	山澤久見招	谷風轉淒薄
	胡事乃躊躇	春醪解飢劬　12
	直爲親舊故	弱女雖非男
4	未忍言索居	慰情良勝無
	良辰入奇懷	栖栖世中事
	挈杖還西廬	歲月共相疎　16
	荒塗無歸人	耕織稱其用
8	時時見廢墟	過此奚所須
	茅茨已就治	去去百年外
	新疇復應畬	身名同翳如　20

Additional Notes

LINE 1. Many commentators have understood T'ao's 'call' to have come from Liu I-min to join him on Lu-shan, but clearly in the context his call is to retirement from the world, and the 'hills and valleys', which symbolize this, should be taken as the subject, cf. *Written when Passing Through Ch'ü-o*, l.14: 'My mind recalls my life amid hills and valleys.'

LINE 4. *So-chü* 'a solitary life' derives from *Li-chi* 3 (2, 10a): 吾離羣而索居亦已久矣 'It is long indeed since I left the company of men and lived alone.'

LINE 8. Cf. Tung Chung-shu, *Shih pu-yü fu* (translated vol. 1, pp. 181–83) line 48: 'I suspect the overgrown ways will be hard to tread.' T'ao may be implying that the way to retirement is hard and few take it.

LINE 10. This line makes use of the *Erh-ya* definitions (9, p. 21, 6): 田 ...
二歲曰新田 , 三歲曰畬 'Fields ... in their second year are called "new fields";
in their third year are called "yü".' The definitions are for *Song* 276, 2 and *I*,
hexagram 25.

LINE 11. 'The valley wind' is the east wind, see *Erh-ya* 8, p. 19. 7 (definition
for *Song* 35).

LINES 13–14. It seems difficult to understand these lines literally and they
have generally been read metaphorically, i.e. spring wine is better than no
wine at all. It is interesting to note, however, that Po Chü-i imitated T'ao's
words with a literal sense in *Nien Chin-luan-tzu* 念金鑾子, Poem I (*Po
Hsiang-shan shih-chi*, *Ch'ang-ch'ing chi* 10, 5a; for a translation see Waley,
Chinese Poems, p.154).

LINE 15. *Hsi-hsi*: the meaning 'bustling', which the Sung commentator Hsing
Ping applies to the famous occurrence in *Lun-yü* 14, 34, seems already to
have been established in the Han period, e.g. Pan Ku, *Ta pin-hsi* 答賓戲
(*Wen-hsüan* 45, 17b; there written 棲棲).

23   IN RETURN FOR A POEM BY LIU CH'AI-SANG

酬劉柴桑

窮居寡人用　　　　　嘉穀養南疇
時忘四運周　　　　　今我不爲樂
門庭多落葉*　　　　　知有來歲不　　8
4 慨然知已秋　　　　命室攜童弱
新葵鬱北牖　　　　　良日登遠遊

* 門，各本作欄，曾集本註云一作門。今從之。

Additional Notes

LINES 7–8. These lines are founded on the refrain of *Song* 114: 蟋蟀在堂，
歲聿其莫 , 今我不樂, 日月其除 'The cricket is in the hall;/The year now comes
to its end./If now we are not happy,/The days and months will have passed
by.'

24 ANSWERING A POEM BY REGISTRAR KUO

和郭主簿二首

I

藹藹堂前林

中夏貯清陰

凱風因時來

4　回飆開我襟

息交遊閒業

臥起弄書琴

園蔬有餘滋

8　舊穀猶儲今

營己良有極

過足非所欽

春秫作美酒

酒熟吾自斟　12

弱子戲我側

學語未成音

此事真復樂

聊用忘華簪　16

遙遙望白雲

懷古一何深

II

和澤周三春

清涼素秋節 *

露凝無游氛

4　天高肅景澈

陵岑聳逸峯

遙瞻皆奇絕

芳菊開林耀

青松冠巖列　8

懷此貞秀姿

卓爲霜下傑

銜觴念幽人

千載撫爾訣　12

檢素不獲展

厭厭竟良月

* 此句曾集本作華華涼秋節，註云又作清涼素秋節。今從之。

⁺ 肅，曾集本作風，註云一作肅。今從之。

Additional Notes

I, 2. *Chung-hsia* is the second of the three summer months, i.e. the fifth month of the lunar calendar.

I, 3. *K'ai-feng* is defined as the south wind in *Erh-ya* 8, p. 19.7 (definition for *Song* 32).

I, 5. The terminology of this line is used in *Return Home!*, 1.34 and *Singing of Poor Scholars*, VI, 3. I accept the reading 息交遊閒業 (臥起弄書琴). Ku

Chih suggests that *hsien-yeh* is the opposite of *cheng-yeh* 正業 in *Li-chi* 18 (11, 2b), where it is defined by K'ung Ying-ta in his sub-commentary as 'the correct books of the former kings (i.e. the Confucian books) and not the hundred schools of the philosophers' (先王正典，非諸子百家). Since this definition seems to arise from a misunderstanding of the original text, I am doubtful whether we can apply its converse to T'ao's line and understand that the poet here refers to the study of books like *Lao-tzu*, *Chuang-tzu* and *Shan-hai-ching*, as Wang Yao and others have done.

II, 3. The expression *yu-fen* 'drifting mists' occurs in P'an Yüeh's *Ch'iu-hsing fu* 秋興賦 (*Wen-hsüan* 13, 6b), a poem with which T'ao was fairly certainly familiar.

II, 14. T'ao may have intended the tenth month by *liang-yüeh* on account of *Tso-chuan*, Chuang sixteenth year: 使以十月入，曰良月，就盈數焉 'He made him enter [the city] in the tenth month, saying that it was "the happy month" because ten is a number of completeness.'

25 SEEING OFF A GUEST AT GENERAL WANG'S BANQUET

於王撫軍座送客

	秋日淒且厲	瞻夕欣良讌
	百卉具已腓	離言聿云悲
	爰以履霜節	晨鳥暮來還
4	登高餞將歸	懸車歛餘暉 12
	寒氣冒山澤	逝止判殊路 #
	游雲倏無依	旋駕悵遲遲
	洲渚四緬邈 *	目送回舟遠
8	風水互乖違	情隨萬化遺 16

* 四緬，曾集本作思綿，註云一作四緬。今從之。
 欣，曾集本作欲，註云一作欣。今從之。
逝，曾集本作遊，註云一作逝。今從之。

Additional Commentary

The first extant source to connect this poem with Hsieh Chan's *On a Parting Feast with General Wang and Yü Hsi-yang* 王撫軍庾西陽集別 (*Wen-hsüan* 20, 44a) is the commentary of Li Kung-huan, although he states: 'According to the *nien-p'u* this poem was written in the autumn of the second year of Yung-chu, *hsin-yu* of the Sung Emperor Wu.' This *nien-p'u* (neither Wang Chih's nor Wu Jen-chieh's) can no longer be identified. Hsieh Chan's poem, which has the words 'At the time I was Prefect of Yü-chang and Yü had been summoned back to the east' as part of the title, reads:

Respecting the summons, you return to the northern capital;
Caring for my office, I go back to the southern domain.
In boats side by side, we break off our old friendship;
On mats set opposite, we part from the wise governor.
We raise our cups and make our farewell toasts;
We point to the road, mindful of 'going out and passing the night'.

[Allusion to *Song* 39, 2]

To the time of return there is no certain clue,
But the hour of parting will surely come soon.
The declining light illumines the crossing place;
The evening shades obscure the level land.
The boatman straightens the moving bows;
To the light carriage the return driver is called.
I let go your hand at the gate in the eastern wall;
The oar is started in the cove of the western river.
Though partings and meetings are mingled together,
The stream that has passed, how shall it return again?
Who shall say that feelings may be written?
Their complete expression is not in letters.

[The last couplet is founded on *I*, *Hsi-tz'u chuan* A, 12: 書不盡言，言不盡意, 'Writing does not completely express words; words do not completely express thoughts.']

Hsieh's poem must come from 421, since in this year he became Prefect of Yü-chang and while in this office became ill and died (see his short biography in *Sung shu* 56, 1b). Li Shan (see Hu K'o-chia [ed.], *Wen-hsüan* 20, 35a) in a prefatory comment to the poem has collected from *Sung shu* various pieces of information on Wang Hung, Hsieh Chan and Yü Teng-chih, the Prefect of Hsi-yang, who was summoned from this post to be Chief Secretary to the Heir-apparent (*T'ai-tzu shu-tzu*; see *Sung shu* 53, 4b), and also the statement from a preface in Hsieh Chan's collected works that: 'When Hsieh returned to Yü-chang and Yü was called back to the capital, General Wang escorted them as far as P'en-k'ou [at the junction of the P'en river with the Yangtze, west of Hsün-yang, also called P'en-p'u 湓浦]. Composed in the Southern Tower.' Li Kung-huan in his comment has a substantially similar statement to this and continues: 'Hsiu-yüan (Wang Hung) must have asked Ching-chieh (T'ao Yüan-ming) to arrange the farewell banquet. This is why Hsieh Chan's *Chi-hsi chi-pieh shih* 即席集別詩 in the *Wen-hsüan* in its heading records four guests.' Whether there was once an edition of the *Wen-hsüan* which conformed with Li's statement, there is no longer. In any case it is obvious that T'ao's name did not actually appear in it, so that in fact Li Kung-huan's statement is only a firmly asserted guess and has no independent support.

When one turns back to a comparison of the two poems, the differences seem more significant than the similarities. T'ao's poem is very clearly written in autumn and might well be a Double Ninth poem. If this were the case, it could hardly fail to evoke some reference in Hsieh's poem, but in fact the latter has no indication of the season.

Additional Notes

LINES 1–2. These opening lines are a virtual quotation of *Song* 204, 2: 秋日淒淒, 百卉具腓 'The autumn days are chill;/The hundred plants all wither.' Cf. *The Ninth Day of the Ninth Month of the Year Chi-yu*, ll.2–3, p. 82.

LINE 3. *Li-shuang* 'treading on frost' is found in *Songs* 107, 1 and 203. 2 and in the *Wen-yen* commentary to *I*, hexagram 2.

LINE 4. Here, as in *Living in Retirement on the Ninth Day*, p. 36 and *The Ninth Day of the Ninth Month of the Year Chi-yu*, p. 82, T'ao thinks of *Chiu-pien* I (*Ch'u-tz'u* 8, 1bff). In this case he adapts the line: 登山臨水兮送將歸 'We climb the hill and gaze over the water, seeing off him who is going home.'

LINE 12. *Hsüan-ch'e* 'the unyoked chariot' as an expression for 'sunset' derives from *Huai-nan-tzu* 3, 9b.

26 PARTING FROM YIN CHIN-AN

與殷晉安別

序　殷先作晉安南府長史掾，因居潯陽。後作太尉參軍，移
　　家東下，作此以贈。

遊好非少長*	負杖肆遊從	
一遇盡殷勤	淹留忘宵晨	8
信宿酬清話	語黙自殊勢	
4　益復知爲親	亦知當乖分	
去歲家南里	未謂事己及	
薄作少時鄰	興言在茲春	12

*　少，曾集本作久，註云一作少。今從之。

飄飄西來風　　　　　良才不隱世
悠悠東去雲　　　　　江湖多賤貧
山川千里外　　　　　脱有經過便
16　言笑難爲因　　　　念來存故人　　20

Additional Commentary

Ssu-ma Kuang brought together Liu Yü's acceptance of the office of Grand Commandant (*t'ai-wei*) and Yin's appointment as acting *t'ai-wei ts'an-chün* under the third month of 411 (*Tzu-chih t'ung-chien* 116, p. 3644). Liu Yü had had this office conferred on him in the ninth month of 409 but had declined it (*Sung shu* 1, 12a). It was this earlier conferring which led Liang Ch'i-ch'ao (p. 53; he was followed by Li Ch'en-tung, p. 18, although the latter refers to a second attempt to confer the title on Liu Yü in the sixth month of 410) to date T'ao's poem in 410. Yin Ching-jen's biography in *Sung shu* 63, 4a, while giving no date for his appointment with Liu Yü, mentions an earlier post as Aide to Liu I 劉毅 as General of the Rear Army. Liu I was degraded to this rank in 410 (see his biography in *Chin shu* 85, 2b). He was also at this time Governor of Yü-chou 豫州 with his headquarters at Ku-shu 姑孰 (modern Tang-t'u, Anhui). For Yin to have been Aide to Liu I in 410, to have held the post at Hsün-yang, mentioned in T'ao's preface and to have left early in 411, there would seem to have been hardly sufficient time. Lu Ch'in-li (p. 232) suggested that Yin continued with Liu I, when the latter became concurrently Governor of Chiang-chou in 411 and that he resigned and remained at Hsün-yang, when Liu I went to Chiang-ling as Governor-General of Ching-chou in the fourth month of 412. He then went east to serve Liu Yü on the latter's return from Chiang-ling to the capital in the second month of 413.

While it is possible to approve Lu Ch'in-li's conclusion as fitting the content of T'ao's poem, there are some points of detail which require further attention. Liu I's biography in *Chin shu* (loc. cit.) states that after being degraded to General of the Rear Army he subsequently became Guard General (*wei chiang-chün*; this was the military rank he had previously had) and Governor-General of Chiang-chou. This would seem to imply that Liu I was restored to the higher rank, when he became Governor-General of Chiang-chou in 411. *Sung shu* 2, 1a, recording Liu I's transfer to Ching-chou in the fourth month of 412, refers to him as General of the Rear Army, while *Sung shu* 67 (Biography of Hsieh Ling-yün; Hsieh, like Yin Ching-jen, went from Liu I's service to that of Liu Yü), 1a specifies that Liu I was Guard General during 412, when he was at Chiang-ling. The probability is that Liu I was still General of the Rear Army on taking up his governor-generalship of Chiang-chou and that there is an error in the *Chin shu* biography.

Lu Ch'in-li seems to equate Yin Ching-jen's post as Aide to Liu I, General of the Rear Army and the *Chin-an nan-fu ch'ang-shih yüan* of T'ao's preface.

But it must be noted that Liu I on taking over Chiang-chou in addition to his former province of Yü-chou, did not move to Hsün-yang, but set up his headquarters at Yü-chang 豫章 (modern Nan-ch'ang, Kiangsi). This is made clear by a memorial, recorded in his biography in *Chin shu* 85, 3a and also in *Sung shu* 52 (Biography of Yü Yüeh), 2a. It may be that Yin Ching-jen gave up his post as Aide to Liu I on or before becoming *Chin-an nan-fu ch'ang-shih yüan*.

There are two Buddhist pieces in the collection *Kuang hung-ming chi* (ch. 15, p. 198–99), which bear Yin's name in the form Yin Chin-an. These may very well have been written during Yin's stay in Hsün-yang. This leads us to an aspect of the present problem, which, so far as I am aware, has gone unnoticed. We know from the statement which appears at the end of Hui-yüan's *Wan-fo-ying ming* 萬佛影銘 (*Inscription on the Buddha's Shadow*) in *Kuang hung-ming chi*, chapter 15, p. 198, 2 that on the first day of the fifth month of 412 Hui-yüan had a Fo-ying t'ai (Buddha's Shadow Terrace) erected on Lu-shan and that his inscription was cut in stone on the third day of the ninth month of 413. The *Lu-shan chi* of Ch'en Shun-yü (ch. 1, p. 1029, 3) quotes a similar statement as coming from Hui-yüan's *K'uang[-Lu]-shan chi* and follows it with the words: 孟江州懷玉，王別駕喬之，張常侍野，殷晉安隱，毛黃門修之，宗隱士炳，孟散騎，孟司馬二人名闕，殷主簿蔚，范孝廉悦之，王參軍穆夜等咸賦銘讚 'Meng (Chiang-chou) Huai-yü, Wang (*pieh-chia*) Ch'iao-chih, Chang (*ch'ang-shih*) Yeh, Yin (Chin-an) Yin, Mao (*Huang-men*) Hsiu-chih, Tsung (*yin-shih*) Ping, Meng (*san-ch'i*), Meng (*ssu-ma*), the personal names of these men are missing, Yin (*chu-pu*) Wei, Fan (*hsiao-lien*) Yüeh-chih and Wang (*ts'an-chün*) Mu-yeh all composed inscriptions and eulogies.' *Fo-tsu t'ung-chi*, chapter 26, p. 261, 2 has the same names with the exception of Meng *san-ch'i* and Meng *ssu-ma*. The author Chih-p'an, however, changed the form of the names. Thus Yin Yin appears as 晉安太守殷隱, 'the Prefect of Chin-an Yin Yin'. This is simply an incorrect assumption on Chih-p'an's part from 'Chin-an'. He also makes Meng Huai-yü, the Governor of Chiang-chou (*ts'e-shih*) 'Prefect of Chiang-chou' (*t'ai-shou*).

We have here apparently a further valuable piece of evidence for dating T'ao's poem. Nevertheless a new difficulty arises. Li Kung-huan's edition of the works has under the title of the poem the comment 景仁名鐵 'Ching-jen, personal name T'ieh'. Liu Chih-chi in his *Shih-t'ung* (8, 5a) also established that the personal name of Yin Ching-jen (Ching-jen being his courtesy-name under which he was generally known) was T'ieh by reference to *Sung shu* (Biography of Liu Chan) 2b and *Nan shih* 33 (Biography of Fan T'ai), 2b. Unless we are to believe that Yin Ching-jen and Yin Yin are not the same person and that there were at Hsün-yang at almost the same time two persons both referred to as Yin Chin-an within the same general group, then we must probably conclude that Yin changed his personal name from Yin to T'ieh. There of course remains the possibility of error in one of the two.

I believe that we may safely take this Yin Yin to be Yin Ching-jen. We have thus a confirmation of Yin's presence at Hsün-yang in 412, and the dating of T'ao's poem in 413 is indirectly strengthened.

Additional Notes

LINE 1. The variant readings 少 and 久 may simply be the result of graphic confusion. *Shao* is probably to be preferred as giving a slightly less usual expression. Ku Chih notes a close parallel in *Chin shu* 83 (Biography of Yüan Ch'iao), 3b (Yüan Ch'iao's letter breaking off relations with General of the Army of the Left Ch'u P'ou).

LINE 3. *Hsin-su:* this expression has its earliest example in *Song* 159, 3: 於女信宿 'With you I shall pass two nights' (cf. also *Song* 284).

LINE 6. *Po* seems to be the *Songs* particle (*Song* 2 *et passim*), commonly used in the regular four-word poems of this period.

LINE 9. For *yü-mo*, see Additional Note to *Charge to My Son*, IV, 5, p. 26.

LINE 12. *Hsing yen* (*yen* is a particle) is from *Song* 207, 3 (a song of the troubles of office): 興言出宿 'I rise, go out and spend the night.'

27 TO CHIEF OF STAFF YANG

贈羊長史

序　左軍羊長史，銜使秦川。作此與之。

愚生三季後	路若經商山
慨然念黃虞	爲我少躊躇
得知千載外	多謝綺與甪
4　正賴古人書	精爽今何如　16
賢聖留餘迹	紫芝誰復採
事事在中都	深谷久應蕪
豈忘游心目	駟馬無貰患
8　關河不可踰	貧賤有交娛　20
九域甫已一	清謠結心曲
逝將理舟輿	人乖運見疏
聞君當先邁	擁懷累代下
12　負痾不獲俱	言盡意不舒　24

Additional Notes

LINE 1. For the expression *san-chi hou*, cf. *Han shu* 100B, 5b.

LINE 2. Cf. *The Revolution of the Seasons*, IV, 7–8, p.3.

LINE 15. Besides Ch'i-li Chi 綺里季 and Lu-li hsien-sheng 用里先生, whom T'ao mentions, the 'Four White-heads' included Tung-yüan kung 東園公 and Hsia-huang kung 夏黃公: see Huang-fu Mi's *Kao-shih chuan* 7a–b, where their song (often referred to as *Tzu-chih ko* 紫芝歌 'The Purple Agaric Song'), on which T'ao draws heavily in his poem, may be found.

LINE 16. The *locus classicus* for the term *ching-shuang* is *Tso-chuan*, Chao seventh year.

LINE 21. For the expression *chieh hsin-ch'ü*, cf. Chang Hsieh, *Tsa-shih*, I (*Wen-hsüan* 29, 35b). The phrase *hsin-ch'ü* appears first in *Song* 128, 1.

28 AT THE END OF THE YEAR ANSWERING A POEM BY ATTENDANT CHANG

歲暮和張常侍

市朝懷舊人	厲厲氣遂嚴
驟驥感悲泉	紛紛飛鳥還　12
明旦非今日	民生鮮常在
歲暮余何言　(4)	矧伊愁苦纏
素顏歛光潤	屢闕清酤至
白髮一已繁	無以樂當年　16
闊哉秦穆談	窮通靡攸慮
旅力豈未愆　(8)	顦顇由化遷
向夕長風起	撫己有深懷
寒雲沒西山	履運增慨然　20

Additional Notes

LINE 1. For the use of the expression *shih-ch'ao*, see Additional Note to *Returning to Live in the Country*, IV, 13, p. 40.

LINE 2. *Pei-ch'üan* 'Sad Springs', the last stage in the sun's daily journey, i.e. nightfall, will suggest death, just as 'year's end' in line 4 suggests life's end.

LINES 7–8. The text of the *Shu* (*Ch'in-shih*) to which T'ao refers reads: 耆耆 [= 皤] 良士, 旅力既愆, 我尚有之 'The white-haired excellent officers, whose strength has failed, I prefer to have them.'

LINE 20. There is a closely similar line in a poem by a contemporary of T'ao, Hsieh Chan: 履運傷荏苒 'Following the cycle of the seasons, I grieve at their alternation' (*Yü An-ch'eng ta Ling-yün* 於安城答靈運 *At An-ch'eng In Reply to Hsieh Ling-yün*, *Wen-hsüan* 25, 29b).

29 ANSWERING A POEM BY PERSONNEL SECRETARY HU ADDRESSED TO LEGAL SECRETARY KU

和胡西曹示顧賊曹

蕤賓五月中	於今甚可愛
清朝起南颸	奈何當復衰
不駛亦不遲	感物願及時
4 飄飄吹我衣	每恨靡所揮 12
重雲蔽白日	悠悠待秋稼
閒雨紛微微	寥落將賒遲
流目視西園	逸想不可淹
8 曄曄榮紫葵	猖狂獨長悲 16

Additional Notes

TITLE. The Personnel Secretary seems to have been a subordinate of the governor of a province (*chou ts'e-shih*), while the Legal Secretary was a subordinate of the prefect of a commandery (*chün t'ai-shou*), see *T'ung-tien* 32 sub *tsung-lun chou-tso*, p. 185 and ibid. 33 sub *tsung-lun chün-tso*, p. 189.

LINE 5. This line is a reminiscence of *Old Poem*, I, 11: 浮雲蔽白日.

LINE 11. In the context I think that it is more probably T'ao's favourite *Old Poem*, XV, 5–6: 為樂當及時, 何能待來茲 'To be happy one must match the time;/How can one wait for the coming years?' which underlies *chi-shih* rather than the possible alternative reference to *Wen-yen* commentary to *I*, hexagram 1: 君子進德修業，欲及時也 'The gentleman promotes his moral power and cultivates his studies, because he wishes to match the time, i.e. be equal to opportunities.' Those who follow Wang Yao in thinking that this is a poem of self-exhortation to achievement would prefer the latter.

LINE 12. *Hui* stands for *hui-pei* 揮杯, cf. *The Revolution of the Seasons*, II, 7, p. 4.

30 GRIEVING FOR MY COUSIN CHUNG-TE

悲從弟仲德

街哀過舊宅		二胤纏數齡	12
悲淚應心零		雙位委空館 +	
借問為誰悲		朝夕無哭聲	
懷人在九冥	4	流塵集虛坐	
禮服名羣從		宿草旅前庭	16
恩愛若同生		階除曠遊迹	
門前執手時		園林獨餘情	
何意爾先傾	8	翳然乘化去	
在數竟不免 *		終天不復形	20
為山不及成		遲遲將回步	
慈母沉哀疚		惻惻悲襟盈	

* 數，曾集本作毀，註云一作數。今從之。
+ 位，曾集本作泣，註云一作位。今從之。

Additional Notes

LINE 1. The opening line is possibly reminiscent of the first line of Hsi K'ang's poem *Yü Juan Te-ju* 與阮德如 (*Works* 1, 11b): 含哀還舊廬 'Filled with sorrow, I return to my old house.'

LINE 2. For an earlier example of this figure see P'an Yüeh's *Tao-wang shih* 悼亡詩, III (*Wen-hsüan* 23, 26b).

LINE 11. It does not seem necessary to understand *tz'u-mu* as 'foster-mother' here, as some have done. There are many instances of *tz'u* as a more or less conventional epithet for *mu*.

3

DATED AND OTHER POEMS

31 WRITTEN WHEN PASSING THROUGH CH'Ü-O WHILE BEGINNING MY SERVICE AS AIDE TO THE GENERAL OF THE STABILIZATION ARMY

始作鎮軍參軍經曲阿

弱齡寄事外		我行豈不遙	
委懷在琴書		登降千里餘 +	12
被褐欣自得		目倦川塗異	
屢空常晏如	4	心念山澤居	
時來苟冥會		望雲慚高鳥	
宛轡憩通衢 *		臨水愧游魚	16
投策命晨裝		真想初在襟	
暫與園田疏	8	誰謂形迹拘	
眇眇孤舟逝		聊且憑化遷	
綿綿歸思紆		終返班生廬	20

* 宛轡，陶注云，各本作婉孌，此從文選作宛轡。
+ 降，陶注云，各本作陟，此從文選。

Additional Commentary

Once the idea that T'ao Yüan-ming *would* not have served Liu Yü is dismissed, there can be no reason to identify the Chen-chün general of the title as any other person. Although T'ao Shu's attempt to establish that Liu Lao-chih was the general of the title (see *nien-p'u k'ao-i*, sub Lung-an 5 for his later argument) has still found acceptance by some recent writers, it remains a piece of unsupported speculation. (An early protest against T'ao Shu and the belief that Yüan-ming would not have served Liu Yü is to be found in Pao Shih-ch'en's *I-chou shuang-chi*, 9, 28b, under the heading *Shu Han wen hou hsia-p'ien* 書韓文後下篇 .) While there is no reason to doubt that Liu Yü became acting Chen-chün General in the third month of 404 as stated in *Chin shu* 10 (An-ti Annals), 4a, there is a considerable objection to dating this poem 404. As Chang Chih (p. 36) specifically pointed out, *Written in the Third Month of the Year I-ssu* (405) begins with the words: 'Since last I trod this ground,/A good many years and months have piled up.' Since these words, if taken literally, refer to a part of the Yangtze near modern Kuei-ch'ih, i.e. lying between Hsün-yang (modern Kiukiang) and the capital (modern Nanking), it seems impossible that T'ao could have passed down the Yangtze in the previous year, as he would have had to have done to reach Ch'ü-o, which is downriver from Nanking. Even if these words were understood metaphorically, as they might possibly be, i.e. 'It is a good many years since I was in the position of going on service', the difficulty would not be lessened. Young Yong (*Chiao-chien*, p. 432), although he does not refer to the difficulty in his discussion of this poem, does make an attempt to solve it under *Written in the Third Month of the Year I-ssu* by suggesting that in 404 (on the way to Ch'ü-o) he was travelling hurriedly, but in 405 he could make a close inspection. This is very unconvincing.

The solution which I have suggested in the Commentary (see vol. 1, p. 81) has not hitherto been looked for, because the early biographies of T'ao have largely been accepted too uncritically. The detailed examination I have provided ought to show that this is unwarranted. My reversal of the order of T'ao's two appointments as Aide requires that Liu Yü should have continued to have the rank of Chen-chün after the third month of 405. In fact this seems to have been the case. Although the emperor conferred on Liu Yü in the third month of 405 the new military rank of General of Chariots and Cavalry (*Ch'e-ch'i chiang-chün* 車騎將軍) together with high civil office, according to the *Sung shu* (1, 7b) he firmly declined and continued to refuse in the face of determined attempts to secure his acceptance. According to the same source, the same rank was re-conferred and again refused more than a year and a half later.

Additional Notes

LINES 1–2. Cf. *Drinking Wine*, XVI, 1–2. For 'lute and books' as symbols of retirement see Additional Note to *Reply to Aide P'ang*, I,2, p. 17.

LINE 4. 'Often empty' may be described as a favourite quotation for T'ao. It occurs also in *Drinking Wine*, XI, 3 and in *Biography of the Gentleman of the Five Willows*, where as here it is followed by the expression *yen ju* 'at peace'. It may also be noted that *yen ju* is used to describe the attitude of Yang Hsiung in his poverty (see *Han shu* 87A, 2a). Yang Hsiung was certainly one of T'ao's models.

LINES 15–16. Ku Chih cites *Chuang-tzu* 23 (8A, 3b–4a): 鳥獸不厭高，
魚鼈不厭深．夫全其形生之人藏其身也不厭深眇而已矣 'Birds and beasts do
not weary of the heights; fish and turtles do not weary of the depths. So the
man who would complete his body's life hides his person and simply does not
weary of deep retirement' and remarks that the idea of T'ao's poem is based
on this. While one may agree that this passage could have been in the poet's
mind, his own thought seems to proceed to a different conclusion. Although
he is made ashamed by the birds and fish which keep to their natural element,
while he has left his, yet he goes on to maintain in the following lines that his
true self is unchanged.

LINE 20. 'Master Pan's dwelling' is a reference to Pan Ku's *Yu-t'ung fu*
幽通賦 (*Wen-hsüan* 14, 14b) where he says of his father: 終保己而貽則兮里上
仁之所廬 'Finally he preserved himself and handed down an example./He
dwelt where the highest goodness resided.' This in turn contains a reference
to *Lun-yü* 4, 1.

32 DETAINED BY CONTRARY WINDS AT KUEI-LIN WHILE RETURNING FROM THE CAPITAL DURING THE FIFTH MONTH OF THE YEAR KENG-TZU

庚子歲五月中從都還阻風於規林

I

行行循歸路	凱風負我心	
計日望舊居	戢枻守窮湖	
一欣侍溫顏	高莽眇無界	
4　再喜見友于	夏木獨森疎	12
鼓棹路崎曲	誰言客舟遠	
指景限西隅	近瞻百里餘	
江山豈不險	延目識南嶺	
8　歸子念前塗	空歎將焉如	16

II

自古歎行役	久游戀所生	
我今始知之	如何淹在茲	8
山川一何曠	靜念園林好	
4　巽坎難與期	人間良可辭	
崩浪聒天響	當年詎有幾	
長風無息時	縱心復何疑	12

Additional Notes

TITLE. Kuei-lin has not been identified.

I, 3. Wang Yao would see the word *wen* as referring to a son's duty to see that his parents are warm in winter (and cool in summer). I should prefer the sense of 'genial', 'kind' (characteristic quality of parents).

I, 4. The use of the expression *yu yü* (originally 'friendly to sc. brothers') does not originate here in the extended use of 'brothers'. As T'ao Shu noted, it was already so used by Ts'ao Chih in his memorial *Ch'iu-t'ung ch'in-ch'in piao* 求通親親表 (*San-kuo chih, Wei shu* 19, 12b).

I, 9. *K'ai-feng* 'the Joyous [South] Wind' must be intended to suggest the desire of his mother to see him and his desire to see her, in addition to the literal meaning that it is the south wind which holds him up. For *k'ai-feng* from *Song* 32 (the Mao and other schools differed about the intention of this song, see Wang Hsien-ch'ien, *Shih san-chia i chi-shu* 3A, 22aff.) is quite commonly used during the Han and Six Dynasties periods (for examples see Wang Hsien-ch'ien, loc. cit.) to represent the grief of a mother and her son's concern; cf. T'ao's own use of the allusion in *Biography of His Excellency Meng*, p. 145. It appears from all the examples that the view of the Lu and Ch'i schools rather than that of the Mao was accepted, and that T'ao accorded with the general practice.

II, 1. 'From of old' . . . T'ao possibly had in mind *Song* 110 which is a lament for a man going on military service.

II, 7. This line is reminiscent of a Han *yüeh-fu*, *Ch'ang-ko hsing* 長歌行 No. 3, l.4 (*Yüeh-fu shih chi* 30, 3b): 遊子戀所生 'The wanderer longs for her who bore him.' This *yüeh-fu* contains the same allusive *k'ai-feng* as I, 9 above.

33   WRITTEN IN THE SEVENTH MONTH OF THE YEAR HSIN-CH'OU WHILE PASSING THROUGH T'U-K'OU AT NIGHT WHEN RETURNING TO CHIANG-LING FROM LEAVE

辛丑歲七月赴假還江陵夜行塗口*

閒居三十載	如何舍此去
遂與塵事冥	遙遙至西荊+
詩書敦宿好	叩枻新秋月
林園無俗情	臨流別友生

4   8

* 塗口，陶注云，各本作塗中，此從文選。
+ 西，陶注云，各本作南。非。

涼風起將夕
夜景湛虛明
昭昭天宇闊
皛皛川上平
懷役不遑寐
中宵尚孤征
商歌非吾事
依依在耦耕
投冠旋舊墟
不爲好爵縈
養眞衡茅下
庶以善自名

Additional Notes

LINES 1–2. Li Shan in his commentary to this poem, which was included in the *Wen-hsüan* (26, 28b), quotes the *Shuo-wen* which glosses 冥 as 窈 'remote', and his understanding has been generally followed. Thus the first two lines have generally been read: 'I lived in retirement for thirty years, thus I was remote from dusty affairs.' This reading does not accord very well with the poet's actual situation in 401 or with the following lines in the poem. I believe that the lines should be understood as in my translation. Good support for understanding *ming* in the sense of 'confused', 'blinded' can be found in *Song* 206, 2 無將大車，維塵冥冥 'Do not lead on the big chariot!/The dust will blind you.' This is certainly a *Song* which T'ao could have had in his mind in the mood of this poem.

LINE 6. *Hsi-Ching*, the reading of the *Wen-hsüan* text, 'Ching-chou in the west' is certainly correct. The *nan-Ching* of the collected works must be the result of an erroneous correction made at a period when, in a reunified empire, Ching-chou resumed its relatively southern position.

LINE 15. The most complete versions of the story of Ning Ch'i's gaining the notice of Duke Huan of Ch'i occur in *Lü-shih ch'un-ch'iu* 19, 20a–b and *Huai-nan-tzu* 12, 5b (which has in its current text Ning Yüeh 越 in error for Ning Ch'i). 'Ning Ch'i wished to bring himself to the notice of Duke Huan of Ch'i, but he was in want and had no means of putting himself forward. So he became a travelling merchant and came to Ch'i in a cart. In the evening he stopped for the night outside the gate in the outer wall. Duke Huan was welcoming a guest on the outskirts of the city. During the night the gate was opened and the ruler rode out in a carriage. The torch lights were very numerous; the followers were a great crowd. Ning Ch'i was feeding his ox beneath his cart. He looked at Duke Huan from a distance and grieved. He struck the ox's horn and sang a sad Shang [*Lü-shih ch'un-ch'iu* lacks 'Shang'] song. [According to some versions of the story Ning Ch'i sang *Song* 113, see Kao Yu's commentary to *Lü-shih ch'un-ch'iu.*] When Duke Huan heard him, he grasped his driver's hand and said: "It is strange! This singer is an unusual man." He ordered one of the rear carriages to fetch him.'

LINE 16. 'To be a plough-mate' will refer to the story of Ch'ang-chü and Chieh-ni for which see Additional Note to *At the Beginning of Spring in the Year Kuei-mao*, II, 12, p. 74. Cf. also *To Encourage Farming*, IV, 4.

LINE 18. There would seem probably to be some reference here to *I*, hexagram 61: 我有好爵，吾與爾靡之 'I have an excellent wine-cup; you and I will share it.' Since *chüeh* acquired the secondary meaning of 'noble rank' and thus 'office', a pun could be made with *hao-chüeh* (excellent wine-cup — important office). In view of the similarity of 縻 and 爢 which occurs as a variant for the 靡 of the *I* text, I wonder whether T'ao could have written 不爲好爵爢 , i.e. and not practise excellent wine-cup (office) sharing. The sense of the line would not in any case be altered.

34 AT THE BEGINNING OF SPRING IN THE YEAR KUEI-MAO THINKING OF THE ANCIENTS ON MY FARM

癸卯歲始春懷古田舍

I

在昔聞南畝　　　　　冷風送餘寒* 8
當年竟未踐　　　　　寒竹被荒蹊
屢空既有人　　　　　地爲罕人遠
春興豈自免 4　　　　是以植杖翁
夙晨裝吾駕　　　　　悠然不復返 12
啓塗情已緬　　　　　即理愧通識
鳥哢歡新節　　　　　所保詎乃淺

* 餘寒，各本作餘善，今改作餘寒。

II

先師有遺訓　　　　　雖未量歲功
憂道不憂貧　　　　　即事多所欣
瞻望邈難逮　　　　　耕種有時息
轉欲志長勤 4　　　　行者無問津 12
秉耒歡時務　　　　　日入相與歸
解顏勸農人　　　　　壺漿勞近鄰
平疇交遠風　　　　　長吟掩柴門
良苗亦懷新 8　　　　聊爲隴畝民 16

Additional Notes

I, 1. *Nan-mou* 'southern acres' is from the line 饁彼南畝 'we carry food to those southern acres' which occurs in *Songs* 154, 1; 211, 3 and 212.

I, 8. There appears to be a slight corruption of the text here. Most texts read 鳥哢歡新節, 冷風送餘善 and note as a variant 鳥哢新節冷, 風送餘寒善. 送餘善 would seem a slightly strange expression (?'brings superabundant delights'). I think the true reading of line 8 is probably 冷風送餘寒; the first line of *The Day of the Cha Sacrifice* would provide a good parallel. It is not easy to explain how 善 came in. It is just possible perhaps that it was accidentally interpolated from an editor's quotation of the well-known passage in *Chuang-tzu* 1 (1A, 9b): 列子御風而行, 冷然善也 to illustrate 冷風.

I, 11. Chih-chang weng (in Hsi K'ang's *Sheng-hsien kao-shih chuan* he became Ho-tiao chang-jen 荷蓧丈人, see Yen K'o-chün, *Ch'üan San-kuo wen* 52, 5b) comes from *Lun-yü* 18, 7. 'When Tzu-lu was following [the Master], he fell behind and met an old man, carrying a basket on his staff. Tzu-lu asked him: "Have you seen my master?" The old man said: "You who do not toil with your four limbs, who do not distinguish the five grains — who is your master?" And he planted his staff and started to weed; Tzu-lu stood with folded hands. He kept Tzu-lu for the night, killed a fowl and prepared millet to make him a meal, and introduced his two sons to him. The next day Tzu-lu went on and told what had taken place. The Master said: "He is a recluse," and he told Tzu-lu to go back and see him again. When he reached the place, the old man had gone.' The received text of the *Lun-yü* continues with the following sentences which are probably displaced from the above conversation: 'Tzu-lu said: "Not to take service is not right. If the rules that apply to old and young cannot be disregarded, how should the duties of prince and minister be disregarded? By wishing to keep his person pure, he puts the great relationship in confusion. The gentleman in his service carries out his duty. That the Way is not practised, he knows beforehand."''

II, 2. *Lun-yü* 15, 31 reads: 'The Master said: "The gentleman takes thought about the Way, he does not take thought about a livelihood. In farming want may be involved, in learning emolument may be involved. But the gentleman is anxious about the Way; he is not anxious about poverty."''

II, 3. T'ao very possibly had Yen Yüan's lament on the difficulty of following Confucius' doctrines in mind. *Lun-yü* 9, 10: 'Yen Yüan said with a deep sigh: "When I look up at them, they become still loftier; when I bore into them, they become still harder. When I gaze at them in front of me, suddenly they are behind me. The Master step by step skilfully entices one on. He broadens me with culture, he restrains me with ritual. Though I wish to stop, I am not able. When I have exhausted all my ability, it is as though there were something towering up before me, and though I want to follow it, I am quite without means." '

II, 12. The story of Ch'ang-chü and Chieh-ni (they also were included in Hsi K'ang's *Sheng-hsien kao-shih chuan*, see loc. cit., 5a) in *Lun-yü* 18, 6 reads: 'Ch'ang-chü and Chieh-ni were ploughing together as plough-mates. Master K'ung passed by them and sent Tzu-lu to ask where there was a ford. Ch'ang-chü said: "For whom are you driving?" Tzu-lu said: "For K'ung Ch'iu." He said: "Is it not that K'ung Ch'iu of Lu?" Tzu-lu said: "It is." He said: "He already knows the ford." Tzu-lu asked Chieh-ni. Chieh-ni said: "Who are you?" He said: "I am Chung Yu." Chieh-ni said: "Are you not a follower of K'ung Ch'iu?" He said: "That is so." Chieh-ni said: "Everyone in the empire is swept away. Who can change it? Rather than follow one who withdraws from particular men, would it not be better to follow one who withdraws from the whole generation?" And he continued covering the seed. Tzu-lu went and told the Master, who said with a sigh: "One cannot flock together with birds and beasts. If I cannot associate with such men as there are, with whom can I associate? If the empire possessed the Way, I should not be trying to change it." '

35 WRITTEN IN THE TWELFTH MONTH OF THE YEAR KUEI-MAO FOR MY COUSIN CHING-YUAN

癸卯歲十二月中作與從弟敬遠

寢迹衡門下
邈與世相絶
顧眄莫誰知
荊扉晝常閉 (4)
淒淒歲暮風
翳翳經日雪
傾耳無希聲
在目皓已潔 (8)
勁氣侵襟袖
箪瓢謝屢設

蕭索空宇中
了無一可悦 (12)
歷覽千載書
時時見遺烈
高操非所攀
謬得固窮節 (16)
平津茍不由
栖遲詎爲拙
寄意一言外
茲契誰能別 (20)

Additional Notes

LINE 1. *Heng-men hsia* 'under a cross-beam door' is from *Song* 138, cf. *In Reply to Aide P'ang*, I, 1, p. 14.

LINE 4. Cf. *Returning to Live in the Country*, II, 3. This present line is imitated by T'ao's friend Yen Yen-chih in his poem *To Minister of the Imperial Sacrifices Wang* (Wang Seng-ta 王僧達 d. 458; *Wen-hsüan* 26, 1b): 郊扉常晝閒 'The suburban door is constantly shut by day.'

LINE 10. Cf. *Biography of the Gentleman of the Five Willows*, where 'dishes and gourds' are combined with 'often empty'. Both expressions are from the *Lun-yü* and both relate to the disciple Yen Hui: *Lun-yü* 6, 9: 'The Master said: "Worthy indeed was Hui! A single dish of food, a single gourd of drink and living in a mean lane — others could not endure the distress of it. It did not alter his happiness. Worthy indeed was Hui!"' and ibid. 11, 18: 'The Master said: "Hui comes very near [sc. to Goodness] indeed! He is often empty."'

LINE 11. This line is identical in sense with one in Tso Ssu's *Yung-shih* 詠史, Poem IV (*Wen-hsüan* 21, 4b). I have suggested (vol. 1, p. 134) that this series of Tso Ssu provided a model for T'ao's *Singing of Poor Scholars*.

LINE 13. *Ch'ien-tsai shu* 'thousand-year-old books' are probably the Confucian scriptures; cf. *To Chief of Staff Yang*, ll.3–4.

LINE 14. *I-lieh* also occurs in Tso Ssu's *Yung-shih* series (Poem VII, translated vol. 1, p. 134–35).

LINE 16. *Ku-ch'iung* 'firmness in adversity', an expression of which T'ao shows himself to be peculiarly fond, is from *Lun-yü* 15, 1: 'When he [Confucius] was in Ch'en, provisions ran out and his followers became so ill that they could not get up. Tzu-lu indignantly came to see the Master and said: "Does the gentleman also suffer adversity?" The Master said: "The gentleman stands firm in adversity, but the small man when he is in adversity goes to excess."' The Western Chin poet Chang Hsieh had already used this expression in a similar manner; see *Tsa-shih* X (*Wen-hsüan* 29, 43b): 'The gentleman preserves "firmness in adversity".'

LINE 17. P'ing-chin, if it is a proper name as most commentators have thought, will be Kung-sun Hung, Chancellor of Han Wu-ti, who was enfeoffed as Marquis of P'ing-chin in 124 BC. T'ao would then be saying that he cannot follow Kung-sun Hung in his diplomatic attitude to the ruler, which in spite of his moral qualities earned him the name of flatterer. An alternative interpretation, which I have adopted, is to understand *p'ing-chin* as the 'highway' of public life, cf. *t'ung-chin* in *Singing of the Three Good Men*, l.1, p. 125.

LINE 18. *Hsi-ch'ih* 'to be at rest' is again from *Song* 138, see Additional Note to line 1 above.

LINE 19. Cf. *In Sacrifice for My Cousin Ching-yüan*, 1.52, p. 160.

36   WRITTEN IN THE THIRD MONTH OF THE YEAR I-SSU WHEN PASSING CH'IEN-CH'I WHILE ON A MISSION TO THE CAPITAL AS AIDE TO THE ESTABLISHING MAJESTY GENERAL

乙巳歲三月爲建威參軍使都經錢溪

我不踐斯境	伊余何爲者	
歲月好已積	勉勵從茲役	
晨夕看山川	一形似有制	
4 事事悉如昔	素襟不可易	12
微雨洗高林	園田日夢想	
清飇矯雲翮	安得久離析	
眷彼品物存	終懷在壑舟 *	
8 義風都未隔	諒哉宜霜柏	16

* 壑，各本作歸，陶注本從何校宣和本作壑。

Additional Commentary

The Chien-wei General of the title was identified as Liu Huai-su 劉懷肅 (367–407) by Wu Jen-chieh, who also mistakenly made him Governor of Chiang-chou. *Chin shu* 10, 5a states: 'In the third month of 405 Huan Chen 桓振 again made a surprise attack on Chiang-ling. The Governor of Ching-chou, Ssu-ma Hsiu-chih 司馬休之, fled to Hsiang-yang. The Chien-wei General, Liu Huai-su, suppressed Chen and beheaded him.' This statement is repeated in the biography of Huan Chen (*Chin shu* 74, 4a–b), which adds the detail that it was the Kuang-wu General, T'ang Hsing 唐興, who beheaded Chen. It is accepted by Ssu-ma Kuang in *Tzu-chih t'ung-chien* 114, p. 3581.

Wu Chan-t'ai, however, cited a remark from Liu Huai-su's biography in *Sung shu* 47, 1b, which seems to imply that Liu was at this time not Chien-wei General but Fu-kuo General. Wu then suggested a new identification which was accepted by T'ao Shu and by most modern critics (Young Yong, *Chiao-chien*, pp. 431–33, is an exception in defending Wu Jen-chieh even to the extent of arguing that Liu Huai-su was Governor of Chiang-chou, which is certainly wrong), viz. that the Chien-wei General of T'ao's title was Liu Ching-hsüan 劉敬宣, the eldest son of the former northern commander Liu Lao-chih. In Liu Ching-hsüan's biography in *Chin shu* 84, 6a and *Sung shu* 47, 5b there is the statement that he was transferred to the posts of Chien-wei General and Governor of Chiang-chou. From the context it would seem probable that Liu Ching-hsüan's appointment to Chiang-chou dated from the fourth month of 404; Ssu-ma Kuang (*Tzu-chih t'ung-chien* 113, p. 3570) placed it under this month. According to both *Chin shu* 84 and *Sung shu* 47 Liu Ching-hsüan had the rank of Fu-kuo General before this new appointment.

Now, there is a further reference to Liu Huai-su as Chien-wei General, which is probably to be dated the fifth month of 404. *Chin shu* 99 (Biography of Huan Hsüan), 10a states that Liu T'ung 劉統 and Feng Chih 馮稚, former generals of Huan Hsüan, collected four hundred partisans, attacked and broke into Hsün-yang. Liu I 劉毅 sent the Chien-wei General Liu Huai-su to suppress them. *Chin shu* 85 (Biography of Liu I), 1b in referring to the same event reads for 'Chien-wei' an impossible 'Wu-wei' 武威 which must be a graphic error for the former term. Ssu-ma Kuang (ibid., p. 3571) placed these events under the fifth month of 404. There seems thus to be some confusion in the histories over the titles of Liu Huai-su and Liu Ching-hsüan. The problem can, however, be taken a little further than has yet been done by the commentators on T'ao Yüan-ming.

If we consider first the title of Fu-kuo General, we find evidence that this rank was held by Ho Wu-chi 何無忌, a cousin of Liu Ching-hsüan, from the fourth month of 404 (see *Chin shu* 10, 4a; ibid. 85, Biography of Ho Wu-chi, 6b and fragment of Hsü Yüan's *Sung shu* ap. *T'ai-p'ing yü-lan* 128, 2b) until he became General of the Right in the new conferring of titles after the return of Emperor An to the capital in the third month of 405 (see *Chin shu* 85, 7a). At this time, the title of Fu-kuo General passed to Liu Tao-kuei 劉道規, Liu Yü's youngest brother (see *Sung shu* 51, 7a). It would thus seem that when Liu Ching-hsüan was appointed to be Governor of Chiang-chou in the fourth month of 404, his title of Fu-kuo General passed to Ho Wu-chi. As Governor of Chiang-chou it is very probable that he would have had a title as a general, but it is unlikely that he would have gone from Fu-kuo to Chien-wei General, as this would have been a demotion. It was presumably his belief that the histories must be incorrect on this point that led Ssu-ma Kuang to omit any mention of it.

From the above it seems that Wu Chan-t'ai's objection to Wu Jen-chieh's identification is not valid and that the view that T'ao was Aide to Liu Ching-hsüan may be discarded. The evidence would seem definitely to point to Liu Huai-su having been Chien-wei General in the third month of 405, the time when this poem was written. At what point T'ao joined Liu Huai-su cannot be determined.

Additional Notes

LINE 7. The *locus classicus* for *p'in-wu* 'all things in their kinds' is in the *t'uan* commentary to *I*, hexagram 1.

LINE 15. This line, if the reading *ho* 壑 is adopted, will contain a reference to the saying in *Chuang-tzu* 6 (3A, 11a): 'You may hide a boat in a gully, you may hide a fish-trap [reading 山 as 汕, as suggested by Yü Yüeh, *Chu-tzu p'ing-i* 17, p. 338] in a marsh, but at midnight a strong man may come and bear them away on his back. The stupid do not realize.' T'ao seems to understand this in the sense of Kuo Hsiang's commentary, i.e. that one must accept and submit to change. 'Of forces without apparent force none is greater than that of change.... The old does not gradually cease, but all of a sudden has passed into the new.... Therefore the I that I was a little while ago is not still the I that I am now. I and now go together. Surely one cannot always preserve the old.' Cf. also *Miscellaneous Poem*, V, 11, p. 115.

LINE 16. *Shuang-po* 'the frosty cypress' could be an allusion either to *Lun-yü* 9, 27 or *Chuang-tzu* 28 (9B, 11b). The two passages are obviously connected, although the interpretation of the metaphor of the 'frosty cypress' as expressing the quality of the gentleman, which stands out in troubled times, in the case of the *Lun-yü* only appears in later commentary to the original text. *Lun-yü* 9, 27, which has no context reads: 'It is only when the year turns cold that we know that the pine and cypress are the last to fade.' (For the relation of the metaphor to the gentleman see *Lun-yü chi-chieh i-shu* 5, p. 128) The *Chuang-tzu* passage occurs in a context where Confucius explains to Tzu-lu and Tzu-kung why he bore his various ordeals with equanimity. 'Confucius said: "... The gentleman calls succeeding in the Way success and failure in the Way failure. Now I cherish the Way of Goodness and Righteousness and through it I have met with the misfortunes of a disorderly age. Why should I regard it as failure? So it is that I look within and find no failure in the Way and in the face of difficulties I do not lose its power. When the great [reading 大 as proposed by Yü Yüeh, *Chu-tzu p'ing-i* 19, p. 379] cold has come and the frost and snow have descended, it is then that we know the vigour of the pine and cypress."' For another version of this *Chuang-tzu* passage, see *Lü-shih ch'un-ch'iu* 14, 17b–18a.

37 RETURNING TO MY OLD HOME

還 舊 居

<table>
<tr><td>疇昔家上京</td><td>今日始復來</td></tr>
<tr><td>六載去還歸</td><td>惻愴多所悲　　4</td></tr>
</table>

阡陌不移舊　　　　流幻百年中
邑屋或時非　　　　寒暑日相推　　12
履歷周故居　　　　常恐大化盡
鄰老罕復遺　　　　氣力不及衰
步步尋往迹　　　　撥置且莫念
有處特依依　　　　一觴聊可揮　　16

8

Additional Commentary

Li Kung-huan in his commentary to this poem quotes from a *Nan-k'ang chih* 南康志, the statement that 'five *li* from the town there is a locality named Shang-ching, where there is a former dwelling of Yüan-ming'. This *Nan-k'ang chih* was probably the work of that name by Chu Tuan-chang, who was Prefect of Nan-k'ang in the Ch'ien-tao period (1165–73) of Southern Sung (Ch'en Chen-sun, *Chih-chai shu-lu chieh-t'i* 8, p. 242 dates it 1175). Chu Tuan-chang's work has not survived. From a probably not very much later date (Chu Hsi was Prefect of Nan-k'ang 1179–82) comes the statement in *Chu-tzu yü-lei* 138, 6b, which has been extensively quoted and often slightly misquoted by the commentators: 'On Lu-shan there is a place with relics of Yüan-ming named Shang-ching. Yüan-ming's collected works read "ching" as in "ching-shih" [capital], but now the local people consider it to be "ching" as in "Ching-Ch'u". In the river there is a flat rock and on the rock may be traced: Yüan-ming in drunkenness slept on this rock. It is called the Rock of Yüan-ming's Drunkenness.' The very words Chu Hsi uses have the air of a legend. In their turn they obviously gave rise to a new reading in T'ao's text, the reading 荊 as a variant for 京. This is not found in the Southern Sung editions of the collected works, but occurs in Mao Chin's Lu-chün t'ing 綠君亭 edition, cited by T'ao Shu. This led Liang Ch'i-ch'ao (p. 48) to propose its adoption as the correct reading and to refer it to Chiang-ling (Ching-chou). This can fairly be described as a ridiculous proposal.

In spite of the general acceptance of Shang-ching as a place on Lu-shan from Li Kung-huan onwards, there has been considerable disagreement about how to understand the title and the first three lines of the poem. T'ao Shu, who dates the poem 405 and understands the 'old home' of the title as Shang-ching, reads the second line as 'for six years I went away and returned again', i.e. in the six years 399–405 (this in Chinese methods of counting would be more likely to be considered seven years) he several times left and returned to Shang-ching. Among modern critics there has been some tendency to understand the second line in the manner of T'ao Shu but to find a different reference for the 'old home' of the title. Thus Ku Chih and Wang Yao would read:

RETURNING TO MY OLD HOME [Ku = Li-li; Wang = Ch'ai-sang]
Formerly while I lived with my family at Shang-ching,
For six years I went to and fro [to my old home].
Today [a later date] I have visited it [my old home] again.

Both Ku (*nien-p'u* sub I-hsi 7) and Wang (p. 71) take the six years which they think T'ao lived at Shang-ching as immediately preceding his move to the 'Southern Village' (see vol. 1, p. 65), which they date 410. Ku counts the six years back to 404 and Wang to 405. Wang gives 417 as a provisional date for the writing of this poem. Change Chih (pp. 51–53) alone, of modern commentators, understands 'shang-ching' as 'the capital'. While I believe that he was correct in this, I believe that his dating of the poem 405, his taking of the 'old home' of the title as Chien-k'ang and his understanding the first two lines as 'Formerly I lived in the capital [he adopts the variant 居];/After six years I have come back to it' is not satisfactory.

Additional Notes

LINE 12. This is a reminiscence of *I, Hsi-tz'u chuan* B, 3: 'The sun goes and the moon comes; the moon goes and the sun comes. Sun and moon replace one another and brightness is thereby produced. The cold goes and the heat comes; the heat goes and the cold comes. Cold and heat replace one another and the year is thereby completed.'

LINE 13. For *ta hua* see *Body, Shadow and Soul*, III, 21, vol. 1, p. 35 n.8.

LINE 14. The decline of vigour associated with the fiftieth year; cf. *Li-chi* 5 (4, 16a): 'In one's fiftieth year one begins to decline.'

38   SUFFERING A FIRE IN THE SIXTH MONTH OF THE YEAR WU-WU

戊午歲六月中遇火＊

草廬寄窮巷	一宅無遺宇
甘以辭華軒	舫舟蔭門前
正夏長風急	迢迢新秋夕
林室頓燒燔	亭亭月將圓

4   8

＊ 戊午，各本作戊申，陶澍所引江州志作戊午，今從之。

	果菜始復生	貞剛自有質	
	驚鳥尚未還	玉石乃非堅	
	中宵竚遙念	仰想東戶時	
12	一盼周九天	餘糧宿中田	20
	緫髮抱孤介	鼓腹無所思	
	奄出四十年	朝起暮歸眠	
	形迹憑化往	既已不遇茲	
16	靈府長獨閒	且遂灌我園	24

Additional Commentary

The *Chiang-chou chih*, quoted by T'ao Shu (*nien-p'u k'ao-i* A, 10b) is probably the work extensively cited in the *Yung-lo ta-tien*, but now no longer extant. Chang Kuo-kan, *Chung-kuo ku fang-chih k'ao*, p. 559, from the contents of the citations in the surviving parts of the *Yung-lo ta-tien*, judges it to have been compiled after the Ch'un-yu period (1241–52) of Southern Sung. T'ao Shu himself thought that the reading *wu-wu* was an error.

Additional Notes

LINE 1. For *ch'iung-hsiang* 'narrow lane' see Additional Note to *Returning to Live in the Country*, II, 2, p. 40.

LINE 16. *Ling-fu* 'spirit's abode' is an elegant substitute for *hsin* 心, taken from *Chuang-tzu* 5 (2C, 14b).

LINES 19–20. The statement that in the time of Tung-hu surplus grain was left overnight in the fields appears in *Huai-nan-tzu* 10, 7b and in a fragment of *Tzu-ssu-tzu* 子思子 in *Ch'u-hsüeh chi* 9, p. 208. Tung-hu, described by Kao Yu in his commentary to the *Huai-nan-tzu* passage as an ancient ruler, is placed by Pan Ku in *Han shu* 20, 5a (*Table of Persons of the Past and Present*; Tung-hu is there written 東扈) under the reign of the first of the legendary emperors T'ai-hao (Fu-hsi).

LINE 21. *Ku fu* 'drummed their bellies' is from *Chuang-tzu* 9 (4B, 6a): 'In the time of Ho-hsü the people were in a state of not knowing what they were doing, of walking without knowing where they were going. They filled their mouths and were glad. They drummed their bellies and took their ease.' In Pan Ku's table (see last note) Ho-hsü is also placed under T'ai-hao.

39 THE NINTH DAY OF THE NINTH MONTH OF THE YEAR CHI-YU

己酉歲九月九日

靡靡秋已夕	萬化相尋繹[+]
淒淒風露交	人生豈不勞
蔓草不復榮	從古皆有沒
4 園木空自凋	念之中心焦 12
清氣澄餘滓	何以稱我情
杳然天界高	濁酒且自陶
哀蟬無留響 [*]	千載非所知
8 叢雁鳴雲霄	聊以永今朝 16

[*] 留，曾集本作歸，註云一作留，陶注本作留。
[+] 繹，陶注云，各本作繹，從何校宣和本作異。

Additional Notes

LINES 1–8. In the first half of the poem in which the external scene is described T'ao drew heavily on *Chiu-pien* I (*Ch'u-tz'u* 8, 1bff), which was clearly a favourite with him and especially associated by him with the Double Ninth, cf. Additional Notes to *Living in Retirement on the Ninth Day*, l.18, p. 36 and *Seeing off a Guest at General Wang's Banquet*, 1.4, p. 59. 悲哉秋之 為氣也，蕭瑟兮草木搖落而變衰 … 沉寥兮天高而氣清 … 蟬寂寞而無聲，雁雝雝而南遊兮，… 'Grievous is autumn's air;/Mournful, plants and trees shed their leaves, change and decay.... Vast and empty, the heavens are high and the air is clear.... The cicadas are silent and make no sound;/The wild geese, crying, travel south.'

LINES 9–10. These lines may contain a reminiscence of *Chuang-tzu* 6 (3A, 10b–12a): 'Now the Great Mass [Nature] contains me with form, makes me labour by life, gives me ease with old age and makes me cease by death.... As for man's form, it undergoes ten thousand transformations and has never a limit.'

LINE 16. The last four characters of this line derive from *Song* 186, 1.

40 HARVESTING THE DRY RICE IN THE WESTERN FIELD IN THE NINTH MONTH OF THE YEAR KENG-HSÜ

庚戌歲九月中於西田穫旱稻*

人生歸有道	田家豈不苦
衣食固其端	弗獲辭此難　　　12
孰是都不營	四體誠乃疲
4　而以求自安	庶無異患干
開春理常業	盥濯息簷下
歲功聊可觀	斗酒散襟顏　　　16
晨出肆微勤	遙遙沮溺心
8　日入負禾還⁺	千載乃相關
山中饒霜露	但願長如此
風氣亦先寒	躬耕非所歎　　　20

* 旱，各本作早，今從丁箋注作旱。
⁺ 禾，曾集本作禾，註云一作耒。

Additional Notes

TITLE. The transmitted title which reads 'early rice' presents a problem, since rice harvested in the ninth month is not early rice. This consideration prompted Lu Ch'in-li to suggest that 'ninth month' should perhaps read 'seventh month' on account of line 10 of the poem (he would seem to understand *hsien han* as 'prematurely cold'). Lines 9–10, however, do not seem a probable description of the seventh month. It seems better to emend *tsao* 早 to *han* 旱 'dry rice' (i.e. rice grown in dry fields), as Ting Fu-pao proposed.

LINES 1–2. Behind these lines would seem to lie the concept enunciated in *Han shu* 24A, 4b: 衣食足而知榮辱，廉讓生而爭訟息 'When clothing and food are sufficient, the people will know honour and disgrace; incorruptibility and giving way to others will arise and contention and litigation cease.'

LINE 8. The variant readings 耒 and 禾 are clearly an example of graphic confusion. The choice between them must be determined by one's understanding of the context, whether T'ao is thought to be describing spring tasks, which would require *lei* or the harvesting which is the subject of the poem, for which *ho* would be appropriate. I have preferred the latter.

LINE 11. There is a probable reminiscence here as in the next poem (*Harvesting on the Farm at Hsia-sun*) of Yang Yün's 楊惲 letter in reply to Sun Hui-tsung 孫會宗, preserved in his biography in *Han shu* 66, 11b: 田家作苦 'As a farmer I perform harsh tasks.'

LINE 13. With 'four limbs" T'ao is probably playing on the rebuke of the Old Man Who Planted His Staff to Tzu-lu in *Lun-yü* 18, 7; see Additional Note to *At the Beginning of Spring in the Year Kuei-mao*, I, 11, p. 73.

LINE 14. Cf. *Returning to Live in the Country*, III, 8 and the next poem, *Harvesting on the Farm at Hsia-sun*, l.4.

LINE 20. Cf. *Moving House*, II, 12.

41 HARVESTING ON THE FARM AT HSIA-SUN IN THE EIGHTH MONTH OF THE YEAR PING-CH'EN

丙辰歲八月中於下潠田舍穫

貧居依稼穡		鬱鬱荒山裏	
勵力東林隈		猿聲閑且哀	12
不言春作苦		悲風愛靜夜	
常恐負所懷	4	林鳥喜晨開	
司田眷有秋		曰余作此來	
寄聲與我諧		三四星火頹	16
飢者歡初飽		姿年逝已老	
束帶候鳴雞	8	其事未云乖	
揚楫越平湖		遙謝荷篠翁	
汎隨清壑迴		聊得從君栖	20

Additional Notes

LINES 2–3. There are reminiscences here of Yang Yün's letter in reply to Sun Hui-tsung (see Additional Note to l.11 of the preceding poem): 身率妻子 戮力耕桑 'I myself lead my wife and children; we unite our efforts in ploughing and mulberry-culture' and 田家作苦 'As a farmer I perform harsh tasks'.

LINE 4. Cf. *Returning to Live in the Country*, III, 8 and the preceding poem, l.14.

LINE 16. T'ao would have had in his mind the line from *Song* 154, 1, 2&3: 七月流火 'In the seventh month there is the declining Fire-star.'

42 DRINKING WINE

飲酒二十首

序 余閒居寡歡，兼比夜已長。偶有名酒，無夕不飲。顧影獨盡，忽焉復醉。既醉之後，輒題數句自娛。紙墨遂多，辭無詮次。聊命故人書之，以爲歡笑爾。

I

衰榮無定在　　人道每如茲
彼此更共之　　達人解其會
邵生瓜田中　　逝將不復疑　8
寧似東陵時　　勿與一觴酒
寒暑有代謝　　日夕歡相持

（4）

II

積善云有報　　九十行帶索
夷叔在西山　　飢寒況當年
善惡苟不應　　不賴固窮節
何事空立言　　百世當誰傳　8

（4）

III

道喪向千載　　豈不在一生
人人惜其情　　一生能有幾
有酒不肯飲　　倏如流電驚　8
但顧世間名　　鼎鼎百年內
所以貴我身　　持此欲何成

（4）

IV

栖栖失羣鳥
日暮猶獨飛
裴回無定止
夜夜聲轉悲
厲響思清遠
去來何依依*

因值孤生松
歛翮遙來歸
勁風無榮木
此蔭獨不衰
託身已得所
千載不相違

* 五六兩句曾集本註云一作厲響思清晨，遠去何所依。

V

結廬在人境
而無車馬喧
問君何能爾
心遠地自偏
采菊東籬下

悠然見南山*
山氣日夕佳
飛鳥相與還
此中有真意⁺
欲辯已忘言

* 見，文選作望。
⁺ 中，文選作還，王叔岷案疑涉上相與還而誤。

VI

行止千萬端
誰知非與是
是非苟相形
雷同共譽毀

三季多此事
達士似不爾
咄咄俗中愚
且當從黃綺

VII

秋菊有佳色
裛露掇其英
汎此忘憂物
遠我遺世情
一觴雖獨進

杯盡壺自傾
日入羣動息
歸鳥趨林鳴
嘯傲東軒下
聊復得此生

VIII

青松在東園
眾草沒其姿
凝霜殄異類
卓然見高枝 (4)
連林人不覺
獨樹眾乃奇
提壺挂寒柯
遠望時復爲 (8)
吾生夢幻間
何事紲塵羈

IX

清晨聞叩門
倒裳往自開
問子爲誰與
田父有好懷 (4)
壺漿遠見候
疑我與時乖
繿縷茅簷下
未足爲高棲 (8)
一世皆尚同
願君汨其泥
深感父老言
稟氣寡所諧 (12)
紆轡誠可學
違己詎非迷
且共歡此飲
吾駕不可回 (16)

X

在昔曾遠遊
直至東海隅
道路迥且長
風波阻中塗 (4)
此行誰使然
似爲飢所驅
傾身營一飽
少許便有餘 (8)
恐此非名計
息駕歸閑居

XI

顏生稱爲仁
榮公言有道
屢空不獲年
長飢至于老 (4)
雖留身後名
一生亦枯槁
死去何所知
稱心固爲好 (8)
客養千金軀
臨化消其寶
裸葬何必惡
人當解意表 (12)

XII

長公曾一仕
壯節忽失時
杜門不復出
終身與世辭　　4
仲理歸大澤
高風始在茲

一往便當已
何爲復狐疑　　8
去去當奚道
世俗久相欺
擺落悠悠談
請從余所之　　12

XIII

有客常同止
取捨邈異境
一士長獨醉
一夫終年醒　　4
醒醉還相笑

發言各不領
規規一何愚
兀傲差若穎　　8
寄言酣中客
日沒燭當秉

XIV

故人賞我趣
挈壺相與至
班荊坐松下
數斟已復醉　　4
父老雜亂言

觴酌失行次
不覺知有我
安知物爲貴　　8
悠悠迷所留
酒中有深味

XV

貧居乏人工
灌木荒余宅
班班有翔鳥
寂寂無行迹　　4
宇宙一何悠

人生少至百
歲月相催逼
鬢邊早已白　　8
若不委窮達
素抱深可惜

XVI

少年罕人事
遊好在六經

行行向不惑
淹留自無成　　4

竟抱固窮節
飢寒飽所更
敝廬交悲風
荒草沒前庭　8

披褐守長夜
晨雞不肯鳴
孟公不在茲
終以翳吾情　12

XVII

幽蘭生前庭
含薰待清風
清風脫然至
見別蕭艾中　4

行行失故路
任道或能通
覺悟當念還
鳥盡廢良弓　8

XVIII

子雲性嗜酒
家貧無由得
時賴好事人
載醪祛所惑　4
觴來為之盡

是諮無不塞
有時不肯言
豈不在伐國
仁者用其心　8
何嘗失顯默

XIX

疇昔苦長飢
投耒去學仕
將養不得節
凍餒固纏己　4
是時向立年
志意多所恥
遂盡介然分

拂衣歸田里 *　8
冉冉星氣流
亭亭復一紀
世路廓悠悠
楊朱所以止　12
雖無揮金事
濁酒聊可恃

* 拂衣，曾集本作終死，註云一作拂衣，陶注本作拂衣。

XX

羲農去我久
舉世少復真
汲汲魯中叟
彌縫使其淳　4

鳳鳥雖不至
禮樂暫得新
洙泗輟微響
漂流逮狂秦　8

詩書復何罪　　終日馳車走
一朝成灰塵　　不見所問津　　16
區區諸老翁　　若復不快飲
為事誠殷勤　　空負頭上巾
如何絕世下　　但恨多謬誤
六籍無一親　　君當恕醉人　　20

12

Additional Notes

I, 3–4. The story of Shao P'ing is recorded in the biography of Hsiao Ho 蕭何, Chancellor of Han Kao-tsu, see *Shih-chi* 53, pp. 9–10; *Han shu* 39, 4a.

II, 1–4. *I*, hexagram 2, *Wen-yen chuan* has: 'A family which piles up good will certainly have abundant blessings; a family which piles up evil will certainly have abundant misfortunes', but T'ao's immediate source for his lines will lie in the comments which Ssu-ma Ch'ien makes after his biography of Po-i and Shu-ch'i in *Shih-chi* 61 and which I have translated in the Commentary to *Body, Shadow and Soul*, vol. 1, pp. 37–38.

II, 5. The longest and most circumstantial account of the nonagenarian Jung Ch'i-ch'i occurs in *Lieh-tzu* 1, pp. 13–14; there is a shorter version in a fragment of Hsi K'ang's *Sheng-hsien kao-shih chuan* (a work with which T'ao was certainly also familiar), preserved in *T'ai-p'ing yü-lan* 509, 4a. Since T'ao makes several references to Jung Ch'i-ch'i, I translate the *Lieh-tzu* version in full here:

> Confucius was on an excursion to T'ai-shan, when he met Jung Ch'i-ch'i walking on the heath of Ch'eng. Jung Ch'i-ch'i was wearing a deerskin with a rope for a girdle; he was playing on a lute and singing. Confucius asked him: 'What is the reason for your happiness, sir?' He replied: 'My joys are very many. Heaven gives birth to the Ten Thousand Things, but man alone is noble. I had the luck to become a man; this is my first joy. In the distinction of male and female, the male is noble and the female base, therefore to be a male is considered honourable. Since I had the luck to become a male, this is my second joy. Among those who are born are some who do not see a day or a month or do not live beyond babyhood. Since I have lived for ninety years, this is my third joy. Poverty is the constant lot of the scholar; death is the end of man. Abiding in the constant and awaiting [reading 俟] my end, how should I be anxious?' Confucius said: 'Excellent is he who can liberate himself.'

II, 7. Cf. *Written in the Twelfth Month of the Year Kuei-mao for My Cousin Ching-yüan*, l.16 and Additional Note thereto.

III, 1. Cf. *To Secretary Chou, Tsu and Hsieh*, l.9. The identical line in that poem makes it clear that the Way must be that of Confucius.

III, 3. Cf. *Body, Shadow and Soul*, I, 16, p. 31.

III, 9. *Ting-ting* has its *locus classicus* in *Li-chi* 3 (2, 16a), where Cheng Hsüan glosses it 大舒 'too extended'. Many commentators and translators have felt that this meaning was inappropriate and have thought that the context demands the sense of 'swiftly passing'. The supported meaning of 'great', 'flourishing', 'extended' can be retained if one imagines that T'ao was using the word with irony.

IV, 1. For *hsi-hsi* see Additional Note to *Answering a Poem by Liu Ch'ai-sang*, 1.15, p. 55.

IV, 5–6. The reading 厲響思清遠, 去來何依依 is not only to be preferred on the principle of *lectio difficilior* but also as fitting much better into the allegory of himself, which the poet is presenting.

IV, 7–8. Cf. *The Bird Which Has Come Home*, IV, 2, p. 29. For the 'solitary pine', cf. *Return Home!*, 1.32, p. 138.

V, 1–2. Though T'ao no doubt was describing the location of his hermitage, which he kept in the environs of the city and not remote from it, quite factually, he was at the same time stressing its difference from the accepted convention. Since he was certainly familiar with the work of the Western Chin poet Chang Hsieh, he may have been writing a deliberately opposite line to the latter's 結宇窮岡曲 'I have built my house in the fold of a remote hill'. (*Miscellaneous Poem*, IX, 1; *Wen-hsüan* 29, 41a.) Equally the second line cannot fail to be doubly suggestive. On the one hand it suggests that the hermit's isolation is achieved without the hermit's normal remote locality, but it must also carry undertones of a positive separation from the political world, since 'carriages and horses' so often come to call the hermit to the king's service (cf. the story of Ch'ien Lou, translated in the Additional Note to *Singing of Poor Scholars* IV, p. 122).

V, 5–6. Since the chrysanthemum is always a symbol of the seeking of long life, it may well be, as Wang Yao suggested, that the 'southern mountains' (physically Lu-shan) have a similar symbolic reference through allusion to *Song* 166, 6; 如南山之壽 'like the longevity of the southern mountains'. Su Shih and other critics have strongly animadverted against the variant 望 which appears in the *Wen-hsüan* version of this poem instead of 見 as destroying the quality and expression of the poem (see *T'ao Yüan-ming shih-wen hui-p'ing*, p. 167 ff.)

V, 9–10. T'ao is here using the Taoist idea that the True Way is inexpressible in words, which continually recurs in *Lao-tzu* and *Chuang-tzu*. His form of words is verbally close to *Chuang-tzu* 22 (7B, 15a): (in response to the three questions of Knowledge on how to know the Way, how to rest in the Way, how to achieve the Way) 'K'uang-ch'ü said: "Oh! I know it and will tell you," but as he was about to speak, he forgot what he was going to say.'

VI, 3. Ku Chih and many modern commentators following him have seen the reference of 'right' and 'wrong' as being to the argument on the relativity of these terms in *Chuang-tzu* 2. To me, however, T'ao's nuance seems somewhat different. He is not here so much concerned with the ultimate relativity of 'right' and 'wrong' (it is very doubtful that he would have assented to the proposition) as with the thought that contemporary ideas of right and wrong were a matter of slavish agreement for the many. Thus the recognition of the reminiscence of *Chiu-pien*, IX (*Ch'u-tz'u* 8, 12b) in the next line, also noticed by Ku Chih, is the significant indication of T'ao's thought.

VI, 4. Reminiscence of *Chiu-pien*, IX: 世雷同而炫曜兮，何毀譽之昧昧 'The men of the age are alike as thunderclaps and full of display./How confused are their censure and praise.'

VII, 1–2. Cf. *Li-sao* st. 17 (*Ch'u-tz'u* 1, 10a): 'In the morning I drink the dew fallen on the magnolias;/In the evening I feed on the fallen blossoms of the autumn chrysanthemums.' The chrysanthemums again suggest the search for long life, and while, if T'ao indeed had these lines of the *Li-sao* in mind, they are certainly to be connected with the search for long life, the association with Ch'ü Yüan will probably evoke a further suggestion of withdrawal from the world and a desire to preserve purity.

VII, 3. The periphrasis *tz'u wang yu wu* 'this thing which makes me forget care' for wine may be founded on the Mao commentary to *Song* 26, 1: 微我無酒，以敖以遊 'It is not that I have no wine/For pleasure and diversion.' Mao glosses: 非我無酒可以敖遊忘憂也 'It is not that I have no wine with which I can find diversion and forget care.' Cf. also Additional Note to *Body, Shadow and Soul*, II, 15, p. 33. Li Shan in his commnentary to this present poem in *Wen-hsüan* 30, 2b, besides citing this reference to the Mao commentary, notes a parallel to the action in T'ao's line in P'an Yüeh's *Ch'iu-chü fu* 秋菊賦 (fragment only extant; elsewhere ascribed to P'an Ni, see Yen K'o-chün, *Ch'üan Chin-wen* 91, 8b): 汎流英於清醴，似浮萍之隨波 'I float drifting blossoms on the clear sweet wine;/They are like floating duckweed going with the waves.'

VIII, 1–4. Behind these lines lies the symbolic use of the green pine to represent the quality of the gentleman, which stands out in times of difficulty;

see Additional Note to *Written in the Third Month of the Year I-ssu*, l.16, p. 78. Cf. also *Answering a Poem by Registrar Kuo*, II, 8–10 ,p. 56.

VIII, 10. With *ch'en-chi* 'dusty halter', cf. *ch'en-wang* in *Returning to Live in the Country*, I, 3, p. 36.

IX, 1–2. These lines are founded on and allude to *Song* 100, 1 (the same lines are repeated in st. 2 with one small change): 'The east is not yet bright,/When he jumbles on his clothes;/He jumbles them on;/From the court he is summoned.'

IX, 9–10. These lines are clearly intended to evoke the words of the fisherman in the piece of that title (*Yü-fu*) in *Ch'u-tz'u* 7, 1b–2a: 'The fisherman said: "The sage is not bound by material things, but is able to change with his age. If the men of the age are filthy, why not wallow in their mud and raise their waves? If the multitude are all drunk, why not eat their dregs and drink their lees?"' Once this allusion is recognized, it becomes clear that the *Yü-fu* is the source of T'ao's conception of this poem and that the fisherman is the model for the peasant (*t'ien-fu*). It is important also to note that Wang I glosses the final words of the passage quoted 食其祿 'feed on their salary'. The identity of opinion and desires among the mass of men is also a common idea in the *Ch'u-tz'u*; cf. the *Li-sao* lines cited in the Additional Note to Poem XVII, 1–4 below.

X, 3. This line is an echo of *Old Poem* I, 5.

XI, 1. Cf. *Lun-yü* 6, 5: 'As for Hui, his mind for three months did not depart from Goodness.' and also *K'ung-tzu chia-yü* 38 (9, 1a): 'Confucius praised him [Hui] for his Goodness.'

XI, 3. 'Often empty' is from the description of Yen'Hui by Confucius in *Lun-yü* 11, 18. T'ao's line is close to *Shih-chi* 61, p. 12: '... yet Hui was often empty. He did not weary of rotten husks and yet in the end he died early.' (The complete passage is translated in the Commentary to *Body, Shadow and Soul*, see vol. 1, p. 37). According to *K'ung-tzu chia-yü* 38 (9, 1a) he died in his thirty-first year.

XI, 5. The phrase *shen-hou ming*, which T'ao also uses in *Resentful Poem in the Ch'u Mode*, 1.17, p. 47, was used by Chang Han 張翰 (third century) in a famous remark, which might well have been known to T'ao: 'To make me have a name after death is not as good as a cup of wine here and now.' (*Shih-shuo hsin-yü* C/A, 40a–b; included also in Chang's biography in *Chin shu* 92, 9a.) In view of *k'u-kao* in the following line T'ao may also have had in his mind *Chuang-tzu* 24 (8B, 8b): 枯槁士宿名 'Men who are dead and withered hold to fame.'

XI, 8. The expression *ch'en-hsin* 'to accord with the heart' occurs also in *Revolution of the Seasons*, II, 6, p.3.

XI, 9. There has been a tendency to understand *k'o yang* as 'to treat [our body] as an honoured guest', but in view of the very many places where T'ao and others treat life as a brief sojourning, like a stay at an inn, it seems to me better to refer *k'o* to the subject rather than to the verb. Hence my translation. Ting Fu-pao perhaps had somewhat the same idea, but he referred *k'o* directly to Yang Wang-sun, whose naked burial is alluded to in line 11. I should regard this as making the last four lines too specific.

XI, 11. For Yang Wang-sun 楊王孫 (first century BC), who finally prevailed on his son, despite the latter's reluctance, that he should be buried naked 'in order to return to his true [natural] state' (see *Han shu* 67, 1aff.).

XII, 1. Chang Chih has a brief notice at the end of the biography of his father Chang Shih-chih 張釋之 in *Shih-chi* 102, p. 11 (repeated in *Han shu* 50, 4a). For a translation, see *Written after Reading History*, IX, vol. 1, p. 218.

XII, 5–6. Yang Lun has a biography among the Confucian scholars in *Hou-Han shu* 109A (13aff.), but T'ao's knowledge of him must derive from some earlier source.

XIII, 9–10. These lines contain an echo of T'ao's favourite *Old Poem*, XV, 3–4: 'Since the day is short and we grieve at the night's length,/Why not take a candle and enjoy oneself?'

XIV, 3. *Pan ching* 'spreading brushwood' has a *locus classicus* in *Tso-chuan*, Hsiang twenty-sixth year, from which context it may carry a connotation of friendship.

XIV, 8. Underlying this line seems to be *Chuang-tzu* 17 (6B, 8b–9a): 'From the point of view of the Way nothing is noble or base; from the point of view of things they themselves are noble and others are base.' Without a sense of self these distinctions are not made and the position of the Way is achieved.

XV, 2. *Kuan-mu* 'thick-growing trees' has its origin in *Song* 2, 1.

XV, 3. *Pan-pan* (clear) must be used in opposition to the dark disorder of the trees and perhaps plays on the sense of 'order' in the unreduplicated *pan*.

XV, 7–8. Cf. *Miscellaneous Poem*, VII, 2 and 6, p. 115.

XVI, 1–2. Cf. *Written when Passing through Ch'ü-o*, ll.1–2, p. 67.

XVI, 3–4. Since 'no doubts' as a substitute for 'forty years old' derives from *Lun-yü*, it seems probable that in 'without achieving anything' T'ao will have had in mind *Lun-yü* 9, 22: 'The Master said: "A younger man may be respected. How do we know that in the future he may not be what we are now. But if a man is forty or fifty and has no reputation, then certainly he cannot be respected."' Nevertheless, the form of words seems to come from *Chiu-pien* I (*Ch'u-tz'u* 8, 3a), also used by T'ao in *Living in Retirement on the Ninth Day*, l.18, p. 35. Cf. also *The Tree in Blossom*, IV, p. 5.

XVI, 5. Cf. Poem II, 7 above.

XVI, 11. Li Kung-huan was followed by many other commentators in identifying Meng-kung as Ch'en Tsun 陳遵 (biography in *Han shu* 92) who was 'fond of wine. Whenever he gave a great drinking party and the guests filled the hall, he had the gates shut and the linch-pins of the guests' carriages taken and thrown into the well so that even if it were urgent, they could not go' (8b). But Ku Chih was certainly correct in identifying him as Liu Kung whose courtesy-name was also Meng-kung and who was the only man who recognized the merits of Chang Chung-wei; see *Singing of Poor Scholars*, VI, vol. 1, p. 139 n. 76.

XVII, 1–4. These lines contain an allusion to *Li-sao*, st. 68 (*Ch'u-tz'u* 1, 28a): 'Men's likes and dislikes do not agree;/These cliques alone are different./They all fill their belts with artemesia,/And say the shady orchid is not fit for girdle-hangings.'

XVII, 8. This line derives from an anonymous rhyme which has been preserved in two separate contexts in *Shih-chi* with slight variations. It appears in a letter from Fan Li, general of King Kou-chien of Yüeh, to the great officer Chung (*Shih-chi* 41, p. 15): 'When the flying birds are all gone,/The good bow is put away;/When the wily hare has been killed,/The hound is boiled.' It is quoted with a further couplet by Han Hsin (ibid., 92, p. 36): 'Truly it is as men say: "When the wily hare is killed,/The good dog is boiled;/When the high flying birds are all gone,/The good bow is put away;/When the enemy state is destroyed,/The minister who gave counsel is no more."'

XVIII, 1–4. T'ao's source for these lines is the appraisal at the end of Yang Hsiung's biography in *Han shu* 87B, 17a: 'His family was always poor, and he was fond of wine. Few men came to his gate, but at this time there were those interested in affairs, who brought him wine and delicacies and joined him in diversion and study.' The close parallel in the *Biography of the Gentleman of the Five Willows* (see p. 147), both in thought and actual language, with these four lines and the following one may be noted.

XVIII, 8. The unwillingness to speak of attacking other states cannot be traced directly to Yang Hsiung, but seems to derive from a remark attributed to Liu-hsia Hui in the biography of Tung Chung-shu (*Han shu* 56, 17b): 'I have heard that in the past the ruler of Lu asked Liu-hsia Hui: "I wish to attack Ch'i, how am I to do it?" Liu-hsia Hui said: "It is not permissible." When he returned home, he had a troubled look. He said: "I have heard that the Good Man is not asked about attacking other states. Why were these words directed to me?"' T'ao Shu, to whom Yang Hsiung was not a worthy person because of his support of Wang Mang, believes that the poet, writing the whole poem as an allegory of himself, in fact shifted his model from Yang Hsiung to Liu-hsia Hui at line 7. But this would produce a rather awkward reading. Ku Chih argues against T'ao Shu that Yang Hsiung was regarded as a sage in the Han, Wei and Liu-ch'ao periods. For T'ao Yüan-ming here Yang Hsiung seems to be above all an example of withdrawal, as in Tso Ssu's *Yung-shih*, IV (*Wen-hsüan* 21, 4b).

XVIII, 10. *Hsien* and *mo* are elliptic for *hsien-yin, yü-mo* 顯隱, 語黙 Ting Fu-pao cites an example of the full expression in the *San-kuo ming-ch'en hsü tsan* 三國名臣序贊 of Yüan Hung 袁宏 (328–76) (*Wen-hsüan* 47, 35a): 'When the times are upside down, revealing oneself is not as good as going into retirement; when all things are in order, silence is not as good as speech.' The expression is only a variation on *I, Hsi-tz'u chuan* A, 6; see Additional Note to *Charge to My Son*, IV, 5, p. 26.

XIX, 2. *Hsüeh shih* 'study and service' (which really became a circumlocution for service) derives from *Lun-yü* 19, 13: 'When one has served sufficiently, one studies; when one has studied sufficiently, one serves.'

XIX, 11–12. Li Kung-huan and most subsequent commentators trace this reference to Yang Chu to *Huai-nan-tzu* 17, 14b: 'Master Yang wept when he saw a crossroads, because he could go south or go north.' T'ao certainly uses this reference in the preface to his five-word poem *In Reply to Aide P'ang* (see p. 49 and Additional Note, p. 50), but there it is used to imply parting. If the same reference is intended here, it must have a different connotation. 'Stopping' here must mean withdrawing from the world, as it does in *Stopping Wine* below.

XIX, 13. In his reference to the Two Shus here T'ao seems to be directly influenced by Chang Hsieh's lines in *Singing of the Two Shus* (*Wen-hsüan* 21, 9b): 'Scattering the gold, they delighted in the present;/For their years' end they kept no store.' (Chang Hsieh's complete poem is translated in the Commentary to *Singing of the Two Shus*, see vol. 1, p. 144).

XX, 2. For a definition of 'return to the true', see *Chuang-tzu* 17 (6B, 16a–b):

故曰，無以人滅天，無以故滅命 ... 謹守而勿失，是謂反其真 'Therefore I say: Do not by the human destroy the natural, do not by the conventional destroy the inborn ... Carefully preserve and do not lose. This I call returning to the true.'

XX, 3. *Chi-chi* (anxious, hurried) is applied contemptuously to the Way of Confucius by the robber Chih in *Chuang-tzu* 29 (9B, 22b), but T'ao clearly does not intend it unkindly here.

XX, 5. The reference is to *Lun-yü* 9, 8: 'The Master said: "The phoenix does not come; the river does not give forth a chart. All is over with me."'

XX, 6. This is based on a passage in Confucius' biography in *Shih-chi* 47, p. 68, where several sayings from *Lun-yü* are put together in support. 'In Confucius' time, the Chou house had become weak; the *Rites* and the *Music* had been abandoned; the *Songs* and the *Documents* had become defective. He traced back the rites of the three dynasties [Hsia, Shang and Chou] and put in order the documents and records: above recording the time of T'ang and Yü [i.e. Yao and Shun] and below coming to Mu of Ch'in [i.e. covering the time span of the present *Documents*], he arranged their deeds.' Then follow *Lun-yü* 3, 9; 3, 14; 3, 23 and 9, 14, which are interpreted as demonstrating Confucius' editorship of the *Documents*, the *Songs*, the *Rites* and the *Music*.

XX, 7. Confucius is said to have taught his disciples between the Chu and Ssu, cf. *Li-chi* 3 (2, 10a), where Tseng-tzu says to Tzu-hsia: " ... You and I served the Master between the Chu and Ssu." *Ch'o wei hsiang* 'his subtle tones ceased' is probably a reminiscence of the beginning of the *I-wen chih* chapter (30) of the *Han shu*: 'Formerly Chung-ni died and his subtle words ceased', or of *Han shu* 36 (Biography of Liu Hsin), 28b, where virtually the same words occur.

43 STOPPING WINE

止 酒

居止次城邑	好味止園葵
逍遙自閑止	大歡止稚子
坐止高陰下	平生不止酒
步止蓽門裏	止酒情無喜

4

8

暮止不安寢　　　　始覺止爲善
晨止不能起　　　　今朝眞止矣　16
日日欲止之*　　　從此一止去
12　營衛止不理　　　將止扶桑涘
徒知止不樂　　　　清顏止宿容
未信止利己+　　　奚止千萬祀　20

* 日日，湯注本作日月。
+ 未信，湯注本作未知。

44　TELLING OF WINE

述 酒

重離照南陸　　　　成名猶不勤　16
鳴鳥聲相聞　　　　卜生善斯牧
秋草雖未黃　　　　安樂不爲君
4　融風久已分　　　平王去舊京#
素礫晶脩渚　　　　峽中納遺薰　20
南嶽無餘雲　　　　雙陵甫云育
豫章抗高門　　　　三趾顯奇文
8　重華固靈墳　　　王子愛清吹
流淚抱中歎　　　　日中翔河汾　24
傾耳聽司晨　　　　朱公練九齒
神州獻嘉粟　　　　閒居離世紛
12　西零爲我馴*　　峨峨西嶺內　28
諸梁董師旅　　　　偃息常所親
羋勝喪其身+　　　天容自永固
山陽歸下國　　　　彭殤非等倫

* 零，各本作靈，何校宣和本作零。
+ 羋，各本作羊，李注黃山谷（庭堅）云羊勝當是羋勝。
# 王，湯注從韓子蒼（駒）本，舊作生。

Additional Notes

LINE 1. T'ang Han made the line allude to the founding of Eastern Chin by equating 重離 with 重黎, i.e. Ch'ung and Li, two early mythical heroes (sometimes wrongly made into one person) who were accounted ancestors of the ruling Ssu-ma family of Chin. The reference to hexagram 30 is, however, sufficient by itself to give this suggestion. It may be noted that Kuo P'u made use of the *hsiang* explanation to hexagram 30 in his lament for the first emperor of Eastern Chin, *Yüan huang-ti ai-ts'e wen* 元皇帝哀策文 (ap. *I-wen lei-chü* 13, 6b): 大人承運, 重明繼作 'The great man carried on the destiny, doubled brightness was in continuity created.'

LINE 2. Wu Shih-tao believed that T'ao's line was founded on *Shu, Chün-shih* (10, 4a): 我則鳴鳥不聞 'By us the singing bird [Ma Jung explains as the phoenix] will not be heard.' The preceding clause is in fact: 'If the old and those of accomplished virtue do not give their support'. Thus T'ao was referring to the abundance of worthy men when the Chin first moved to the south. Wu's proposal seems preferable to T'ao Shu's reference of the line to *Ch'u-tz'u, Li-sao*, st. 75 (1, 30b–31a): 恐鵜鴃之先鳴, 使夫百草爲之不芳 'Lest the shrike cry before and make all plants unfragrant.' T'ao Shu noted that the shrike is supposed to cry at the summer solstice. Ku Chih goes too far in suggesting that both Wu Shih-tao and T'ao Shu are correct.

LINE 4. *Jung feng* (defined by *Shuo-wen, sub* 風 as the north-east wind) is equated with the *t'iao feng* 條風, stated in *Huai-nan-tzu* 3, 4a to come forty-five days after the winter solstice. If lines 3 and 4 have a metaphorical as well as their surface meaning, they would perhaps imply that though the Chin managed to re-establish its dynasty south of the Yangtze, its initial vigour had been lost.

LINE 5. T'ao Shu compared this line to Tu Fu's 渚清沙白鳥飛迴 in his poem 登高 (411/26/39) and said it was a metaphor for the partial dynasty in South China. Both Ch'u Wan-feng and Lu Ch'in-li take it as a reference to the usurpation of Huan Hsüan. Ch'u would establish the reference through Pai-shih 白石, the place where Huan in the eighth month of 398 gained the victory which started him on the road to his brief overthrow of the dynasty (see *Chin shu* 10, 1b). Lu makes a somewhat more convincing case by equating *hsiu-chu* with Chiang-ling, Huan Hsüan's base, via 渚宮. He also shows by examples that *li* (pebbles) can be a symbol of 'worthlessness'. I believe, however, that Ku Chih's interpretation, which would relate the line to an omen, is to be preferred, as helping to produce a consistency of reading in the first section of the poem (lines 1–12). Ku thought that *su-li* (white stone) was an omen for the Chin's gaining the mandate of Heaven. He cites a quotation from the *Han-Chin ch'un-ch'iu* in P'ei Sung-chih's commentary to

San-kuo chih, Wei shu, 3, 12a, which relates the story of a large blue stone 蒼石 which appeared in a river in the Chang-yeh area of modern Kansu. This stone was decorated with white stone 白石 representations of horses and other animals, the Eight Trigrams and other signs, and carried the ambiguous inscription *Ta t'ao Ts'ao* 大討曹. P'ei Sung-chih quotes other versions of the story with varying details from *Wei-shih ch'un-ch'iu* and *Sou-shen chi.* These make it clear that although the stone was regarded as an auspicious omen by the Wei, it was also used as a portent by the Chin. The *Han-Chin ch'un-ch'iu* quotation ends with the words: 'At the beginning of Chin the inscription became brighter and the representations of the horses all became as luminous as jade.' Cf. also *Chin shu* 27, 7a and *Sung shu* 27, 14a–b.

LINES 7–8. T'ang Han's association of *Ch'ung-hua* in line 8 with the abdication of Emperor Kung has been one of the main props of the received interpretation of the poem. The emperor on his abdication became Prince of Ling-ling 零陵 and in Ling-ling was the Chiu-i shan 九疑山, the site of the tomb of the legendary emperor Shun (Ch'ung-hua). Line 8 is thus understood: 'Ch'ung-hua [= Emperor Kung] has only a sacred grave' (固 being read as 顧 = 但). In line 7 Yü-chang is then taken as Liu Yü from his first ennoblement in 406 as Yü-chang chün kung (see *Chin shu* 10, 5b). The rest of the line is thought to be based on *Song* 237, 7: 'Then he [the old duke Tan-fu, grandfather of King Wen of Chou] raised the outer gate;/The outer gate was high.' Thus Liu Yü's gradual progress towards usurpation is implied. In spite of the general acceptance of this sort of interpretation, the couplet seems to me strangely constructed, if it is to be so understood. I have made a new approach by connecting these lines with the story in Lei Tz'u-tsung's *Yü-chang chi.* I therefore understand *yü-chang* in line 7 not as a place-name but as the name of the camphor laurel tree (= 樟木). As something of a parallel for *fen* (line 8) in the sense in which I have understood it, cf. Ts'ao Chiung, *Liu-tai lun* (*Wen-hsüan* 52, 20b): 譬之種樹 ... 雖壅之以黑墳 ... 猶不救於枯槁 'It may be compared to planting trees ... although one banks them up with black mould ... one still does not save them from withering.'

LINE 12. T'ang Han has been generally followed in emending the reading 西靈 to 四靈, i.e. the four auspicious beasts, the unicorn, phoenix, tortoise and dragon. T'ang noted that the expression 四靈效徵 'the four auspicious beasts have given testimony' occurs in the documents relating to Kung's abdication (see *Sung shu* 2, 11b; the emperor's edict of abdication has the words: 四靈效瑞 'the four auspicious beasts have given good augury', ibid., 2, 11a). Most commentators have therefore understood this line: 'the four auspicious beasts have submitted to us' and have taken it, as they have the previous one, as describing the portents for Liu Yü's succession.
There is an alternative approach which has remained unconsidered. There are two variant readings for 靈 noted in the Southern Sung texts, viz. 雲 and 零. If

零 is adopted, there is no need to emend 西, since 西零 will provide a possible reading. Hsi-ling (cf. 先零) is used as a name for the Ch'iang, cf. Shih Ts'en, *Ch'u-shih sung* 出師頌 (*Wen-hsüan* 47, 9a): 西零不順 'The Hsi-ling are not submissive.' Shih Ts'en's piece could indeed have been the source of the present line. If line 11 is interpreted as referring to Liu Yü's defeat of the Later Ch'in forces in 417, as I have suggested, then this reading of line 12 has certainly an appropriate context.

LINES 13–14. There is general agreement among the commentators to read 芈 Mi (suggested by Huang T'ing-chien as an emendation and appearing in the Southern Sung texts as a variant) for 羊 Yang. It seems better to assume this comparatively easy graphic confusion rather than take the reading Yang Sheng to be correct and try to emend line 13 in some way. This course would not be unreasonable, since there is a Yang Sheng who was a 'bad adviser' to the Former Han Prince Hsiao of *Liang*, whose armies played a major part in the suppression of the revolt of the 'Seven Kingdoms' in 154 BC and whose son Ting became Prince of *Shan-yang*. This Yang Sheng was eventually forced to commit suicide (see *Shih-chi* 58, p. 8 and 108, p. 7). In spite of such perplexing uncertainties, some modern commentators have attempted to demonstrate that these lines were intended to be a suggestive analogy of events in the poet's own time. Thus Ku Chih thought that Mi Sheng represents Ssu-ma Hsiu-chih, who after being defeated by Liu Yü in 415, had fled to Yao Hung in Ch'in (see *Chin shu* 10, 7b). In 417, after the destruction of Yao Hung's kingdom by Liu Yü's forces, Ssu-ma Hsiu-chih fled again, this time to the Toba state of Wei, but apparently died on the way (see *Chin shu* 37, 17b). Ku was really putting a name to T'ang Han's suggestion that the couplet referred to Liu Yü's suppression of members of the ruling house with a reputation for ability. Lu Ch'in-li disputes the logic of Ku's proposal and makes the counter-suggestion that Mi Sheng represents Huan Hsüan. Liu Yü, like the Duke of She, put down a usurper and restored the previously reigning monarch. Neither proposal provides events which are wholly analogous to the Mi Sheng affair.

LINES 15–16. Almost all commentators have believed that 'Shan-yang' whom they have taken to be the last ruler of Later Han is an allegory for Emperor Kung. In noting that line 16 derives from *I Chou shu*, *Rules for Posthumous Titles*, T'ang Han remarked that 'Ling' was a name given to ancient rulers who did not come to a good end. A subtle connection was made between the two lines by Ku Chih on the basis of this. The last ruler of Han may be said to have come to a good end, since he lived for fourteen years after his abdication and when he died was canonized as Emperor Hsiao-hsien of Han and buried according to the Han rites (see *San-kuo chih, Wei shu* 3, 8b). Emperor Kung on the other hand was murdered.
An alternative identification for 'Shan-yang' was made by Lu Ch'in-li. He

thinks the reference may be to Liu Ho 劉賀, who succeeded Emperor Chao of Han for a period of twenty-seven days in 74 BC and was then removed because of the impropriety of his conduct. His former kingdom of Ch'ang-i 昌邑 was abolished and became Shan-yang commandery (see *Han shu* 63, 14a). There are serious objections to Lu's proposal. Liu Ho, after his dismissal, had for a long time no title. Although he returned to what then became Shan-yang commandery, he held no official position which would justify his being referred to as 'Shan-yang'. Lu points out that his story is often alluded to in the Wei-Chin period, but he seems always to be described as the Prince of Ch'ang-i. On these grounds Lu's proposal seems to fail. It would seem very probable that Shan-yang is Han Hsien-ti, but there is no real necessity to take the couplet allegorically. I believe that it is possible to understand this couplet and the preceding one as describing typical political situations, i.e. sometimes a bid to seize power fails (Mi Sheng), sometimes a legitimate ruler is overthrown (Han Hsien-ti).

LINES 17–18. There is a great division of opinion on this couplet into two main lines of interpretation. The crux of the problem is whether the first two characters of each line are to be considered proper names or not. The early proposal of T'ang Han to identify Pu sheng as Confucius' disciple Tzu-hsia (Pu Shang 卜商) and because Tzu-hsia was regarded by Marquis Wen of Wei as his teacher, to postulate by this very roundabout means a reference to Wei Wen-ti is impossibly forced. The contrivance seems to have suggested itself to T'ang, because he first identified the An-lo of the following line as Liu Chan 劉禪, the last ruler of Shu Han, who in 264 was given the title of An-lo kung (see *San-kuo chih, Shu shu* 3, 7a). T'ang remarked: 'Since [Ts'ao] P'i had usurped the dynasty of Han, An-lo was not able to become a ruler.' Ku Chih accepted T'ang's identification of An-lo as Liu Chan, but proposed the emendation of 卜生 to 卜年, i.e. 'to divine the life span of a dynasty', a phrase which appears in Emperor Kung's letter at the time of his abdication: 故有國必亡，卜年著其數 'Therefore where there are states, they will certainly fall; by divining their life, their destiny is revealed' (*Sung shu* 2, 12a). Ku thought that the lines were critical of Emperor Kung for being willing to submit like Liu Chan. Lu Ch'in-li takes both Pu sheng and An Lo as proper names but proposes different identifications. Pu sheng is Pu Shih 卜式 (biography in *Han shu* 58, 7a–8b, the material being derived from *Shih-chi* 30, p. 25ff.), a successful sheep-breeder who attracted the notice of Han Wu-ti and rose to be Grand Secretary (*yü-shih ta-fu*) in 111 BC. An Lo (see *Han shu* 89, 10a) is the Chancellor of Liu Ho, Prince of Ch'ang-i (see on lines 15–16 above). Lu would seem to understand the line: 'An Lo did not act [well] for his prince.' This is a rather strained reading for the line. A further possible objection to Lu's interpretation is that the general pattern of the poem is for a couplet to treat a single person or single episode.

The other main approach is to understand neither 卜生 nor 安樂 as proper names. Huang Wen-huan connected the couplet with the *Chuang-tzu* 2 (1B, 33a) saying: 君子牧乎. He said: 'To be emperor and unable to preserve one's own life, then how indeed can one succeed in seeking to be a shepherd of men? He who divines for himself this life, how should he consider it to be good to be a shepherd of men? If he practises what can make for ease and pleasure, he will not desire to be a prince.' (See *T'ao Yüan-ming shih-wen hui-p'ing*, p. 205.) Huang, since he uses the expression 人牧, appears to understand the *chün* and *mu* of the *Chuang-tzu* saying as synonyms, whereas in the Kuo Hsiang commentary to *Chuang-tzu* they are taken to be antonyms. If one is to interpret this couplet without proper names, and this seems perhaps to be the more satisfactory course, it is probably preferable to render *mu* as the opposite of *chün*. The preceding 斯 has not received any consideration. I suggest that it stands here in the sense of 厮 and was intended to reinforce the meaning of *mu*. I think that there may perhaps be a reference to the saying attributed to Duke Wen of Chin (reigned 635–28 BC) in *Kuo-yü*, *Chin-yü* 4 (10, 2a) and elsewhere: 人生安樂, 誰知其他 'Man's life is ease and pleasure; who wishes for anything else?' Wen, at the time when he is supposed to have uttered this saying, had come in the course of exile to Ch'i and was content to end his life there.

LINES 19–20. The reading 平王 has been generally adopted in preference to 平生. This reading was noted by T'ang Han as appearing in the edition of Han Chü 韓駒 (Tzu-ts'ang 子蒼, †1135). King P'ing has been taken to be the founder of Eastern Chou. T'ang Han understood the first line of this couplet to be an allegory of Liu Yü's removal of the Chin emperor but could offer no solution for the second line. T'ao Shu, however, put forward an explanation which has won fairly wide acceptance. T'ao Shu equated 峽 with 郟鄏 Chia-ju, the site where King Ch'eng of Chou 'established the tripods' (see *Tso-chuan*, Hsüan third year) and so used to represent Lo-yang. 薰 is 獯鬻 (cf. 葷粥, 薰育), i.e. the Hsiung-nu 匈奴. He thought that the couplet was intended to describe the transfer of the Chin dynasty south of the Yangtze and the abandonment of North China to the Hsien-pi (he presumably did not intend the term to be precise, since Lo-yang and later Ch'ang-an fell to the Hsiung-nu). Ku Chih added a slight refinement to T'ao Shu's argument by pointing out that Liu Ts'ung 劉聰 (†318), to whom Lo-yang fell, was a descendant of the Hsiung-nu of the Han period (see *Chin shu* 101, 1a, Biography of Liu Yüan-hai 劉元海) and thus one might explain the 遺.
To all this there is a substantial objection, that the surface meaning of the text is not maintained. If the first line outwardly refers to King P'ing of Chou, the second should not outwardly refer to an event a thousand years later. Some element of this interpretation seems to be incorrect. The least satisfactory seems to me to be the explanation of *i-hsün*. It is perhaps particularly unfortunate that 納 is a word which may embrace opposite meanings. I think, however, that *i-hsün* may be understood literally and the line read: 'In Chia

he received the surviving fragrance.' The whole couplet may thus be taken as describing the establishment of Eastern Chou. For I think that what is being introduced here is the subject of a number of capitals. This interpretation requires the equation of 峽 with 郟, but there are at any rate several examples of 郟 standing by itself to represent the Eastern Chou capital, e.g. *Tso-chuan*, Huan seventh year, Hsiang twenty-fourth year.

LINES 21–22. A variety of possible explanations is opened up by the ambiguity of *san-chih*. *San-chih* might represent a portent or might be taken to signify a messenger through reference to the bird messengers of the Queen Mother of the West (see *Reading the Shan-hai-ching*, V, p. 127). These birds are described as three-footed crows in Ssu-ma Hsiang-ju's *Ta-jen fu* (*Shih-chi* 117, p. 88). Several commentators have felt that *shuang-ling* in line 21 has a connection with the two ridges of Hsiao-shan 殽山 or 崤山 in Honan, mentioned in *Tso-chuan*, Hsi thirty-second year. It is clear from Tso Ssu's *Shu-tu fu* (*Wen-hsüan* 4, 17b) that Hsiao-shan may be used to indicate Ch'ang-an. Contrivance, however, has once again been pressed rather far. T'ao Shu appears to think that by *shuang-ling* reference is really intended to the five tombs of the Chin emperors at Lo-yang, but the poet, not daring to speak openly of the five tombs, wrote *shuang-ling* and so used the *Tso-chuan* reference as a sort of camouflage. T'ao Shu understood *san-chih* as an omen of Liu Yü's accession.

Ku Chih also refers to the two ridges of Hsiao-shan but explains the line: 'Kuan [i.e. Ch'ang-an] and Lo[-yang] have been pacified and the people for the first time are able to grow.' For *san-chih* he adopts the messenger idea and refers line 22 to Liu Yü's chief of staff Wang Hung returning to Chien-k'ang after the recovery of Lo-yang to request the conferring of the *Chiu-hsi* 九錫 in recognition of Liu's services. Ku includes in the *ch'i-wen* ('unusual documents') the document conferring the *Chiu-hsi* and the documents of Emperor Kung's abdication. This kind of subtlety in interpretation, which does not cohere into any logical surface reading of the poem, I find unacceptable.

My own attempt at a solution would be on the following lines. I start with the belief that this couplet is to be connected with the preceding one and that the probable link is to be found in the subject of capital cities. I would suggest that the poet treats the occupation of Lo-yang by King P'ing of Chou as the beginning of the pattern of a western and an eastern capital, a pattern which the Han dynasty followed but the three-fold division of the Three Kingdoms broke.

LINES 23–24. Wang-tzu Ch'iao was supposed to have been the heir-apparent of King Ling of Chou (571–45 BC). His personal name was Chin 晉, which led T'ang Han and others to see a further cryptic reference to the fall of the Chin dynasty. If they were right, it seems to be an extremely clumsy device.

In my opinion, Wang-tzu Ch'iao is a fairly obvious example of a prince who gave up the world and there is no need to look further than this.

LINES 25–26. The poet may have had in mind here *Chan-kuo ts'e* 3, 74a (Chin-ts'e 3): 范蠡 ... 超然避世, 長爲陶朱君 'Fan Li ... distantly withdrew from the world and for long was Lord Chu of T'ao', or *Shih-chi* 79 (Biography of Ts'ai Tse), p. 46, which contains the same text. 九齒 has to be read as 久齡. Here T'ang Han again discovered a cryptogram, this time for T'ao Yüan-ming himself, but again I find the suggestion very weak.

LINES 27–28. T'ang Han takes *hsi-ling* to represent the place where Emperor Kung was buried. Ku Chih and Ch'u Wan-feng refer it to the K'un-lun mountains as the abode of the immortals. For Lu Ch'in-li it is the 'Western Hill' (Shou-yang shan) to which Po-i and Shu-ch'i retired (see *Drinking Wine*, II, p. 85). Lu believes that T'ao is describing his emulation of Po-i and Shu-ch'i in being ashamed to serve a new dynasty.

LINES 29–30. T'ao Shu thought that 天容 should be read closely parallel to 彭殤 and so suggested that T'ien-lao 天老 and Jung-ch'eng 容成, who were supposed to be ministers of the Yellow Emperor, were intended. T'ien-lao and Jung-ch'eng would represent position, while P'eng-shang would represent long life. This seems extremely forced. T'ang Han (apparently understanding *T'ien-jung* as 'the emperor's features') again referred the lines to Kung-ti who was murdered in his thirty-sixth year; he interpreted the last line: 'Long life does not need to be considered [in Kung-ti's case].'
It seems to me that these two lines express an idea usual enough in T'ao Yüan-ming (cf. for example the opening lines of *Body, Shadow and Soul*, p. 31) that the natural order endures, while man, however long-lived, does not.

45   REPROVING MY SONS

責 子

白髮被兩鬢　　　而不愛文術　　8
肌膚不復實　　　雍端年十三
雖有五男兒　　　不識六與七
4　總不好紙筆　　通子垂九齡
阿舒已二八　　　但覓梨與栗　　12
懶惰故無匹　　　天運苟如此
阿宣行志學　　　且進杯中物

46   WRITTEN WHEN I HAD A PERCEPTION

有會而作

序　舊穀既沒，新穀未登，頗爲老農，而值年災，日月尚悠，
　　爲患未已。登歲之功，既不可希，朝夕所資，煙火裁通。
　　旬日已來，始念飢乏。歲云夕矣，慨然永懷。今我不述，
　　後生何聞哉。

	弱年逢家乏	常善粥者心	
	老至更長飢	深念蒙袂非	
	菽麥實所羨	嗟來何足吝	
4	孰敢慕甘肥	徒沒空自遺	12
	惄如亞九飯	斯濫豈攸志	
	當暑厭寒衣	固窮夙所歸	
	歲月將欲暮	餒也已矣夫	
8	如何辛苦悲	在昔余多師	16

Additional Notes

PREFACE. In the opening sentence T'ao borrows from *Lun-yü* 17, 21: 舊穀既
沒，新穀既升 'the old grain is exhausted; the new grain has come up!' 'My
years come to their evening': the form of words comes originally from *Song*
207, 2&3, where the reference is to the calendar year. In this context T'ao
would seem rather to intend the years of his life.

LINE 5. *Ni-ju* is perhaps a reminiscence of *Song* 10, 1: 惄如調飢 'My craving
is like morning hunger', although T'ao has given *ju* a different function. The
statement about Tzu-ssu's nine meals occurs in *Shuo-yüan* 4, 3b, where the
current text reads: 子思居衛縕袍無表，二旬而九食 'When Tzu-ssu was living
in Wei, he wore a hempen robe without an outer garment, and in twenty days
he had nine meals.' Lu Wen-ch'ao, *Shuo-yüan chiao-pu*, p. 478 emended 二旬
'twenty days' to 三旬 'thirty days' because of the reading in T'ao's *After an
Old Poem*, V (see p. 110).

LINE 15. T'ao may have had in mind *Lun-yü* 15, 31: 'The Master said: "The
gentleman takes thought for the Way, he does not take thought for food. As
for farming, hunger may lie in it; as for study, it may bring a salary with it.
The gentleman is anxious about the Way, he is not anxious about poverty."'

47 THE DAY OF THE CHA SACRIFICE

蜡 日

風雪送餘運
無妨時已和
梅柳夾門植
4 一條有佳花

我唱爾言得
酒中適何多
未能明多少
章山有奇歌 8

THE POEMS IN SERIES

48　AFTER AN OLD POEM

擬古九首

I

榮榮窗下蘭
密密堂前柳
初與君別時
不謂行當久
出門萬里客
中道逢嘉友
未言心先醉*
不在接杯酒
蘭枯柳亦衰
遂令此言負
多謝諸少年
相知不忠厚
意氣傾人命
離隔復何有

* 先，各本作相，洪邁容齋三筆卷三引作先。

II

辭家凤嚴駕
當往至無終*
問君今何行
非商復非戎
聞有田子春+
節義爲士雄
斯人久已死
鄉里習其風
生有高世名
既沒傳無窮
不學狂馳子
直在百年中

* 至，陶注各本作志，汲古閣本云一作至，今從之。
+ 春，湯本作泰，陶澍等從之。

III

仲春遘時雨，始雷發東隅。
眾蟄各潛駭，草木縱橫舒。
翩翩新來燕，雙雙入我廬。
先巢故尚在，相將還舊居。
自從分別來，門庭日荒蕪。
我心固匪石，君情定何如。

IV

迢迢百尺樓，分明望四荒。
暮作歸雲宅，朝為飛鳥堂。
山河滿目中，平原獨茫茫。
古時功名士，慷慨爭此場。
一旦百歲後，相與還北邙。
松柏為人伐，高墳互低昂。
頹基無遺主，游魂在何方。
榮華誠足貴，亦復可憐傷。

V

東方有一士，被服常不完。
三旬九遇食，十年著一冠。
辛勤無此比，常有好容顏。
我欲觀其人，晨去越河關。
青松夾路生，白雲宿簷端。
知我故來意，取琴為我彈。
上絃驚別鶴，下絃操孤鸞。
願留就君住，從今至歲寒。

VI

蒼蒼谷中樹，冬夏常如茲。
年年見霜雪，誰謂不知時。
厭聞世上語，結友到臨淄。
稷下多談士，指彼決吾疑。

裝束既有日　　　　　但畏人我欺
已與家人辭　　　　　萬一不合意
行行停出門　　　　　永爲世笑嗤* 　16
還坐更自思　　　　　伊懷難具道
12
不怨道里長　　　　　爲君作此詩

* 嗤，陶注各本作之，從焦本作嗤。

VII

日暮天無雲　　　　　持此感人多
春風扇微和　　　　　皎皎雲間月
佳人美清夜　　　　　灼灼葉中華 　8
達曙酣且歌
4
歌竟長歎息　　　　　豈無一時好
　　　　　　　　　　不久當如何

VIII

少時壯且厲　　　　　不見相知人
撫劍獨行遊　　　　　惟見古時丘 　8
誰言行遊近　　　　　路邊兩高墳
張掖至幽州　　　　　伯牙與莊周
4
飢食首陽薇　　　　　此士難再得
渴飲易水流　　　　　吾行欲何求 　12

IX

種桑長江邊　　　　　根株浮滄海
三年望當採　　　　　春蠶既無食
枝條始欲茂　　　　　寒衣欲誰待 　8
忽值山河改
4
柯葉自摧折　　　　　本不植高原
　　　　　　　　　　今日復何悔

Additional Notes

I, 1–2. The description of nature in the opening couplet to create an atmosphere for a poem is a technique which reaches back through the

Nineteen Old Poems to the *Book of Songs*. Here a reminiscence may be felt of *Old Poem*, II: 青青河畔草, 鬱鬱園中柳 'Green is the herbage on the river bank;/Thick are the willows in the garden.' As Wang Shu-min has noted, the orchids have a sense of purity, while willows always suggest sorrow at parting. In view of the opposition with l.9, there may also be a faint reminiscence of *Song* 167, 6: 昔我往矣, 楊柳依依, 今我來思, 雨雪霏霏 'Before when we went out,/The willows were thick;/Now when we come back,/The falling snow is heavy.'

I, 7. For the expression *hsin . . . tsui*, cf. *Chuang-tzu* 7 (3B, 6a): 鄭有神巫曰季咸 . . . 列子見之而心醉 'In Cheng there was a holy shaman named Chi Hsien . . . When Master Lieh saw him his heart was drunk.'

II, 4. There is an alternative understanding of this line, stemming from Ch'eng Mu-heng (ap. Ting Fu-pao): 'It is not to Shang I am going, nor to the Jung', i.e. I am not following in the footsteps of Confucius who went to Sung (which was former Shang territory) or of Lao-tzu who is said to have gone to the Western Jung tribes. This seems to me oversubtle and not to fit the context particularly well.

II, 5. T'ien Ch'ou's biography appears in *San-kuo chih, Wei shu* 11, 10bff. In the current text T'ien Ch'ou's courtesy name is given as Tzu-t'ai 子泰 but the reading Tzu-ch'un, as Ku Chih noted, appears also in a quotation of the biography in Li Hsien's commentary to *Hou-Han shu* 103 (Biography of Liu Yü), 2b. It seems probable therefore that Li Kung-huan's reading of Tzu-ch'un is correct and that the reading Tzu-t'ai in the T'ang Han and other texts is the result of correction to accord with the current *San-kuo chih* text.

III, 1–6. The essential ideas of the first half of this poem are drawn from the *Yüeh-ling* 月令 text which is found both in *Lü-shih ch'un-ch'iu* 2, 1a–2a and *Li-chi* 6 (5, 4b–5b): 仲春之月 . . . 始雨水 . . . 是月也, 玄鳥至 . . . 是月也 . . . 雷乃發聲, 始電, 蟄蟲咸動 'In the middle spring month . . . the rains begin . . . In this month the swallow comes . . . In this month . . . the thunder bursts; there is the first lightning; hibernating insects all stir.'

IV, 1–2. Cf. *Old Poem*, V, 1–2: 西北有高樓, 上與浮雲齊 'In the north-west there is a lofty tower;/Its top is level with the floating clouds.'

IV, 9–10. These lines are reminiscent of *Song* 124, 4/5: 百歲之後，歸于其居 (室) 'After a hundred years/I shall return to his dwelling (i.e. the tomb).'

IV, 11–12. Cf. *Old Poem*, XIV, 5–6: 古墓犁爲田, 松柏摧爲薪 'The old tombs are ploughed into fields;/The pines and cypresses are broken for firewood.'

IV, 15–16. These lines have some look of being a kind of comment on the later lines of *Old Poem*, XI: 人生非金石，豈能長壽考，奄忽隨物化，榮名以爲寶 'Man's life is not metal or stone;/How can it lengthen its span?/Swiftly it follows nature's changes./Glory and fame are to be prized.'

V, 13. The *Parted Crane* appears in Hsi K'ang's *Ch'in-fu* ('Essay on the Lute'; *Wen-hsüan* 18, 27a) as the *Ch'ien-li pieh-ho* ('The Crane Parted by a Thousand *Li*'). Li Shan, commentary to *Wen-hsüan* ibid., quotes Ts'ai Yung's *Ch'in-tsao*: 'Shang-ling Mu-tzu took a wife and in five years she had no son. His father and elder brother wished him to take another wife. Mu-tzu took his lute and played on it the *Lament for the Parted Crane* to express his vexation.' A similar account appears in *Ku-chin chu* B, p. 11.

V, 14. The *Solitary Phoenix* (*Ku-luan*) has been identified by Wen Ju-neng, followed by several modern critics, as the *Li-luan* 離鸞 tune mentioned in *Hsi-ching tsa-chi* 2, 3b.

VI, 1–4. The 'trees in the valley' would seem to be the pine and cypress of *Chuang-tzu* 5 (2C, 4b): 受命於地，唯松栢獨也正．在冬夏青青． 'Of those things which receive their allotment from Earth, only the pine and cypress are constant. In winter and summer they are green.' At the same time T'ao seems to have in mind *Chuang-tzu* 28 (9B, 11b): 霜雪既降，吾是以知松栢之茂也 'When the frost and snow have descended, it is then that we know the vigour of the pine and cypress.' For he is certainly referring to the pine and cypress as symbols of the constancy of the gentleman in difficult times. Cf. Additional Note to *Written in the Third Month of the Year I-ssu*, 1.16, p. 78.

VII, 7. This line might, because of the similarity of subject, be a deliberate reminiscence of *Pai-t'ou yin* ('Song of the White Heads'; *Yü-t'ai hsin-yung* 1, 7a), sometimes attributed to Cho Wen-chün, wife of the Han *fu*-writer Ssu-ma Hsiang-ju. The second line reads: 皎若雲間月．

VII, 8. This line might be built on *Song* 6, 1 桃之夭夭，灼灼其華 'How beautiful is the peach;/Brilliant are its blossoms.' (The lines are a simile for a beautiful young bride.)

VIII, 10. The combination of Po-ya and Chung Tzu-ch'i with Chuang-tzu and Hui Shih as examples of devoted friends is found in *Huai-nan-tzu* 19, 11a and *Shuo-yüan* 16, 17a. For Po-ya and Chung Tzu-ch'i see also Additional Note to *Resentful Poem in the Ch'u Mode*, 1.20, pp. 48–49. The story of Chuang-tzu and Hui Shih starts from *Chuang-tzu* 24 (8B, 12a–13a): 'When Master Chuang was taking part in a burial procession, he passed by the tomb of Hui Shih. He turned and said to his companions: "... Since the master died, I have had none to be my witness, none with whom to talk."'

49 MISCELLANEOUS POEMS

雜詩十二首

I

人生無根蒂　　　　　　得歡當作樂
飄如陌上塵　　　　　　斗酒聚比鄰　　8
分散逐風轉　　　　　　盛年不重來
此已非常身　　　　　　一日難再晨
落地爲兄弟　　　　　　及時當勉勵
何必骨肉親　　　　　　歲月不待人　　12

II

白日淪西阿　　　　　　不眠知夕永　　8
素月出東嶺　　　　　　欲言無予和
遙遙萬里輝　　　　　　揮杯勸孤影
蕩蕩空中景　　　　　　日月擲人去
風來入房戶　　　　　　有志不獲騁　　12
中夜枕席冷　　　　　　念此懷悲悽
氣變悟時易　　　　　　終曉不能靜

III

榮華難久居　　　　　　枯悴未遽央
盛衰不可量　　　　　　日月有環周
昔爲三春蕖　　　　　　我去不再陽　　8
今作秋蓮房　　　　　　眷眷往昔時
嚴霜結野草　　　　　　憶此斷人腸

IV

丈夫志四海　　　　　　緩帶盡歡娛
我願不知老　　　　　　起晚眠常早　　8
親戚共一處　　　　　　孰若當世士
子孫還相保　　　　　　冰炭滿懷抱
觴絃肆朝日　　　　　　百年歸丘壟
樽中酒不燥　　　　　　用此空名道　　12

V

憶我少壯時
無樂自欣豫
猛志逸四海
騫翮思遠翥
荏苒歲月頹
此心稍已去
值歡無復娛
每每多憂慮
氣力漸衰損
轉覺日不如
壑舟無須臾
引我不得住
前塗當幾許
未知止泊處
古人惜寸陰
念此使人懼

VI

昔聞長者言
掩耳每不喜
奈何五十年
忽已親此事
求我盛年歡
一毫無復意
去去轉欲遠*
此生豈再值
傾家時作樂+
竟此歲月駛
有子不留金
何用身後置

* 遠，陶注本作速。
+ 時，各本作時，陶注本從焦本作持。

VII

日月不肯遲
四時相催迫
寒風拂枯條
落葉掩長陌
弱質與運頹
玄鬢早已白
素標插人頭
前塗漸就窄
家爲逆旅舍
我如當去客
去去欲何之
南山有舊宅

VIII

代耕本非望
所業在田桑
躬親未曾替
寒餒常糟糠
豈期過滿腹
但願飽粳糧
御冬足大布
麤絺以應陽
正爾不能得
哀哉亦可傷

人皆盡獲宜　　　　理也可奈何
12　拙生失其方　　　　且爲陶一觴

IX

遙遙從羈役　　　　蕭條隔天涯
一心處兩端　　　　惆悵念常飡　　8
掩淚汎東逝　　　　慷慨思南歸
4　順流追時遷　　　　路遐無由緣
日沒參與昴*　　　關梁難虧替
勢翳西山嶺　　　　絕音寄斯篇　　12

* 參，各本作星，王叔岷案星蓋參之誤，今從之。

X

閑居執蕩志　　　　我來淹已彌　　8
時駛不可稽　　　　慷慨憶綢繆
驅役無停息　　　　此情久已離
4　軒裳逝東崖　　　　荏苒經十載
沈陰擬薰麝　　　　暫爲人所羈　　12
寒氣激我懷　　　　庭宇翳餘木
歲月有常御　　　　倏忽日月虧

XI

我行未云遠　　　　代謝歸北鄉
回顧慘風涼　　　　離鵾鳴清池
春燕應節起　　　　涉暑經秋霜　　8
4　高飛拂塵梁　　　　愁人難爲辭
邊雁悲無所　　　　遙遙春夜長

XII

嫋嫋松標崖　　　　喬柯何可倚　　4
婉孌柔童子　　　　養色含津氣*
年始三五間　　　　粲然有心理

* 津，陶注本作精。

Additional Notes

I, 1. Because of the expression *ken-ti* there is a possibility of an oblique reference to *Lao-tzu* 59: 是謂深根固柢，長生久視之道 'This is called making deep the roots and making firm the foundation; it is the way of long life and enduring existence.' If any such oblique reference is present, T'ao would intend a rejection of the *Lao-tzu* proposition. All texts of T'ao's works read 蔕 which will stand as loan for 柢; many texts of *Lao-tzu* 59 also read 蔕 for 柢 (see Chiang Hsi-ch'ang, *Lao-tzu chiao-ku*, p. 367).

III, 1. There is a possible reminiscence here of Ts'ao Chih's *Miscellaneous Poem*, IV (*Wen-hsüan* 29, 23b): 榮耀難久恃 'Honour and glory are hard to depend on for long.'

III, 3–4. These lines are T'ao's particular variation on a very common formula: 昔爲 'once was' ... 今 'now' ... The earliest surviving example seems to be in the children's song of Han Ch'eng-ti's reign (32–7 BC), preserved in *Han shu* 27 中上, 24b: 故爲人所羨，今爲人所憐 'Of old it was the object of men's envy;/Now it is the object of their pity.' (This poem is one of the earliest examples of the five-word old poem.)

IV, 10. *Ping-t'an* (ice and charcoal); examples of this expression of incompatibility may be found in *Han-Fei-tzu*, but possibly T'ao could have had *Huai-nan-tzu* 11, 14a–b in his mind, since this seems particularly relevant to his thought in this poem. It reads: 'Now those who prize life do not injure themselves for the sake of profit; those who establish principles, when faced with difficulties, do not improperly avoid them; those who covet emoluments, when they see profit do not consider their persons; and those who love fame do not improperly obtain it without righteousness. For these to be discussed together may be compared with ice and charcoal, curve and line; when can they be combined?'

VI, 1–4. Ku Chih has found the source for T'ao's sixth poem in the *T'an-shih fu* 'Lament upon Death'; *Wen-hsüan* 16, 17a) of Lu Chi, the preface of which reads: 'In the past I always heard my elders going back over their past life and reckoning up that of the relations and friends of their own age some had already declined and died and some only were surviving. I am just forty, but of my close kin and relatives by marriage many have died and few are alive, and of my near associates and intimate friends again not half are living. Some with whom I travelled one road or with whom I feasted in one house came to their end and died more than ten years ago. By these thoughts' sadness, sorrow can indeed be known.' While there is some similarity between this and T'ao's opening lines so that T'ao could have had Lu Chi's work in his mind, he obviously developed his poem rather differently.

VI, 11–12. Most commentators have felt that T'ao had the story of Shu Kuang in mind in writing these lines, see *Singing of the Two Shus* (p. 124, in particular l.22).

VII, 9. The form of words might well be a reminiscence of *Lieh-tzu* 4, p. 81: 'I regard myself just as I regard others; I live in my house as if it were an inn for travellers', though T'ao's thought is of course different.

VII, 10. Cf. the similar image in *Old Poem*, III, 3–4: 'Man's life between Heaven and Earth is brief,/As of a guest who has far to go.'

VIII, 4. *Tsao-k'ang* (husks), the food of the poor scholar; cf. the reference to Yen Hui in *Shih-chi* 61, quoted in the Commentary to *Body, Shadow and Soul*; see vol. 1, p. 37.

VIII, 5. 'More than to fill my belly' is adapted from *Chuang-tzu* 1 (1A, 12b): 'When the mole drinks from the River, it does not more than fill his belly.'

VIII, 7. For the expression *yü tung* (to withstand the winter), cf. *Song* 35, 6: 'I have a good store to serve against the winter.'

IX, 5. All texts read 星與昴. But *Hsing* is a southern constellation, and Ch'eng Mu-heng (see Ting Fu-pao's commentary) suggested that the character should be amended to 胃, which is like *Mao* a western constellation. The proposal of Wang Shu-min to emend to 参 seems preferable, cf. *Song* 21, 2 where *Shen* and *Mao* are combined.

XI. This poem must have been written with *Chiu-pien* I (*Ch'u-tz'u* 8, 2b–3a) very much in mind, in particular:

> The swallows, fluttering, leave for home;
> The cicadas are silent and make no sound.
> The wild geese, crying to one another, fly south;
> The jungle-fowl clucks with a mournful sound.
> Alone, until dawn he does not sleep
> And grieves at the cricket's night wandering.

Whereas the season of the *Chiu-pien* is autumn, the usual time for melancholy, T'ao was writing of spring so that the pathos is heightened.

XI, 7. This line is found entire in Hsi K'ang's *Ch'in-fu* ('Essay on the Lute'; *Wen-hsüan* 18, 25a).

XII, 2. 'A soft child': the softness of the infant is an important condition in the Taoist art of nourishing life, cf. *Lao-tzu* 10: 'By concentrating the breath and achieving the utmost softness, can you be an infant?' 'Can you be an infant?' is the final item in Lao-tzu's canon for preserving life, given in *Chuang-tzu* 23 (8A, 9a–10a).

50 SINGING OF POOR SCHOLARS

詠貧士七首

I

萬族各有託	遲遲出林翮
孤雲獨無依	未夕復來歸 8
曖曖空中滅	量力守故轍
4 何時見餘暉	豈不寒與飢
朝霞開宿霧	知音苟不存
眾鳥相與飛	已矣何所悲 12

II

淒厲歲云暮	詩書塞座外
擁褐曝前軒	日昃不遑研 8
南圃無遺秀	閒居非陳厄
4 枯條盈北園	竊有慍見言
傾壺絕餘瀝	何以慰吾懷
闚竈不見煙	賴古多此賢 12

III

榮叟老帶索	弊襟不掩肘
欣然方彈琴	藜羹常乏斟 8
原生納決履	豈忘襲輕裘
4 清歌暢商音	苟得非所欽
重華去我久	賜也徒能辯
貧士世相尋	乃不見吾心 12

IV

安貧守賤者
自古有黔婁
好爵吾不榮
厚饋吾不酬
一旦壽命盡
弊服仍不周

豈不知其極
非道故無憂　8
從來將千載
未復見斯儔
朝與仁義生
夕死復何求　12

V

袁安困積雪*
逸然不可干
阮公見錢入
即日棄其官
芻藁有常溫
採莒足朝飡

豈不實辛苦
所懼非飢寒　8
貧富常交戰
道勝無戚顏
至德冠邦閭
清節映西關　12

* 困，各本作困，陶注本從何校宣和本作閈。

VI

仲蔚愛窮居
遶宅生蒿蓬
翳然絶交游
賦詩頗能工
舉世無知者
止有一劉龔

此士胡獨然
實由罕所同　8
介焉安其業
所樂非窮通
人事固以拙
聊得長相從　12

VII

昔有黃子廉*
彈冠佐名州
一朝辭吏歸
清貧略難儔
年饑感仁妻
泣涕向我流

丈夫雖有志
固爲兒女憂　8
惠孫一晤歎
腆贈竟莫酬
誰云固窮難
邈哉此前脩　12

* 有，各本作在，湯本註云一作有，今從之。

Additional Notes

I, 11. Cf. *Old Poem*, V, 13–14: 'She does not mind that her song is bitter,/But she is grieved that those who know the notes are few.' The expression 'know the notes' can be referred ultimately to the story of Po-ya and Chung Tzu-ch'i, see Additional Note to *Resentful Poem in the Ch'u Mode*, pp. 48–49.

II, 1. Cf. *Old Poem*, XVI, 1: 凜凜歲云暮 .

II, 8. The line is modelled on *Shu, Wu-i* (9, 10a–b): 'King Wen ... from morning to midday and to evening had no leisure to eat.' Cf. also *Written in the Seventh Month of the Year Hsin-ch'ou*, 1.13, p. 71.

III, 3–4. The source of T'ao's reference to Yüan Hsien could lie in *Chuang-tzu* 28 (9B, 7aff), *Han-shih wai-chuan* 1, 5a or *Hsin-hsü* 7, 8b, which have nearly identical texts. The encounter is also related in *Shih-chi* 67, pp. 35–36, but much more briefly and without the picturesque details of the other versions, which T'ao has taken into his poem. Line 8 of the poem, however, makes it probable that *Chuang-tzu* 28 is the source, for a little further on in the same chapter there appears: 'When Confucius was in distress between Ch'en and Ts'ai, for seven days he had no cooked food and with the goosefoot soup there were no dumplings.' Shun also makes an appearance in this chapter as a 'ceding ruler'. The *Chuang-tzu* text reads: 'Yüan Hsien lived in Lu in a house with surrounding walls only a few paces long. The thatch was growing grass; the brushwood door was unfinished and had a mulberry tree for a post. Its two rooms had earthenware pots for windows, blocked up with coarse cloth. [The above description corresponds closely with the "type" given for the poor scholar's habitation in *Li-chi* 41 (19, 6a).] The roof leaked and the floor was damp, but seating himself correctly, he would play on his lute and sing. Tzu-kung, driving large horses and wearing an inner robe of deep purple and an outer plain one, in a canopied carriage which could not get into the lane, came to see Yüan Hsien. Yüan Hsien in a [?] straw [the *hua* "elegant" of the present text cannot be correct; Liu Wen-tien's emendation 草 from the quotation in *T'ai-p'ing yü-lan* 998, 3a seems the most probable] hat and slippers without heels and with a staff of thorn, answered the door. Tzu-kung said: "Oh! What sickness have you, sir?" Yüan Hsien replied: "I have heard that to be without property is called poverty and that not to be able to put into practice what one has studied is called sickness. Now I am poor, but I am not sick." Tzu-kung drew back, shamefaced. Yüan Hsien laughed and said: "To act with an eye to the world's opinion, to follow the herd in making friends, to study in order to please others and to teach for the sake of oneself, to conceal goodness and righteousness and make a display of carriages and horses, I cannot bear to do."'

'When Master Yüan [the present text reads 曾子; the reading 原子 is taken from *T'ai-p'ing yü-lan* 686, 5a. This is confirmed by the *Han-shih wai-chuan* and *Hsin-hsü* parallels and also, if *Chuang-tzu* is the source, by T'ao's poem] was living in Wei, he wore a robe, quilted with hemp, without an outer garment. His face was swollen and his hands and feet were calloused. For three days he did not light a fire; in ten years he did not make new clothes. When he straightened his cap, the strings broke; when he drew tight the lapel of his robe, his elbows could be seen; when he put on his shoes, the heels burst. Yet dragging his shoes along, he sang the *Hymns of Shang*. His voice filled heaven and earth, as though coming from an instrument of metal or stone.'

III, 8. Besides *Chuang-tzu* 28 (9B, 10b), the statement about Confucius having no dumplings with the goosefoot soup during the 'Distress in Ch'en' occurs in *Hsün-tzu* 28, p. 345 (糂), *Han-shih wai-chuan* 7, 3b (糝), *Shuo-yüan* 17, 11b (糝) and *Lü-shih ch'un-ch'iu* 14, 15b (糝) and 17, 8a (current text 斟 as current T'ao; Pi Yüan would emend to 糂). It would seem on the weight of evidence that the current text of T'ao should be emended.

III, 10. The underlying idea of this line is *Lun-yü* 4, 5: 'The Master said: "Riches and honour are what men desire, but if it is not possible by the proper way, one does not abide in them. Poverty and humble position, these are what men hate, but if it is not possible by the proper way, one does not avoid them."'

IV, 1–6. The *Lieh-nü chuan* story of Ch'ien Lou reads: 'There was the wife of Master Ch'ien Lou of Lu. When he died, Master Tseng and his disciples came to condole with her. He ascended the hall and saw her husband's corpse under the window with an unbaked brick for a pillow and a mat of straw. The body was dressed in a hemp-quilted gown without an outer garment, and was covered by a linen coverlet which did not completely cover the hands and feet. If the head was covered, the feet were seen. Master Tseng said: "Spread the coverlet askew and then the body will be covered." The wife said: "Askew and ample is not as good as straight and insufficient. It was because the Master was not askew that he could come to this. When in his life he was not crooked, to make him so in death would not be the Master's wish." Master Tseng could not answer. Then he lamented for him, saying: "Alas! When the Master has died in this way, what shall be his posthumous name?" His wife said: "Let K'ang [Happy] be his posthumous name." Master Tseng said: "When the Master was alive, his food did not fill his mouth, his clothes did not cover his body. Now he is dead, his hands and feet are not covered, and there are no wine and meat by his side. When he was alive, he did not get his due honour. What happiness is there in this, that he should have the posthumous name K'ang?" His wife said: "In the past the Master's ruler desired to confer the government upon him and make him prime minister of the state, but he declined and did not take office. Thus he had abundant honour. The ruler presented him with thirty measures of millet, but the Master declined and did not accept them. Thus he had abundant riches. He delighted in the most insipid tastes in the world, he was content with the most humble position in the world; he did not grieve over poverty and low position, he did not rejoice at riches and high rank; he sought goodness and he found goodness, he sought righteousness and he found righteousness. Is it not indeed appropriate that his posthumous name should be K'ang?'' Master Tseng said: "He was such a man and he had such a wife!"' The brief account of Ch'ien Lou in Huang-fu Mi's *Kao-shih chuan* (B, 5a) identifies the ruler as Duke Kung of Lu.

V, 1–2. The fragment of Chou Fei's *Ju-nan hsien-hsien chuan* which can provide a source for T'ao's lines occurs in Li Hsien's commentary to Yüan An's biography in *Hou-Han shu* 75, 1a: 'At the time there was heavy snow which piled up on the ground to a depth of more than ten feet. The Prefect of Lo-yang himself went out on a tour of inspection and saw everyone clearing away the snow and going out; some were begging for food. When he came to Yüan An's gate, there was no path. He said: "An has died" and ordered men to clear away the snow. He entered the door and saw An lying down. When he asked why he did not go out, An said: "In heavy snow everyone is hungry; it is not right to trouble others." The Prefect considered him to be a worthy man and recommended him as a Filial and Uncorrupt Person.'

V, 3–4. Suzuki Torao suggested that 'Master Juan' was Juan Hsiu 阮修 (third century) nephew of the poet Juan Chi, because of the statement in his short biography in *Chin shu* 49, 5a: 'Hsiu lived in poverty and when he was more than forty, still had no wife. Wang Tun and others who collected money for him to marry, were all famous scholars. At this time his admirers sought to present him with money, but did not succeed.' But this does not provide all the essential details of T'ao's reference so that it cannot command positive acceptance.

V, 6. The fragment of the *Ju-nan hsien-hsien chuan* to which T'ao could be referring is preserved in *T'ai-p'ing yü-lan* 975, 3a: 'Yüan An was appointed Magistrate of Yin-p'ing. The year was one of famine, and the people were all living on vegetables. The tax contribution had not been completed. When An heard of it, he ordered payment to be made in taro, saying: "If the people are suffering hunger, how can the magistrate eat grain?" He himself first accepted the taro, and his subordinates followed his example.' *Shuo-wen* 1A (p. 16) states that *chü* 莒 is a Ch'i word for *yü* 芋 'taro'. If T'ao is referring to this story of Yüan An, Ho Ch'o's suggestion (*I-men tu-shu chi, T'ao Ching-chieh shih*, 6a) that *chü* should be *lü* 稆 (= 'wild rice') can be discarded.

V, 9–10. Besides *Huai-nan-tzu*, this story also occurs in *Han-Fei-tzu* 7, p. 416, where it is used as an illustration for *Lao-tzu* 33. A more elaborate version of the same basic idea is to be found in *Han-shih wai-chuan* 2, 4a–5a, where Min Tzu-ch'ien replaces Tzu-hsia.

VII, 1–2. There seems to be only two surviving early references to Huang Tzu-lien. A fragment of the *Wu shu* of Wei Chao ap. P'ei Sung-chih's commentary to *San-kuo chih*, *Wu shu* 10, 1b (Biography of Huang Kai) states that Huang Kai was a descendant of the former Prefect of Nan-yang, Huang Tzu-lien. The second mention is in a fragment of *Feng-su t'ung-i* ap. *T'ai-p'ing yü-lan* 426, 5a and 836, 4b which states that: 'Whenever Huang Tzu-lien of Ying-ch'uan watered his horse, he threw a coin into the stream.' It may be noted that a rather similar story is told of Ho Tzu-lien 郝子廉 of T'ai-yüan in the current text of *Feng-su t'ung-i* (3, p. 23). Neither of these references allows Huang Tzu-lien to be firmly identified. Huang Chin (1277–1357) in his *Jih-sun chai pi-chi*, 12a, presumably on the basis of a family genealogy, identifies Huang Tzu-lien (regarding Tzu-lien as a courtesy-name) as Huang Shou-liang 守亮, whom he states was a grandson of Huang Hsiang 香 Chief Secretary (*shang-shu ling*) in AD 96. But as Wu Ch'ien pointed out in *Pai-ching lou shih-hua* 3, 3a, no evidence for this can be found in *Hou-Han shu*, which has biographies of Huang Hsiang and his son Ch'iung 瓊, and post-T'ang genealogies contain many forced interpretations and fabrications. It therefore seems unwise to accept Huang Chin's unsupported statement.

51 SINGING OF THE TWO SHUS

詠 二 疏

	大象轉四時	人行感勝事
	功成者自去	譽常豈哉賢
	借問衰周來	歡里閭厭厭
4	幾人得其趣	務近非營所 · 16
	游目漢廷中	老故延席促
	二疏復此舉	素平道觴揮
	高嘯返舊居	心寄終金問
8	長揖儲君傅	悟未曉言清 · 20
	餞送傾皇朝	年餘樂意放
	華軒盈道路	慮後身恤遑
	離別情所悲	亡人其云誰
12	餘榮何足顧	著彌道而久 · 24

52 SINGING OF THE THREE GOOD MEN

詠三良

彈冠乘通津
但懼時我遺
服勤盡歲月
常恐功愈微 4
忠情謬獲露
遂爲君所私
出則陪文輿
入必侍丹帷 8
箴規嚮已從
計議初無虧
一朝長逝後
願言同此歸 12
厚恩固難忘
君命安可違
臨穴罔惟疑
投義志攸希 16
荊棘籠高墳
黃鳥聲正悲
良人不可贖
泫然沾我衣 20

53 SINGING OF CHING K'O

詠荊軻

燕丹善養士
志在報強嬴
招集百夫良
歲暮得荊卿 4
君子死知己
提劍出燕京
素驥鳴廣陌
慷慨送我行 8
雄髮指危冠
猛氣衝長纓
飲餞易水上
四座列群英 12
漸離擊悲筑
宋意唱高聲
蕭蕭哀風逝
淡淡寒波生 16
商音更流涕
羽奏壯士驚
心知去不歸
且有後世名 20
登車何時顧
飛蓋入秦庭
凌厲越萬里
逶迤過千城 24
圖窮事自至
豪主正怔營
惜哉劍術疏
奇功遂不成 28
其人雖已沒
千載有餘情

54 READING THE *SHAN-HAI-CHING*

讀山海經十三首

I

孟夏草木長　　　　歡然酌春酒
遶屋樹扶疏　　　　摘我園中蔬
眾鳥欣有託　　　　微雨從東來
4　吾亦愛吾廬　　　　好風與之俱　12
既耕亦已種　　　　汎覽周王傳
時還讀我書　　　　流觀山海圖
窮巷隔深轍　　　　俯仰終宇宙
8　頗迴故人車　　　　不樂復何如　16

II

玉臺凌霞秀　　　　靈化無窮已
王母怡妙顏　　　　館宇非一山
天地共俱生　　　　高酣發新謠
4　不知幾何年　　　　寧效俗中言　8

III

迢遞槐江嶺　　　　亭亭明玕照
是謂玄圃丘　　　　落落清滛流*
西南望崑墟　　　　恨不及周穆
4　光氣難與儔　　　　託乘一來游　8

* 滛，各本作瑤，今從何義門讀書記作滛。

IV

丹木生何許　　　　白玉凝素液
廼在峚山陽　　　　瑾瑜發奇光
黃花復朱實　　　　豈伊君子寶
4　食之壽命長　　　　見重我軒黃　8

V

翩翩三青鳥
毛色奇可憐
朝爲王母使
暮歸三危山　4
我欲因此鳥
具向王母言
在世無所須
惟酒與長年　8

VI

逍遙蕪皋上
杳然望扶木
洪柯百萬尋
森散覆暘谷　4
靈人侍丹池
朝朝爲日浴
神景一登天
何幽不見燭　8

VII

粲粲三珠樹
寄生赤水陰
亭亭凌風桂
八幹共成林　4
靈鳳撫雲舞
神鸞調玉音
雖非世上寶
爰得王母心　8

VIII

自古皆有沒
何人得靈長
不死復不老
萬歲如平常　4
赤泉給我飲
員丘足我糧
方與三辰游
壽考豈渠央　8

IX

夸父誕宏志
乃與日競走
俱至虞淵下
似若無勝負　4
神力既殊妙
傾河焉足有
餘迹寄鄧林
功竟在身後　8

X

精衛銜微木
將以填滄海
形天舞干戚*
猛志故常在　4
同物既無慮
化去不復悔
徒設在昔心
良晨詎可待　8

＊ 天，曾紘案當作夭。今不從之。又舞干戚，原本作無干歲。今從曾紘作舞干戚。

XI

巨猾肆威暴* 　　明明上天鑒
欽䲹違帝旨 　　為惡不可履
窫窳強能變 　　長梧固已劇⁺
4　祖江遂獨死 　　鵁鵝豈足恃　　8

* 巨猾，各本作巨猾，丁箋注本改作臣危。
⁺ 梧，各本作枯，丁箋注本改作梧。今從之。

XII

鳴鴂見城邑* 　　青丘有奇鳥
其國有放士 　　自言獨見爾
念彼懷王世 　　本為迷者生
4　當時數來止 　　不以喻君子　　8

* 鳴鴂，各本作鵃鵝，湯注云當作鴟鴂。今改作鳴鴂。

XIII

巖巖顯朝市 　　仲父獻誠言
帝者慎用才 　　姜公乃見猜
何以廢共鯀 　　臨沒告飢渴
4　重華為之來 　　當復何及哉　　8

Additional Notes

III, 6. I follow Ho Ch'o in believing that 滛 is the correct reading in both the *Shan-hai-ching* and T'ao's poem, rather than that the *Shan-hai-ching* should be corrected from the current 瑤 of T'ao's poem, as Hao I-hsing and others proposed. (See Ho's *I-men tu-shu chi*, *T'ao Ching-chieh shih*, 6b)

III, 7–8. In the *Mu t'ien-tzu chuan* passage (2, 2b) which is the source for these two lines the *Hsüan* of Hsüan-p'u is written 縣 (=modern 懸) 'hanging', but Kuo P'u's citation of this passage in his commentary to *Shan-hai-ching* 2, 16a has 玄 as in T'ao's poem, line 2. The constant alternation of these two characters in the writing of this name makes decision in favour of one or the other probably arbitrary. The explanation might be that both are used only for their sound values.

IV, 8. With Hsüan-huang 軒黃 (apparently a contraction of Hsüan-yüan Huang-ti 軒轅皇帝 'The Yellow Emperor, Lord of Hsüan-yüan') compare Huang Hsüan 黃軒 of Kuo P'u's Appraisal for the picture of the Red Trees and Liquid Jade.

VI, 5–6. The current text of the *Shan-hai-ching* passage (15, 5a) which provides the source for these lines appears in part to be faulty. The current versions read: 方日浴于甘淵 with the exception of the 1470 text reprinted in the *Ssu-pu ts'ung-k'an* which has 方浴日于甘淵. Various quotations (*I-wen lei-chü* 1, 4a, *Ch'u-hsüeh chi* 1, p. 5, *T'ai-p'ing yü-lan* 3, 6b and Li Hsien's commentary to *Hou-Han shu* 79, 7b) also read: 浴日. Of these only Li Hsien preserves the difficult 方. I suggest that the 為 of T'ao's line might be the original character corrupted into 方 through cursive forms. In that case the order 日浴 would be correct. Ku Chih's suggestion that the *Shan-hai-ching*'s 甘淵 is an error for the 丹淵 of T'ao's line and which is also supported by its occurrence in Juan Chi's *Yung-huai shih*, XXIII seems reasonable.

X, 3. There has been considerable discussion among commentators both to the *Shan-hai-ching* and T'ao's poem as to whether 形天 or 形夭 is the correct reading. An extensive summary of this discussion is given in Hashikawa Tokio's *T'ao-chi pan-pen yüan-liu k'ao*, 47b–49b. The attempt to reconcile T'ao's line with the *Shan-hai-ching* began with Tseng Hung, whose comment is dated 1124. It is clear that the twelfth century reading of T'ao's line was 形夭無干歲, but subsequently many editions have substituted the emendation proposed by Tseng Hung, viz. 刑天舞干戚. The weight of evidence cited by Hashikawa, however, points to 形天 having been the original reading of the *Shan-hai-ching*. I have therefore retained the reading 形天 but accepted the emendation 舞干戚 (Hashikawa would read 無干戚).

XII, 1. In none of the early texts of T'ao's works does the character 鵠 (*chu*) appear; the Tseng Chi text reads 鵾鵠 and notes as variant 鳴鵠, while the Li Kung-han text reads 鵾鵾. T'ang Han proposed the emendation 鷗鵼 in an attempt to make T'ao's text agree with the *Shan-hai-ching*, and this emendation has been generally adopted. Some modern editions in fact print the emendation without noting it as such. Yet 鷗鵼 is not supported as a compound word and it does not seem a very happy formation. I would suggest that the correct reading may be 鳴鵼.

55 IN IMITATION OF BURIAL SONGS

擬挽歌辭三首*

I

有生必有死　　良友撫我哭
早終非命促　　得失不復知
昨暮同爲人　　是非安能覺
今旦在鬼錄　　千秋萬歲後
魂氣散何之　　誰知榮與辱
枯形寄空木　　但恨在世時
嬌兒索父啼　　飲酒不得足

* 陶注云諸本作擬挽歌辭，文選作挽歌詩，無擬字，今從之。

II

在昔無酒飲　　欲語口無音
今但湛空觴　　欲視眼無光
春醪生浮蟻　　昔在高堂寢
何時更能嘗　　今宿荒草鄉
肴案盈我前　　一朝出門去
親舊哭我傍　　歸來良未央

III

荒草何茫茫　　千年不復朝
白楊亦蕭蕭　　千年不復朝
嚴霜九月中　　賢達無奈何
送我出遠郊　　向來相送人
四面無人居　　各自還其家
高墳正嶕嶢　　親戚或餘悲
馬爲仰天鳴　　他人亦已歌
風爲自蕭條　　死去何所道
幽室一已閉　　託體同山阿

Additional Notes

I,1. Cf. the beginning of *To My Sons, Yen and the Others*, p. 153.

I, 5. There could be a reminiscence of the funeral observances of Yen-ling Chi-tzu, described by Confucius in *Li-chi* 4 (3, 17a): 'Then he wailed three times, saying: "Bones and flesh return to the earth. It is their destiny. As for the soul, there is nowhere it will not go, there is nowhere it will not go."'

I, 11–12. These lines seem certainly to be a reminiscence of Juan Chi's *Yung-huai shih*, XV, 9–10: 'After a thousand autumns, ten thousand years,/Glory and fame, where will they have gone?'

II, 10. Following this line the T'ang Han text notes that one edition contained two extra lines: 荒草無人眠, 極視正茫茫 'In the wilds no one sleeps;/To the limit of one's gaze it is simply desolate.' These two lines are actually to be found in the *Yüeh-fu shih chi* version of the poem (ch. 27, 9a), but they seem unlikely to be original and perhaps arose in some manner from the first line of Poem III.

III, 1–2. These lines recall *Old Poem*, XI, 3–4: 'Every way one looks, how vast!/The east wind shakes the hundred plants,' and *Old Poem*, XIII, 3–4: 'The white aspens, how mournful!/Pines and cypresses line the broad road.'

5

THE *FU* POEMS

56 MOVED BY SCHOLARS' NOT MEETING WITH GOOD FORTUNE

感士不遇賦

序　昔董仲舒作士不遇賦，司馬子長又爲之。余嘗以三餘之日，講習之暇，讀其文，慨然惆悵。夫履信思順，生人之善行，抱朴守靜，君子之篤素。自眞風告逝，大偽斯興，閭閻懈廉退之節，市朝驅易進之心。懷正志道之士，或潛玉於當年，潔己清操之人，或沒世以徒勤。故夷皓有安歸之歎，三閭發已矣之哀。悲夫。寓形百年，而瞬息已盡。立行之難，而一城莫賞。此古人所以染翰慷慨，屢伸而不能已者也。夫導達意氣，其惟文乎。撫卷躊躇，遂感而賦之。

咨大塊之受氣　　　　　彼達人之善覺
何斯人之獨靈　　　　　乃逃祿而歸耕
稟神智以藏照　　　　　山嶷嶷而懷影
4　秉三五而垂名　　　　川汪汪而藏聲　16
或擊壤以自歡　　　　　望軒唐而永歎
或大濟於蒼生　　　　　甘貧賤以辭榮
靡潛躍之非分　　　　　淳源汩以長分
8　常傲然以稱情　　　　美惡作以異途　20
世流浪而遂徂　　　　　原百行之攸貴
物羣分以相形　　　　　莫爲善之可娛
密網裁'而魚駭　　　　　奉上天之成命
12　宏羅制而鳥驚　　　師聖人之遺書　24

發忠孝於君親
生信義於鄉閭
推誠心而獲顯
28　不矯然而祈譽
嗟乎雷同毀異
物惡其上
妙算者謂迷
32　直道者云妄
坦至公而無猜
卒蒙恥以受謗
雖懷瓊而握蘭
36　徒芳潔而誰亮
哀哉士之不遇
已不在炎帝帝魁之世
獨祗脩以自勤
40　豈三省之或廢
庶進德以及時
時既至而不惠
無爰生之晤言
44　念張季之終蔽
愍馮叟於郎署
賴魏守以納計
雖僅然於必知
48　亦苦心而曠歲
審夫市之無虎
眩三夫之獻說
悼賈傅之秀朗
52　紆遠轡於促界
悲董相之淵致
屢乘危而幸濟
感哲人之無偶
56　淚淋浪以灑袂

承前王之清誨
曰天道之無親
澄得一以作鑒
恆輔善而佑仁　60
夷投老以長飢
回早夭而又貧
傷請車以備槨
悲茹薇而隕身　64
雖好學與行義
何死生之苦辛
疑報德之若茲
懼斯言之虛陳　68
何曠世之無才
罕無路之不澀
伊古人之慷慨
病奇名之不立　72
廣結髮以從政
不愧賞於萬邑
屈雄志於戚豎
竟尺土之莫及　76
留誠信於身後
動眾人之悲泣
商盡規以拯弊
言始順而患入　80
奚良辰之易傾
胡害勝其乃急
蒼昊遐緬
人事無已　84
有感有昧
疇測其理
寧固窮以濟意
不委曲而累己　88

既軒冕之非榮　　　　且欣然而歸止
豈縕袍之爲恥　　　　擁孤襟以畢歲　　92
誠謬會以取拙　　　　謝良價於朝市

57　QUIETING THE AFFECTIONS

閑 情 賦

序　初張衡作定情賦，蔡邕作靜情賦。檢逸辭而宗澹泊，始則蕩以思慮，而終歸閑正。將以抑流宕之邪心，諒有助於諷諫。綴文之士，奕代繼作，並因* 觸類，廣其辭義，余園閭多暇，復染翰爲之。雖文妙不足，庶不謬作者之意乎。

夫何瓌逸之令姿　　　悲商叩林
獨曠世以秀羣　　　　白雲依山
表傾城之艷色　　　　仰睇天路
4　期有德於傳聞　　　俯促鳴絃　　24
佩鳴玉以比潔　　　　神儀嫵媚
齊幽蘭以爭芬　　　　舉止詳姸
淡柔情於俗內　　　　激清音以感余
8　負雅志於高雲　　　願接膝以交言　　28
悲晨曦之易夕　　　　欲自往以結誓
感人生之長勤　　　　懼冒禮之爲愆
同一盡於百年　　　　待鳳鳥以致辭
12　何歡寡而愁殷　　　恐他人之我先　　32
褰朱幬而正坐　　　　意惶惑而靡寧
汎清瑟以自欣　　　　魂須臾而九遷
送纖指之餘好　　　　願在衣而爲領
16　攘皓袖之繽紛　　　承華首之餘芳　　36
瞬美目以流盼　　　　悲羅襟之宵離
含言笑而不分　　　　怨秋夜之未央
曲調將半　　　　　　願在裳而爲帶
20　景落西軒　　　　　束窈窕之纖身　　40

* 並因，陶注云，從張自烈本作因，各本作固。

嗟溫涼之異氣
或脫故而服新
願在髮而為澤
44 刷玄鬢於頹肩
悲佳人之屢沐
從白水以枯煎
願在眉而為黛
48 隨瞻視以閒揚
悲脂粉之尚鮮
或取毀於華妝
願在莞而為席
52 安弱體於三秋
悲文茵之代御
方經年而見求
願在絲而為履
56 附素足以周旋
悲行止之有節
空委棄於床前
願在晝而為影
60 常依形而西東
悲高樹之多蔭
慨有時而不同
願在夜而為燭
64 照玉容於兩楹
悲扶桑之舒光
奄滅景而藏明
願在竹而為扇
68 含淒飈於柔握
悲白露之晨零
顧襟袖以緬邈
願在木而為琴
72 作膝上之鳴琴

悲樂極以哀來
終推我而輟音
考所願而必違
76 徒契契以苦心
擁勞情而罔訴
步容與於南林
栖木蘭之遺露
80 翳青松之餘陰
儻行行之有覿
交欣懼於中襟
竟寂寞而無見
84 獨悁想以空尋
斂輕裾以復路
瞻夕陽而流歎
步徙倚以忘趣
88 色慘悽而矜顏
葉燮燮以去條
氣淒淒而就寒
日負影以偕沒
92 月媚景於雲端
鳥悽聲以孤歸
獸索偶而不還
悼當年之晚暮
96 恨茲歲之欲殫
思宵夢以從之
神飄颻而不安
若憑舟之失棹
100 譬緣崖而無攀
于時畢昴盈軒
北風淒淒
惆惆不寐
104 眾念徘徊

起攝帶以伺晨
繁霜燦於素階
雞斂翅而未鳴
108 笛流遠以清哀
始妙密以閑和
終寥亮而藏摧
意夫人之在茲
112 託行雲以送懷
行雲逝而無語

時奄冉而就過
徒勤思以自悲
終阻山而帶河 116
迎清風以袪累
寄弱志於歸波
尤蔓草之爲會
誦邵南之餘歌 120
坦萬慮以存誠
憩遙情於八遐

58 RETURN HOME!

歸去來兮辭

序　余家貧,耕植不足以自給。幼稚盈室,缾無儲粟,生生所資,未見其術。親故多勸余爲長吏,脫然有懷,求之靡途。會有四方之事,諸侯以惠愛爲德,家叔以余貧苦,遂見用於小邑。於時風波未靜,心憚遠役,彭澤去家百里,公田之利,足以爲酒,故便求之。及少日,眷然有歸歟之情。何則。質性自然,非矯厲所得。飢凍雖切,違己交病。嘗從人事,皆口腹自役。於是悵然慷慨,深媿平生之志。猶望一稔,當斂裳宵逝。尋程氏妹喪于武昌,情在駿奔,自免去職。仲秋至冬,在官八十餘日。因事順心,命篇曰,歸去來兮。乙巳歲十一月也。

歸去來兮
田園將蕪胡不歸
既自以心爲形役
4 奚惆悵而獨悲
悟已往之不諫
知來者之可追
實迷途其未遠
8 覺今是而昨非

舟遙遙以輕颺
風飄飄而吹衣
問征夫以前路
恨晨光之熹微 12
乃瞻衡宇
載欣載奔
僮僕歡迎
稚子候門 16

三逕就荒　　　　　農人告余以春及
松菊猶存　　　　　將有事於西疇　　40
攜幼入室　　　　　或命巾車
20　有酒盈罇　　　或棹孤舟
引壺觴以自酌　　　既窈窕以尋壑
眄庭柯以怡顏　　　亦崎嶇而經丘　　44
倚南窗以寄傲　　　木欣欣以向榮
24　審容膝之易安　泉涓涓而始流
園日涉以成趣　　　善萬物之得時
門雖設而常關　　　感吾生之行休　　48
策扶老以流憩　　　已矣乎
28　時矯首而遐觀　寓形宇內復幾時
雲無心以出岫　　　曷不委心任去留
鳥倦飛而知還　　　胡爲乎遑遑欲何之　52
景翳翳以將入　　　富貴非吾願
32　撫孤松而盤桓　帝鄉不可期
歸去來兮　　　　　懷良辰以孤往
請息交以絕游　　　或植杖而耘耔　　56
世與我而相遺　　　登東皋以舒嘯
36　復駕言兮焉求　臨清流而賦詩
悦親戚之情話　　　聊乘化以歸盡
樂琴書以消憂　　　樂夫天命復奚疑　60

6

HISTORICAL WRITINGS

59 PEACH-BLOSSOM SOURCE

桃花源記

序　晉太元中，武陵人捕魚爲業，緣溪行，忘路之遠近。忽
逢桃花林，夾岸數百步，中無雜樹。芳草鮮美，落英繽
紛。漁人甚異之，復前行，欲窮其林，林盡水源，便得
一山。山有小口，髣髴若有光。便捨船從口入。初極
狹，纔通人，復行數十步，豁然開朗。土地平曠，屋舍
儼然。有良田、美池、桑竹之屬。阡陌交通，雞犬相
聞。其中往來種作，男女衣著，悉如外人。黃髮垂髫，
並怡然自樂。見漁人，乃大驚，問所從來。具答之，便
要還家，爲設酒，殺雞作食。村中聞有此人，咸來問
訊。自云先世避秦時亂，率妻子邑人來此絕境，不復出
焉。遂與外人間隔。問今是何世，乃不知有漢，無論魏
晉。此人一一爲具言所聞，皆歎惋。餘人各復延至其
家，皆出酒食。停數日，辭去。此中人語云，不足爲外
人道也。既出，得其船，便扶向路，處處誌之。及郡下，
詣太守說如此。太守即遣人隨其往，尋向所誌，遂迷不
復得路。南陽劉子驥，高尚士也。聞之，欣然規往。未
果，尋病終。後遂無問津者。

```
嬴氏亂天紀          往迹寖復湮
賢者避其世          來逕遂蕪廢
黃綺之商山          相命肆農耕
伊人亦云逝          日入從所憩
```

桑竹垂餘蔭　　　　雖無紀曆誌
菽稷隨時藝　　　　四時自成歲
春蠶收長絲　　　　怡然有餘樂
12　秋熟靡王稅　　　于何勞智慧　24
荒路曖交通　　　　奇蹤隱五百
雞犬互鳴吠　　　　一朝敞神界
俎豆猶古法　　　　淳薄既異源
16　衣裳無新製　　　旋復還幽蔽　28
童孺縱行歌　　　　借問游方士
班白歡遊詣　　　　焉測塵囂外
草榮識節和　　　　願言躡輕風
20　木衰知風厲　　　高舉尋吾契　32

Additional Commentary

Ch'en Yin-k'o in his article '*T'ao-hua yüan chi* p'ang-cheng' ('Circumstantial Evidence on *T'ao-hua yüan chi*'), first published in *Tsing-hua hsüeh-pao* XI, no. 1 (1936), has undoubtedly had a considerable effect upon subsequent critics, whether they have accepted or substantially rejected his ideas. Although he saw *Peach-blossom Source* as a combination of allegory and the description of actuality, being foremost an historian, he was clearly more engaged by the latter aspect and his searching out of historical references to groups which withdrew into remote places and maintained themselves as independent communities is probably the most valuable and enduring element of this article.

He was, however, conscious of the need to attempt some explanation of the existence of the collected works and *Sou-shen hou-chi* versions of this piece and he offered a rather curious explanation. He suggested that the *Sou-shen hou-chi* version was T'ao's original rough draft and that the collected works version was his revised, final text. This does not seem to me a very satisfactory description of the two actual texts, and to sustain such an argument would surely require an attempt to explain T'ao's relationship with the *Sou-shen hou-chi*. Ch'en, in fact, doubted whether T'ao had any connection with this work, because of his family's beliefs and his personal ideology, but he dismissed the general question as lying outside the scope of his article. Though he did not try to explain how T'ao's rough draft came to be included in *Sou-shen hou-chi*, he attempted to fit the statements of both versions into his general theory of T'ao's conception of *Peach-blossom Source*. His main conclusions are:

(a) The actual T'ao-hua yüan was at Hung-nung or Shang-lo in the north and not at Wu-ling in the south.

(b) The Ch'in from which the ancestors of the inhabitants of the actual T'ao-hua yüan fled was Fu Ch'in (i.e. the Former Ch'in empire of Fu Chien, 357–85) and not Ying Ch'in (221–208 BC).

(c) The part of *Peach-blossom Source* which is actual description was based on the experiences of Tai Yen-chih and others at the time when Liu Yü led his army into Kuan-chung (i.e. north-west China around Ch'ang-an) in the spring and summer of I-hsi 13 (417).

(d) The allegorical part of *Peach-blossom Source* introduces and combines the story of Liu Lin-chih going into Heng-shan to gather herbs, and also adds the embellishment: 'They did not know that there had been Han, nor of course Wei or Chin.'

(e) Yüan-ming's *After an Old Poem*, II (see p. 109) and *Peach-blossom Source* can support and throw light on each other.

When Ch'en talked of the 'experiences' of Tai Yen-chih and others, his evidence was indeed extremely 'circumstantial'. Tai Tso (courtesy-name Yen-chih), who was a military aide during Liu Yü's northern expedition, wrote a *Hsi-cheng chi* (*Record of the Expedition to the West*) in 2 chüan. None of the fragments of this and several similar works to which the expedition gave rise and which have been preserved in quotation contains any direct reference to people who had been discovered in hidden communities. The most that these sources yields is the occurrence of words for 'fortified encampments', in which such communities could conceivably have dwelt. But having arrived at his very 'circumstantial' speculation, Ch'en proceeded to extend it. He suggested that there might be a correspondence between the fisherman's name, Huang Tao-chen and Yü Tao-yüan, who was sent by Liu Yü up the Lo River in 417 and that the name given for the Prefect of Wu-ling, Liu Hsin is a cover for Liu Yü. These suggestions seem very far-fetched and are perhaps an illustration of how even a very fine Chinese historian can be affected by the universal Chinese belief in the omnipresence of concealed political allusions. Ch'en's view that Liu Hsin did not exist (presumably because he cannot be confirmed from a second source) is surely rash. Above all, it is hard to see what T'ao Yüan-ming would have gained by such substitutions. Would his intention have been to reveal or conceal identity thereby? If one supposes for a moment that Ch'en were correct in his guess, why did T'ao leave out these names in his final version? Ch'en seems somewhat to imply that T'ao moved rather more towards the Liu Lin-chih story in his final version. Yet the reference to Wu-ling is present in both.

In general, Ch'en seems not to have thought out at all precisely the relationship of allegory and what he considers actual description in this work, nor to have given much thought to T'ao's possible viewpoint in producing it. His approach may, I think, be fairly criticized as too external. The hinge of his argument, the transferring of T'ao-hua yüan to the north, is particularly weak and has been attacked by T'ang Ch'ang-ju in his criticism of the article, 'Tu "*T'ao-hua yüan chi* p'ang-cheng" chih-i'. T'ang, by considering some of the material which I have cited in my own Commentary together with some other references, came to the conclusion that the 'Peach-blossom Source' story was a tradition of the Man 蠻 people of Wu-ling and reflected 'their demands'. He argues for taking the fisherman's surname Huang as a Man surname. Ch'en Yin-k'o had, in fact, also taken Huang Tao-chen as a Man in his article '*Wei shu Ssu-ma Jui chuan* Chiang-tung min-tsu t'iao shih-cheng chi t'ui-lun' (in which he argued that T'ao K'an was of the Hsi people). The acceptance of the fisherman as a Man probably reinforces the connection of the story with Wu-ling.

If one accepts that the 'Peach-blossom Source' story is a tradition of the Man people, the question remains of how T'ao Yüan-ming's treatment of it should be viewed. T'ang Ch'ang-ju takes Ch'en Yin-k'o to task for regarding all fugitive communities alike as refugees from warfare and disorder; there were also other groups which fled from oppressive taxation and services. He calls attention to the account of the Man in *Sung shu* 97, 11a, where one reads: 'The Man of Ching-chou and Yung-chou are descendants of P'an Hu. They have established separate tribes and are spread among the various commanderies and districts. . . . Of the Man people the submissive paid several *hu* of grain per household and there were no miscellaneous levies besides, but for the people of Sung the taxes and services were harsh and the poor could no longer bear their lot. Many took flight and joined the Man. For the Man there was no *corvée* labour; the strong also did not pay the government taxes. They formed associations and joined together in bands in which some hundreds or thousands took part. When the forces of the province or commanderies were weak, they rose as bandits. There were many different tribes among them and their population could not be known. Their localities were often remote and inaccessible. Among those dwelling in Wu-ling there were the Hsiung Hsi, the Man Hsi, the Ch'en Hsi, the Yu Hsi and Wu Hsi, who were called the Five Hsi Man.' T'ang stresses that life in such communities would have been hard and suggests that they lived under a form of commune. T'ao's *Peach-blossom Source* represents such a life as these people would have aspired to. It has to be admitted that there are some parallels between the *Sung shu* account of the Man and T'ao's piece, but in general I consider that T'ang, like Ch'en Yin-k'o, has approached the problem as an historian and not as a student of the work of T'ao Yüan-ming. It seems to me doubtful that the story came to T'ao directly as a Man tradition and that it had not already come to be regarded as a story of immortals. If one wished to give a sociological explanation of this phenomenon, it would not be hard to imagine that the 'grotto-dwelling' Man peoples of the south were readily mistaken for 'immortals' and indeed were happy to be taken for such, since this might contribute to their security.

There is certainly an implication in *Peach-blossom Source* that these people are free from the control of officials and the exactions of government. 'Bidding one another they work hard at farming' might perhaps support

T'ang's suggestion of some form of commune. 'On autumn harvest there is no king's tax' is a quite direct statement. It was almost inevitable that sooner or later someone would connect *Peach-blossom Source* with a text which has received a good deal of attention from historians of philosophy in the People's Republic, viz. *Pao-p'u-tzu*, chapter 48 (*Chieh Pao*), 1. In this chapter Ko Hung introduces, as an antagonist, a certain Pao Ching-yen 鮑敬言. Since Pao Ching-yen is otherwise unknown, it is perhaps not impossible that he was a creation of Ko Hung, but lately he has been treated as an important philosopher of the Eastern Chin period and his discourse in the *Pao-p'u-tzu* chapter has been regarded as extracted from a work to which the name 'Wu-chün lun' (On Having No Ruler) is usually given. In an article by T'an Chia-chien, '*T'ao-hua yüan chi* cha-chi', produced during the continuing debate on the evaluation of T'ao Yüan-ming and his works at the end of the 1950s (when *Peach-blossom Source* was sometimes criticized as 'reactionary') this 'Wu-chün lun' was claimed to have influenced T'ao's piece. That T'ao knew *Pao-p'u-tzu* is quite likely, but that the 'Wu-chün lun' exerted any special influence on *Peach-blossom Source* is not easy to demonstrate by a comparison of the texts. The presumed influence stems from an assumption that there is a common ideological standpoint. But T'ao was not engaged in some piece of polemic. As I have maintained in my Commentary, he finally gave to the 'Peach-blossom Source' story a personal application. Here as elsewhere there is a suggestion of Taoist ideas of the simplicity and purity of the uncorrupted age of remote antiquity, but these presumably came from older sources, which *Pao-p'u-tzu*, chapter 48 shared. From the totality of T'ao's writings it would be extremely hard to show that he had any great inclination towards anarchism so that I think that once again this approach may be regarded as too external. It was perhaps motivated by a desire to defend T'ao in a context of ideological evaluation.

60 BIOGRAPHY OF THE FORMER CHIEF OF STAFF TO THE CHIN GENERALISSIMO FOR SUBDUING THE WEST HIS EXCELLENCY MENG

晉故征西大將軍長史孟府君傳

君諱嘉，字萬年，江夏鄳[1] 人也。曾祖父宗，以孝行稱，仕吳司空[2]。祖父揖，元康中爲廬陵太守。宗葬武昌陽新[3] 縣，子孫家焉，遂爲縣人也。君少失父，奉母二弟居。娶大司馬長沙桓公陶侃第十女。閨門孝友，人無能間，鄉閭稱之。沖默有遠量[4]。弱冠，儔類咸敬之。

同郡郭遜，以清操知名，時在君右，常歎君溫雅平曠，自以爲不及。遜從弟立，亦有才志。與君同時齊譽，每推服焉。由是名冠州里，聲流京邑。

太尉潁川庾亮，以帝舅民望，受分陝之重，鎮武昌，並領江州，辟君部廬陵從事。下郡還，亮引見，問風俗得失，對曰，嘉不知，還傳當問從吏。亮以麈尾掩口而笑。諸從事既去，喚弟翼語之曰，孟嘉故是盛德人也。君既辭出外，自除吏名，便步歸家。母在堂，兄弟共相歡樂，怡怡如也。旬有餘日，更版爲勸學從事。時亮崇修學校，高選儒官，以君望實，故應尚德之舉。

太傅河南褚裒[5]，簡穆有器識，時爲豫章太守，出朝宗亮。正旦大會州府人士，率多時彥。君在坐次甚遠。裒[5]問亮，江州有孟嘉，其人何在。亮云，在坐，卿但自覓，裒[5]歷觀，遂指君謂亮曰，將無是耶。亮欣然而笑，喜裒[5]之得君，奇君爲裒[5]之所得，乃益器焉。舉秀才，又爲安西將軍庾翼府功曹，再爲江州別駕，巴邱令，征西大將軍譙國桓溫參軍。

君色和而正，溫甚重之。九月九日，溫游龍山，參佐畢集，四弟二甥咸在坐。時佐吏並著戎服，有風吹君帽墮落，溫目左右及賓客勿言，以觀其舉止。君初不自覺，良久如廁，溫命取以還之。廷尉太原孫盛爲諮議參軍，時在坐，溫命紙筆，令嘲之。文成示溫，溫以著坐處。君歸，見嘲笑，而請筆作答，了不容思，文辭超卓，四座歎之。

奉使京師，除尚書刪定郎，不拜。孝宗穆皇帝聞其名，賜見東堂。君辭以腳疾，不任拜起，詔使人扶入。

君嘗爲刺史謝尚[6]別駕，尚[6]，會稽人，喪亡，君求赴義。路由永興，高陽許詢有雋才，辭榮不仕，每縱心獨往。客居縣界，嘗乘船近行，適逢君過，歎曰，都邑美士，吾盡識之，獨不識此人，唯聞中州有孟嘉者，將非是乎。然亦何由來此。使問君之從者，君謂其使曰，本心相過，今先赴義，尋還就君。及歸遂止信宿，雅相知得，有若舊交。

還至，轉從事中郎，俄遷長史。在朝隤然，仗正順而已。門無雜賓，嘗會神情獨得，便超然命駕，逕之龍山，顧景酣宴，造夕乃歸。溫從容謂君曰，人不可無勢，我乃能駕御卿。後以疾終於家，年五十三[7]。

始自總髮，至于知命，行不苟合，言無夸矜，未嘗有喜
慍之容。好酣飲，逾多不亂。至於任懷得意，融然遠寄，傍
若無人。溫嘗問君，酒有何好，而卿嗜之。君笑而答之，明公
但不得酒中趣爾。又問聽妓，絲不如竹，竹不如肉。答曰，
漸近自然。中散大夫桂陽羅含賦之曰，孟生善酣，不愆其
意。光祿大夫南陽劉耽，昔與君同在溫府，淵明從父太常夔
嘗問耽，君若在，當已作公不。答曰，此本是三司人。爲時
所重如此。淵明先親，君之第四女也。凱風寒泉之思，實鍾厥
心。謹按採行事，撰爲此傳。懼或乖謬，有虧大雅君子之德，
所以戰戰兢兢，若履深薄云爾。

　　贊曰，孔子稱進德修業，以及時也。君清蹈衡門，則令
聞孔昭，振纓公朝，則德音允集。道悠運促，不終遠業。惜
哉，仁者必壽，豈斯言之謬乎。

Additional Notes

1. While all texts of T'ao's works read O 鄡, the quotation in Liu Chün's
commentary to *Shih-shuo hsin-yü* B/A, 41a and the biography of Meng Chia
in *Chin shu* 98, 16b–17a both read Meng 郰. There would appear to have
been a graphic confusion, which is not easily resolved, since both O hsien and
Meng hsien originally belonged to Chiang-hsia commandery. In attempting to
decide the issue, account should also be taken of the description of Chia's
younger brother Meng Lou by Yüan Hung (328–76) in his *Meng Ch'u-shih
ming* 孟處士銘 (preserved in Liu Chün's commentary to *Shih-shuo hsin-yü*
C/A, 17a as a native of Yang-hsin, Wu-ch'ang commandery. This agrees with
T'ao's statement that Meng Tsung, Chia's great-grandfather, was buried at
Yang-hsin and his descendants became natives of the place. It would seem
that T'ao was describing Chia by his family's original registration, since in
Chia's own time, the first half of the fourth century, Meng hsien probably
belonged to I-yang 義陽 commandery (see *T'ai-k'ang ti-chih* ap. *Sung shu* 36,
20b), while O hsien belonged to Wu-ch'ang commandery (see *Sung shu* 37,
7b). The problem may thus be taken back to Chia's great-grandfather's time
in the Wu period, and in this case a decision may be made in favour of reading
Meng rather than O. For in this period the Han O hsien was renamed
Wu-ch'ang, see *Sung shu* 37, 7a–b. In other words, 'Meng hsien, Chiang-hsia
commandery' is a possibility for the Wu period, while 'O hsien, Chiang-hsia
commandery' is not. Naturally, this argument would be strongly supported, if
the hsien of Meng Tsung's registration were known. But the only reference
that appears to have survived (*Wu-lu* ap. P'ei Sung-chih's commentary to *Wu
shu* 3, 14b) only describes him as a man of Chiang-hsia without specifying the
hsien.

2. Li Kung-huan's and many subsequent editions erroneously read *ssu-ma* for the *ssu-k'ung* office of Meng Tsung. The correct reading appears also in the quotation in Liu Chün's commentary to *Shih-shuo hsin-yü*, loc. cit.

3. Yang-hsin has been inverted in all editions of T'ao's works. The correct reading is found in the quotation in Liu Chün's commentary to *Shih-shuo hsin-yü*, loc. cit.

4. *Yu yüan-liang* would seem to be a variant of the well-known expression *yu yüan-lü* 有遠慮, cf. *Tso-chuan*, Hsiang twenty-eighth year and Ai eleventh year, which is also found in a negative form in *Lun-yü* 15, 11.

5. In all texts of T'ao's works Ch'u P'ou's personal name is mistakenly printed as Pao 襃. I have emended to 裒 from *Chin shu* 93 etc.

6. All texts read 永; I emend to 尚.

7. All texts read 五十一; I read 五十三 as *Chin shu* 98.

61 BIOGRAPHY OF THE GENTLEMAN OF THE FIVE WILLOWS

五柳先生傳

先生不知何許人也，亦不詳其姓字。宅邊有五柳樹，因以爲
號焉。閒靖少言，不慕榮利。好讀書，不求甚解。每有會意，
便欣然忘食。性嗜酒，家貧不能常得。親舊知其如此，或置
酒而招之。造飲輒盡，期在必醉。既醉而退，曾不吝情去
留。環堵蕭然，不蔽風日。短褐穿結，簞瓢屢空，晏如也。
常著文章自娛，頗示己志。忘懷得失，以此自終。

　　贊曰，黔婁有言。不戚戚於貧賤，不汲汲於富貴[1]。其
言茲若人之儔乎。酣觴賦詩，以樂其志。無懷氏之民歟。葛
天氏之民歟[2]。

Additional Notes

1. In *Lieh-nü chuan* 2, 18b these words are given to Ch'ien Lou's wife after her husband's death. The Tseng Chi text notes as a variant the addition of 之妻 after 黔婁, which would make the wife the speaker here also. This

variant must be suspected of being an editorial emendation. It is also to be noted that the 汲汲 here and the 忻忻 of the *Lieh-nü chuan* do not agree, but are possible graphic confusions, the one of the other. The reading here, which is supported by an early variant (gloss) 惶惶, is perhaps to be preferred. The same sentence with the two halves reversed, but also reading 汲汲 occurs in the description of Yang Hsiung in his biography in *Han shu* 87A, 2a. This could offer further support for the reading 汲汲, but it also opens the possibility that T'ao took 汲汲 from *Han shu*, whatever the *Lieh-nü chuan* reading, since clearly Yang Hsiung (or rather the *Han shu* account of him) was a principal model for the 'Gentleman of the Five Willows'.

2. Wu-huai shih and Ko-t'ien shih appear in Pan Ku's systematization of the legendary period as minor rulers under the first of the emperors T'ai-hao/Fu-hsi (*Han shu* 20, 4b), but by the time of Huang-fu Mi's *Ti-wang shih-chi* in the third century they have been elevated into the position of emperors between Fu-hsi and Yen-ti (p. 3); cf. Karlgren, 'Legends and Cults in Ancient China.'

62 WRITTEN AFTER READING HISTORY

讀史述九章

序　余讀史記，有所感而述之。

I

夷齊

二子讓國　　　　采薇高歌
相將海隅　　　　慨想黃虞
天人革命　　　　貞風凌俗
4　絕景窮居　　　　爰感懦夫　　　8

II

箕子

去鄉之感　　　　哀哀箕子
猶有遲遲　　　　云胡能夷
矧伊代謝　　　　狡童之歌
4　觸物皆非　　　　悽矣其悲　　　8

III
管鮑

知人未易　相知實難
淡美初交　利乖歲寒　（4）
管生稱心　鮑叔必安
奇情雙亮　令名俱完　（8）

IV
程杵

遺生良難　士爲知己
望義如歸　允伊二子　（4）
程生揮劍　懼茲餘恥
令德永聞　百代見紀　（8）

V
七十二弟子

恂恂舞雩　莫曰匪賢
俱映日月　共餐至言　（4）
慟由才難　感爲情牽
回也早夭　賜獨長年　（8）

VI
屈賈

進德修業　將以及時
如彼稷契　孰不願之　（4）
嗟乎二賢　逢世多疑
候詹寫志　感鵩獻辭　（8）

VII
韓非

豐狐隱穴　以文自殘
君子失時　白首抱關　（4）
巧行居災　忮辯召患
哀矣韓生　竟死說難　（8）

VIII

魯 二 儒

易 代 隨 時　　　　　　　德 不 百 年
迷 變 則 愚　　　　　　　汙 我 詩 書
介 介 若 人　　　　　　　逝 然 不 顧
4　特 爲 貞 夫　　　　　　　被 褐 幽 居　8

IX

張 長 公

遠 哉 長 公　　　　　　　斂 轡 朅 來
蕭 然 何 事　　　　　　　獨 養 其 志
世 路 多 端　　　　　　　寢 跡 窮 年
4　皆 爲 我 異　　　　　　　誰 知 斯 意　8

Additional Notes

II, 1–2. The expression of these lines probably derives from the description of Confucius leaving his native state of Lu in *Meng-tzu* 5B, 1, 4 (same text in ibid., 7B, 17): 'When he left Lu, he said: "Reluctant is my going!" It was the way to leave the state of one's parents.'

II, 6. Modelled on *Song* 90, 1: 云胡不夷 'How should I not be happy?'

IV, 2. Cf. *Singing of Ching K'o*, 1.5, p. 125.

VII, 1–2. The figure of the fox which loses its life because of its fur occurs in *Chuang-tzu* 20 (7A, 20b–21a), *Han-Fei-tzu* 21, p. 387 and *Shuo-yüan* 7, 20a–b. In *Han-Fei-tzu* it appears in the context of a gift of fox and leopard furs to Duke Wen of Chin (ruled 636–628 BC) by a man of Ti; the *Shuo-yüan* adapts what appears to be the same story. In *Chuang-tzu*, while the general import is the same as that of the *Han-Fei-tzu*, the setting is different, being a conversation between the ruler of Lu (probably Duke Ai 494–68 BC) and the great officer I-liao (identified as Hsiung I-liao who appears in *Tso-chuan*, Ai sixteenth year). A comparison of the three passages leads me to believe that *Chuang-tzu* was probably T'ao's source. It reads:

> The ruler of Lu said: 'I have studied the way of the former kings, I have cultivated the teaching of our former princes, I have respected the spirits and honoured the worthy. I have carried this out in person and have not stopped for an instant. Yet I have not avoided misfortune. That is why I am sad.' Master

Shih-nan ['South of the Market-place' = I-liao] said: 'Your method of getting rid of misfortune is indeed shallow. Now the fine fox and the spotted leopard stay among the mountain forests and hide in their rocky lairs; they are still. They go by night and rest by day; they are cautious. Even if they are hungry and thirsty and in distress, they will still go far away [reading 猶且 as the T'ang MS and understanding 胥疏 as a binome in the sense of 'distant'] upon the banks of the Chiang and the lakes and seek their food there; they are determined. Yet still they do not escape from the calamity of the net and trap. What fault have they? Their skin is a misfortune for them. Now is not the state of Lu simply your skin? I desire you to cut open your body and get rid of your skin, cleanse your heart and get rid of your desires and wander in the fields where there is no man.'

VIII, 1. Ho Meng-ch'un noted that the *I-wen lei-chü* (36, 12b) quotation of this piece reads: 易大隨時 and held that this reading was correct, connecting it with *I*, hexagram 17, *chuan* 隨時之義大矣哉 'Great is the significance of the time of following', but this seems to provide a rather strange line and I have not adopted it.

63   APPRAISALS FOR PAINTINGS UPON A FAN

扇上畫贊

荷蓧丈人　長沮桀溺　於陵仲子　張長公　丙曼容　鄭次都　薛孟嘗　周陽珪*

邈逸道五三		溺沮遠遠	
盡日風淳		欣自耕耦	
差參流九		駭不鳥入	
隕推相互	4	羣斯獸雜	16
遷物逐形		陵於矣至	
準常無心		然浩氣養	
人達以是		駟結彼蔑	
隱而時有	8	園灌此甘	20
勤不體四		仕一生張	
分不穀五		還事以曾	
人丈超超		能不我顧	
耘在夕日	12	間人謝高	24

岧 岧 丙 公　　　　　美 哉 周 子 [+]
望 崖 輒 歸　　　　　稱 疾 閒 居
匪 驕 匪 咨　　　　　寄 心 清 尚
28　前 路 威 夷　　　　悠 然 自 娛　40
鄭 叟 不 合　　　　　羃 羃 衡 門
垂 釣 川 湄　　　　　洋 洋 泌 流
交 酌 林 下　　　　　曰 琴 曰 書
32　清 言 究 微　　　　顧 眄 寮 儔 [#]　44
孟 嘗 遊 學　　　　　飲 河 既 足
天 網 時 疏　　　　　自 外 皆 休
眷 言 哲 友　　　　　緬 懷 千 載
36　振 褐 偕 徂　　　　託 契 孤 遊　48

* 周陽珪，藝文類聚第三十六卷引作周妙珪。

+ 美，陶注本作英。

\# 寮，各本作有，藝文類聚第三十六卷引作寮。今從之。

Additional Notes

LINES 29–32. Apart from the brief appearance of Cheng Ching in Fan Yeh's *Hou-Han shu* 59 in the biography of Chih Yün, which is of course too late to be T'ao's source, there are surviving fragments of earlier histories of Later Han which mention Cheng Ching and include reference to his friend Teng Ching (which Fan Yeh's work does not), e.g. the *Hou-Han shu* of Hsieh Shen (*fl.* mid-fourth century), quoted in the commentary to Fan Yeh's *Hou-Han shu* (59, 13a). Either Hsieh Shen's history or that of Hsieh Ch'eng (third century), the fragments of which have also been collected by Wang Wen-t'ai in his *Ch'i-chia Hou-Han shu* (for Cheng Ching, see p. 223), could have been T'ao's source here, while another strong possibility is the *Ju-nan hsien-hsien chuan* (Accounts of Former Worthies of Ju-nan, by Chou Fei, cf. *Singing of Poor Scholars*, V,1–2 and 6, p. 123), in which Cheng Ching's appearance is confirmed by five shorter or longer quotations in *T'ai-p'ing yü-lan*, viz. 12, 8b; 72, 7b; 264, 8b; 709, 8b and 954, 8b. The quotation from Hsieh Shen's *Hou-Han shu* in the commentary to *Hou-Han shu* 59, supplemented by a further quotation in *T'ai-p'ing yü-lan* 502, 2b reads: 'Ching lived in retirement and did not cultivate human relationships. The Commandant [*tu-wei*] of Hsin-ch'ien pressed him to become his Services Secretary [*kung-ts'ao*]. A tree in front of the government offices at that time had a clear sap, which was taken to be Sweet Dew [a favourable omen]. Ching said: "Your Excellency's administration cannot produce Sweet Dew. This is merely clear tree sap." He

pleaded sickness and went away. He became a recluse and engaged in
abstruse studies at O-p'o [Moth Slope]. Yin Chiu and Yü Yen both called him
to appointments but he did not go. Teng Ching of the same commandery
[became Inspector (*tu-yu*) and he passed by and enquired after Ching. Ching
was just fishing at Ta-tse (Great Marsh). He] accordingly broke off
water-chestnut leaves to make seats, offered meat on lotus leaves and filled
gourds with wine. They talked the whole day. In his rustic hut with its wicker
gate he enjoyed himself with his lute and books. [Emperor] Kuang-wu
summoned him to court but he did not go.'

LINES 33–36. Hsüeh Pao is briefly cited in the prefatory section of chapter 69
of Fan Yeh's *Hou-Han shu* as an example of great filial piety, shown towards
his mother. This passage (2a) also tells of his being called to office in the
Chien-kuang period (AD 121), but refusing on a plea of sickness. A
virtually identical version of the passage is quoted in *T'ai-p'ing yü-lan* 414, 1a
as from the *Ju-nan hsien-hsien chuan* (see last note). We may speculate that
this source in its complete form could have contained all the details
concerning Hsüeh Pao necessary for T'ao's reference here. Another possible
source is the *Tung-kuan Han-chi*, which in its current incomplete form
contains a brief notice of Hsüeh Pao (ch. 20, 2a), which is only a shortened
version of the story of his filial piety found in Fan Yeh's *Hou-Han shu*.
Because none of these sources provides the details of T'ao's lines, Ōyane
Bunjirō (p. 683) has suggested that the identification as Hsüeh Pao may be
incorrect and the person intended may be Meng Ch'ang (courtesy-name,
Po-chou), who has a brief biography in Fan Yeh's *Hou-Han shu* 106,
10b–12a. Meng Ch'ang, however, does not seem to fit T'ao's lines very much
better and it is not very likely that he would be referred to so directly by his
surname and personal name.

64 APPRAISAL OF SHANG CH'ANG AND CH'IN CH'ING

尚長禽慶贊

尚子昔薄宦　　　　禽生善周遊
妻孥共早晚　　　　周遊日已遠
貧賤與富貴　　　　去矣尋名山
4　讀易悟益損　　　　上山豈知反*　　8

* 山，陶注本作反。

CAUTIONARY AND SACRIFICIAL PIECES

65 TO MY SONS, YEN AND THE OTHERS

與子儼等疏

告儼俟份佚佟

天地賦命，有生必終[1]。自古聖賢，誰猶能免。子夏有言曰，死生有命，富貴在天。四友之人[2]，親受音旨。發斯談者，將非窮達不可妄求，壽夭永無外請故耶。

吾年過五十，少而窮苦，每以家弊，東西游走。性剛才拙，與物多忤。自量爲己，必貽俗患。僶俛辭世，使汝等幼而飢寒。余嘗感孺仲賢妻之言[3]，敗絮自擁，何慚兒子。此既一事矣。但恨鄰靡二仲[4]，室無萊婦[5]。抱茲苦心，良獨惘惘[6]。

少學琴書，偶愛閒靜，開卷有得，便欣然忘食。見樹木交蔭，時鳥變聲，亦復歡然有喜。常言五六月中，北窗下臥，遇涼風暫至，自謂是羲皇上人。

意淺識陋[7]，謂斯言可保。日月遂往，機巧好疏。緬求在昔，眇然如何。疾患以來，漸就衰損。親舊不遺，每以藥石見救，自恐大分將有限也。

汝輩稚小，家貧無[8]役，柴水之勞，何時可免，念之在心，若何可言。然汝等雖不同生，當思四海皆兄弟之義。鮑叔管仲，分財無猜，歸生伍舉，班荊道舊[9]，遂能以敗爲成，因喪立功。他人尚爾，況同父之人哉。潁川韓元長，漢末名士，身處卿佐，八十而終。兄弟同居至於沒齒[10]。濟北氾稚春，晉時操行人也。七世同財，家人無怨色[11]。詩曰，高山

仰止，景行行止。雖不能爾，至心尚之。汝其慎哉，吾復何
言。

Additional Notes

TITLE. The common formula for the titles of cautionary pieces is *chieh* 誡
(addressee) *shu* 書. *I-wen lei-chü* 23, 9b in quoting T'ao's piece in fact entitles
it 誡子書. This does not need to be an accurate version of the original, but it
does demonstrate the well-established nature of the formula. There must be a
possibility that *chieh* did occur in the original title. The 疏 of the transmitted
title seems merely a variant of 書, for one may note 書疏猶存 in *In Sacrifice
for My Sister Madame Ch'eng*, l.45, where the two are synonyms.

1. The reading of the *Chin-lou-tzu* 有生必終 is supported by the quotation in
T'ai-p'ing yü-lan 593, 8b and the *Sung shu*'s 有往必終 appears to be a
corruption of this reading (? via 往). The collected works reading 生必有死
may be the result of contamination with *In Imitation of Burial Songs*, I, 1.

2. The *Chi sheng-hsien ch'ün-fu lu*, A (T'ao's *Works* 9, 7a) contains the same
list of the four friends and gives as source the *K'ung-ts'ung-tzu*.

3. A version of the story to which T'ao refers can now be seen in the short
biography of Wang Pa's wife in Fan Yeh's *Hou-Han shu* 114, 1b–2a. (Wang
Pa himself has a short notice among the recluses in ibid., 113, 5a–b.) T'ao's
source was probably the same as Fan Yeh's, but it does not appear to have
survived. The source of both may well have been the *Lieh-nü hou-chuan*
列女後傳 of Huang-fu Mi (215–82). The *Hou-Han shu* version reads: 'We
do not know whose daughter the wife of Wang Pa of T'ai-yüan was. Pa in his
youth established lofty principles, and although during the reign of Kuang-wu
[25–57] he was continually called to office, he did not serve. Pa has already
appeared in the *Biographies of the Recluses*. His wife also had excellent ideals
and conduct. In the beginning Pa had been friends with Ling-hu Tzu-po of the
same commandery [i.e. T'ai-yüan]. Later Tzu-po became Chancellor of Ch'u
and his son became Personnel Secretary in the commandery. Tzu-po then
ordered his son to take a letter to Pa. His [the son's] carriage horses were
docile and well-trained. Pa's sons at the time were just ploughing rough
ground. When they heard that a visitor had come, they left off ploughing and
returned home. When they saw Ling-hu's son, they were cast down with
shame and could not look up at him. When Pa observed them, he looked
ashamed. When his visitor left, for a long time he lay down and did not get
up. His wife in surprise asked the reason. At first he would not tell her, but
when his wife asked his pardon, he said: "Tzu-po and I were fundamentally
different. Now I have seen his son whose appearance is very splendid and

whose behaviour is fitting, while my sons have dishevelled hair and missing teeth and do not know the rules of ritual. When they see a visitor, they are shamefaced. A father's affection for his sons is deep. I simply was unaware that I had gone astray." His wife said: "In your youth you cultivated pure principles and did not regard honours or salary. How does Tzu-po's rank now compare with your loftiness? What use is it to forget your old ideals and be ashamed of your children?" Pa sprang up, laughing: "You are right!" So they spent their lives together in retirement.'

4. The *Chi sheng-hsien ch'ün-fu lu*, A (T'ao's *Works* 9, 9b–10a) lists the Two Chungs (求仲, 羊仲) with the following description: 'We do not know of what places the above two men were natives. Both mended carriages as their occupation. They practised purity and shunned fame. When Chiang Yüan-ch'ing [personal name Hsü] left Yen-chou and returned to Tu-ling, brambles blocked his gate, but within his grounds there were three paths. He did not go out and these two men alone strolled with him there. Contemporaries called them "The Two Chungs".' The reference for this account is given as Hsi K'ang's *Kao-shih chuan*. The surviving fragment of Hsi K'ang's account of Chiang Hsü in *T'ai-p'ing yü-lan* 510, 2b, however, contains no reference to the Two Chungs. Li Kung-huan (8, 4b) quotes a *Tung-shu yen-t'an* 東塾燕談 (I have not succeeded in identifying this work), which repeats the above as coming from Hsi K'ang's *Kao-shih chuan*. While it is hard to say definitely whether this is independent evidence or merely a repetition of the *Chi hsien-sheng ch'ün-fu lu* (I am rather inclined to suspect the latter), it is quite likely that Hsi K'ang's work was T'ao's source here as in some number of cases elsewhere.
A similar account of Chiang Hsü and the Two Chungs is found in a fragment of *San-fu chüeh-lu* 三輔決錄, quoted in Li Shan's commentary to T'ao Yüan-ming's *Kuei-ch'ü-lai tz'u*, *Wen-hsüan* 45, 27b and elsewhere.

5. The *Lieh-nü chuan's* account of Lao-lai's wife reads: 'She was the wife of Master Lao-lai of Ch'u. Master Lai withdrew from the world and ploughed on the south side of Meng-shan. He made walls of reeds, a roof of thatch, a bed of wood and a mat of yarrow stalks. He wore clothes of hemp and ate pulse. He opened up new ground on the mountain side and sowed. Someone said of him to the King of Ch'u: "Lao-lai is a worthy gentleman. Your Majesty should invite him with presents of jade and silk, but I fear that he will not come." So the King of Ch'u went in his carriage to Lao-lai's house. Lao-lai just then was weaving a basket. The king said: "I am stupid and unlearned, but have the sole custody of my ancestral temple. I desire you to do me the favour of overseeing it." Master Lao-lai said: "I am a man of the wilds; I am not capable of taking charge of the government." The king went on: "Being alone in charge of the country, I wish to make you change your mind." Master Lao-lai agreed.

'The king left and his wife came with a basket on her head and firewood under her arms. She said: "Why are there so many carriage tracks?" Master Lao-lai said: "The King of Ch'u wishes to put me in charge of the government of the country." His wife said: "Did you agree to it?" He said: "Yes." His wife said: "I have heard that those who may be fed with wine and meat may be subjected to whipping and beating; those who may be given offices and salaries may be subjected to beheading. If now you take others' wine and meat and are given others' offices and salaries, you will be under others' control. Will you be able to escape misfortune? I cannot be under others' control." She threw down her basket and went away. Master Lao-lai said: "Come back! For your sake I shall reconsider it." She then went on and did not look back. When she came to Chiang-nan, she stopped, saying: "The feathers and hair, shed by birds and beasts can be spun into clothes; one can pick up the left-behind grains for food." Master Lao-lai then followed his wife and dwelt with her. The people who followed and lived with them in one year formed a hamlet, in three years formed a village . . . '

6. The 惘惘 of *Chin-lou-tzu* seems to suit the context rather better than the 內愧 of the collected works and is supported by the *Sung shu*'s 罔罔.

7. The reading of the *Sung shu*; the collected works read 罕.

8. The reading of the *Sung shu*; the collected works read 每.

9. On Kuei Sheng and Wu Chü, *Tso-chuan*, Hsiang twenty-sixth year has: 'In the beginning Wu Ts'an of Ch'u was a friend of Tzu-chao, the Grand Tutor of Ts'ai and their sons, Wu Chü and Sheng-tzu, were friendly. Wu Chü married a daughter of Prince Mou. When Prince Mou, who was Duke of Shen, fled the country, the men of Ch'u said: "Wu Chü indeed saw him off." Wu Chü then fled to Cheng and was going to flee from there to Chin. Sheng-tzu on his way to Chin met him in the outskirts of Cheng. They *spread brushwood* and ate together, and spoke of Chü's returning home. Sheng-tzu said: "Go on your way. I shall certainly have you recalled." When Hsiang Hsü of Sung sought to make peace between Chin and Ch'u, Sheng-tzu went as an envoy to Chin, and on his return he went to Ch'u. The chief minister Tzu-mu talked with him and asked him about affairs in Chin. He also asked: "Who are wiser, the great officers of Chin or those of Ch'u?" Sheng-tzu replied: "The ministers of Chin are inferior to those of Ch'u, but the great officers are wiser. They are all material for ministers. Like *ch'i* and *tzu* wood, hides and leather they come from Ch'u, but although Ch'u has the material, Chin actually uses it . . . " Sheng-tzu said: "Now there is something worse than this. Chiao Chü [= Wu Chü] married the daughter of Prince Mou, Duke of Shen. Prince Mou committed a crime and fled the country. The great officers of your ruler said to Chiao Chü: 'You really sent him away.' Chü in alarm fled to Cheng. He gazed longingly towards the south and said: 'May they pardon me!' But here too no thought was given, and he is now in Chin . . . If he gives advice on how to injure Ch'u, how shall it not be a misfortune?" Tzu-mu was alarmed and spoke of it to the king. They increased his emoluments and brought him back.' The story also appears in *Kuo-yü* 17 (*Ch'u-yü* 1), 3a–b, but T'ao's quotation of words not in *Kuo-yü* makes it clear that the *Tso-chuan* was his source.

10. Han Jung has the following brief mention at the end of the short biography of his father Han Shao 韶 in *Hou-Han shu* 92, 9b: 'His son Jung, courtesy-name Yüan-ch'ang, in his youth could distinguish principles, but he did not practise textual studies. His reputation was very great. The Five Authorities [i.e. the chief officials of the central government] all gave him appointments. At the beginning of Emperor Hsien's reign he advanced to the post of Grand Charioteer. He died in his seventieth year.' *Hou-Han shu*'s 'seventieth year' does not agree with T'ao's 'eighty', and Hui Tung, *Hou-Han shu pu-chu* 15, 7b proposed its correction to 'eightieth'; in some texts of T'ao's works the correction has been made in the reverse direction.
The source of T'ao's remarks about Han Jung may well have been the 'commemorative account' of him composed by Ts'ao Jui (Wei Ming-ti). Ts'ao Jui's twenty-four commemorative accounts (*chen-piao chuang* 甄表狀) of late Hou-Han worthies seem to have survived only in quotation in *Chi sheng-hsien ch'ün-fu lu*, B (T'ao's works 10, 1a–2b). According to this source the twenty-four men were designated for commemorative honours by Ts'ao Jui's father Ts'ao P'i (Wei Wen-ti), while he was Chancellor and King of Wei (March-December 220). The account of Han Jung, who appears with the title of Grand Herald (*ta hung-lu*) is: 'Jung was acute of understanding and he knew the workings of things. He was brilliant as a child, and his contemporaries designated him as "penetrating the divine and understanding the changes of the universe". *He and his brothers lived together until they died*. He occupied ministerial position for twenty years. In his life he maintained frugality and did not injure his repute.'

11. Fan Yü has a short biography in *Chin shu* 91, 4a, which begins: 'Fan Yü, courtesy name Chih-ch'un, was a native of Lu in Chi-pei commandery. He was of a family which had been Confucian scholars for many generations, and was always cordial to his whole family. His family had lived in Ch'ing-chou for seven generations up to Yü. The people of the time named it the family where children had no regular fathers, clothes no regular owners.' This characterization of Yü's family had appeared in written form well before T'ao's day, since a fragment of the *Chin shu* of Wang Yin (first half of fourth century), which contains the substance of the above and may be the source of the seventh century *Chin shu* version, has been preserved in Li Shan's commentary to Jen Fang's *Memorial Accusing Liu Cheng* 奏彈劉整 in *Wen-hsüan* 40, 6a.

66 IN SACRIFICE FOR MY SISTER MADAME CH'ENG

祭程氏妹文

序　維晉義熙三年五月甲辰，程氏妹服制再周。淵明以少牢之奠，俛而酹之。嗚呼哀哉。

寒往暑來
日月寢疏
梁塵委積
庭草荒蕪　[4]
寥寥空室
哀哀遺孤
肴觴虛奠
人逝焉如　[8]
誰無兄弟
人亦同生
嗟我與爾
特百常情*　[12]
慈妣早世
時尚孺嬰
我年二六
爾纔九齡　[16]
爰從靡識
撫髫相成
咨爾令妹
有德有操　[20]
靖恭鮮言
聞善則樂
能正能和
惟友惟孝　[24]
行止中閨
可象可儀
我聞為善
慶自己蹈　[28]

彼蒼何偏
而不斯報
昔在江陵
重罹天罰　[32]
兄弟索居
乖隔楚越
伊我與爾
百哀是切　[36]
黯黯高雲
蕭蕭冬月
白雲掩晨
長風悲節　[40]
感惟崩號
興言泣血
尋念平昔
觸事未遠　[44]
書疏猶存
遺孤滿眼
如何一往
終天不返　[48]
寂寂高堂
何時復踐
藐藐孤女
曷依曷恃　[52]
煢煢遊魂
誰主誰祀
奈何程妹
於此永已　[56]

死如有知
相見蒿里
嗚呼哀哉

* 百，曾集本作迫，註云一作百。今從之。

67 IN SACRIFICE FOR MY COUSIN CHING-YÜAN
祭從弟敬遠文

序　歲在辛亥，月惟仲秋，旬有九日，從弟敬遠，卜辰云窆，永寧后土。感平生之遊處，悲一往之不返，情惻惻以摧心，淚愍愍而盈眼。乃以園果時醪，祖其將行。嗚呼哀哉。

於鑠吾弟
有操有槩
孝發幼齡
友自天愛　4
少思寡欲
靡執靡介
後己先人
臨財思惠　8
心遺得失
情不依世
其色能溫
其言則厲　12
樂勝朋高
好是文藝
遙遙帝鄉
爰感奇心　16
絕粒委務
考槃山陰
淙淙懸溜
曖曖荒林　20

晨採上藥
夕閑素琴
曰仁者壽
竊獨信之　24
如何斯言
徒能見欺
年甫過立
奄與世辭　28
長歸蒿里
邈無還期
惟我與爾
匪但親友　32
父則同生
母則從母
相及齠齔
並罹偏咎　36
斯情實深
斯愛實厚
念疇昔日
同房之歡　40

冬無縕葛
夏渴瓢簞
相將以道
相開以顏　44
豈不多乏
忽忘飢寒
余嘗學仕
纏綿人事　48
流浪無成
懼負素志
斂策歸來
爾知我意　52
常願攜手
寘彼眾議
每憶有秋
我將其刈　56
與汝偕行
舫舟同濟
三宿水濱
樂飲川界　60
靜月澄高
溫風始逝
撫杯而言
物久人脆　64
奈何吾弟
先我離世

事不可尋
思亦何極　68
日徂月流
寒暑代息
死生異方
存亡有域　72
候晨永歸
指塗載陟
呱呱遺稚
未能正言　76
哀哀嫠人
禮儀孔閑
庭樹如故
齋宇廓然　80
孰云敬復
何時復還
余惟人斯
昧茲近情　84
著龜有吉
制我祖行
望旐翩翩
執筆涕盈　88
神其有知
昭余中誠
嗚呼哀哉

68　IN SACRIFICE FOR MYSELF

自　祭　文

序　歲惟丁卯，律中無射，天寒夜長，風氣蕭索，鴻雁于征，草木黃落。陶子將辭逆旅之館，永歸於本宅。故人悽其相悲，同祖行於今夕。羞以嘉蔬，薦以清酌。候顏已冥，聆音愈漠。嗚呼哀哉。

茫茫大塊
悠悠高旻
是生萬物
余得爲人　[4]
自余爲人
逢運之貧
簞瓢屢罄
絺綌冬陳　[8]
含歡谷汲
行歌負薪
翳翳柴門
事我宵晨　[12]
春秋代謝
有務中園
載耘載籽
迺育迺繁　[16]
欣以素牘
和以七弦
冬曝其日
夏濯其泉　[20]
勤靡餘勞
心有常閒
樂天委分
以至百年　[24]
惟此百年
夫人愛之
懼彼無成
愒日惜時　[28]
存爲世珍
沒亦見思
嗟我獨邁
曾是異茲　[32]

寵非己榮
涅豈吾緇
捽兀窮廬
酣飲賦詩　[36]
識運知命
疇能罔眷
余今斯化
可以無恨　[40]
壽涉百齡
身慕肥遯
從老得終
奚所復戀　[44]
寒暑逾邁
亡既異存
外姻晨來
良友宵奔　[48]
葬之中野
以安其魂
窅窅我行
蕭蕭墓門　[52]
奢恥宋臣
儉笑王孫
廓兮已滅
慨焉已遐　[56]
不封不樹
日月遂過
匪貴前譽
孰重後歌　[60]
人生實難
死如之何
嗚呼哀哉

THE BIOGRAPHY OF T'AO YÜAN-MING

Three of the Dynastic Histories contain a biography of T'ao Yüan-ming: the *Sung shu* (488), the *Chin shu* (644) and the *Nan shih* (exact date of completion is not known; its author Li Yen-shou died *c.* 679). There is also a biography by Hsiao T'ung (501–31), preserved by being transmitted with T'ao's collected works, and there is a short account in the Buddhist *Lien-she kao-hsien chuan* (Biographies of the Worthies of the Lotus Society, a work of uncertain date, contained in the thirteenth century *Fo-tsu t'ung-chi*). In addition, a number of quotations have been preserved from the various works on the history of the Chin period, from which the present *Chin shu* was compiled.

Below I present these biographies in a critical manner, treating the *Sung shu*, since it is the earliest complete version extant, as the basic text and noting the variants of the other versions. Wherever there is matter in any of the other versions not represented in the *Sung shu*, I have inserted it parenthetically at what I have thought the most appropriate point. The decision has had in a few cases to be merely arbitrary. I have also set the fragments of the early Chin histories against the passages for which they were probably the sources.

Each of the versions subsequent to the *Sung shu* shows knowledge of its predecessors. The *Lien-she kao-hsien chuan* version apart from the Hui-yüan story is derived entirely from the *Chin shu*. The *Nan shih* takes its material from the *Sung shu* and Hsiao T'ung's biography and does not add to it, while the *Chin shu* shows the greatest divergence from the other versions.

For convenience of reference and discussion the text has been divided into sections, lettered alphabetically.

Texts: Basic text *Sung shu*, ch. 93

       H   Hsiao T'ung biography ap. *Collected Works*

       C   *Chin shu*, ch. 94

       N   *Nan shih*, ch. 75

       L   *Lien-she kao-hsien chuan* ap. *Fo-tsu t'ung-chi*, ch. 26

Abbreviations:

       CHC   *Ch'u-hsüeh chi*

IWLC	*I-wen lei-chü*
PSLT	*Po-shih liu-t'ieh shih-lei chi*
PTSC	*Pei-t'ang shu-ch'ao*
TPYL	*T'ai-p'ing yü-lan*
add.	words added
mov.	words transferred to new position
om.	words omitted

I have omitted from the text all quotations from T'ao's works, although I have indicated where the quotations stand and which of the histories include or omit them.

陶淵明傳

〔A〕

陶潛字淵明，或云淵明字元亮，尋陽柴桑人也。曾祖侃，晉大司馬。〈C祖茂武昌太守。〉

陶…亮〕陶淵明，字元亮。或云潛字淵明H；陶潛字元亮C；陶潛字淵明，或云字深明，名元亮N；陶潛字淵明L。
尋…也〕om. CL；潯H。曾…馬〕大司馬侃之曾孫也C；晉大司馬侃之曾孫也NL。

〔B〕

潛少有高趣，〈HC博學善屬文，穎脫不羣，任眞自得。〉〈C爲鄉鄰之所貴。〉〈N宅邊有五柳樹，故〉嘗著**五柳先生傳**以自況，曰…其自序如此，時人謂之實錄。

潛〕淵明H；om. NL。有〕懷CL。趣〕尚CL。羣〕羈C。嘗〕om. L。以自況〕mov. N。曰…〕om. L。其…此〕om. HL；add. 蓋以自況N。謂之〕以爲L。

〔C〕

親老家貧，起爲州祭酒，不堪吏職，少日，自解歸。州召主簿，不就。躬耕自資，遂抱羸疾。

C om. L。親〕以親C。歸〕而歸N。

〔D〕

〈HN江州刺史檀道濟往候之，偃臥瘠餒有日矣。道濟謂曰，賢者處世，天下無道則隱，有道則至。今子生文明之世，奈何自苦如此。對曰，潛也何敢望聖賢，志不及也。道濟饋以粱肉，麾而去之。〉

賢〕 夫賢N。聖〕 om. N。

〔E〕

復爲鎮軍建威參軍，謂親朋曰，聊欲弦歌，以爲三徑之資，可乎。執事者聞之，以爲彭澤令。

復〕 後HN；初L。鎮軍〕 om. L。以〕 om. L。可乎〕 om. L。

〔F〕

〈HN不以家累自隨，送一力給其子，書曰，汝旦夕之費，自給爲難，今遣此力，助汝薪水之勞。此亦人子也，可善遇之。〉

〔G〕

公田悉令吏種秫稻，〈HC曰吾常得醉於酒足矣。〉妻子固請種秔，乃使二頃五十畝種秫，五十畝種秔。

G om. L。公田〕 在縣公田C。吏〕 om. C。稻〕 om. H；穀C。吾〕令吾C。得〕 om. C。秫〕 粳H。二〕 一C；二 C ap. TPYL 839，11a。秫〕 粳H。
檀道鸞 〈續〉晉陽秋 ap. PTSC 78，9a：陶潛除彭澤令。姓好學善酒。在縣使種秫穀，曰，吾常醉足矣。

〔H〕

〈C素簡貴，不私事上官。〉〈H歲終，會〉郡遣督郵至縣，吏白應束帶見之。潛嘆曰，我不能爲五斗米折腰向鄉里小人。即日解印綬去職，賦**歸去來**，〈N以遂其志。〉其詞曰，…

白〕請曰 H。潛〕淵明 H。我〕吾 CL。不〕豈 H。向〕拳拳事 CL。
人〕兒 H；add. 邪 CL。即日〕義熙二年 C；om. L。綬〕om. CL。
職〕縣，add. 乃 CL。其詞曰…〕om. HL；om. 其詞 N。
何法盛**晉中興書** ap. PTSC 78，9a：陶潛爲彭澤令，督郵察縣〔俞本
縣下有縣字〕吏白當板履而就謁。潛曰，吾不能爲五斗米折腰向鄉里小
人〔俞本作賢〕。於是掛冠而去。

〔I〕

義熙末，徵著作佐郎，不就。

I om. L.
義熙末〕om. H；頃之 C。佐〕om. HC。

〔J〕

〈C既絕州郡覲謁，其鄉親張野及周旋人羊松齡龐遵等或有
酒要之，或要之共至酒坐，雖不識主人，亦欣然無忤，酣醉
便反。未嘗有所造詣，所之唯至田舍及廬山游觀而已。刺史
王弘以元熙中臨州，甚欽遲之，後自造焉。潛稱疾不見，既
而語人云，我性不狎世，因疾守閑，幸非絜志慕聲，豈敢以
王公紆軫爲榮邪。夫謬以不賢，此劉公幹所以招謗君子，其
罪不細也。〉

〔K〕

江州刺史王弘欲識之，不能致也。潛嘗往廬山，弘令潛故人
龐通之齎酒具於半道栗里要之。潛有腳疾，使一門生二兒舉
籃輿。既至，欣然便共飲酌。俄頃弘至，亦無忤也。〉

K om. L。
江…潛〕弘每令人候之，密知 C。潛〕淵明 H。嘗〕當 C。弘…潛〕乃
遣其 C；弘命淵明 H。之〕add. 等 C。具〕先 C。栗里〕om. C；add.
之間 H。要〕邀 H。潛〕淵明 H。有…也〕既遇酒，便引酌野亭，欣然
忘進。弘乃出與相見，遂歡宴窮日 C。舉〕舁 H；轝 N。既〕及 N。忤〕
迕 H。

〔L〕
〈C潛無履，弘顧左右爲之造履，左右請履度，潛便於坐申腳令度焉。〉

檀道鸞**續晉陽秋** ap. TPYL 692，2b：江州刺史王弘造陶淵明，〈淵明〉無履，弘從人脫履以給之，語左右爲彭澤作履，左右請履度，淵明於衆坐伸腳令度，及履至，著而不疑。

〔M〕
〈C弘要之還州，問其所乘，答云，素有腳疾，向乘籃輿，亦足自反。乃令一門生二兒共輿之，至州而言笑賞適，不覺有羨於華軒也。〉

〔N〕
〈C弘後欲見，輒於林澤間候之。至於酒米乏絕，亦時相贍。〉

〔O〕
先是，顏延之爲劉柳後軍功曹，在尋陽，與潛情款。後爲始安郡，經過，日日造潛，每往必酣飲致醉。〈H N弘欲邀延之坐，彌日不得。延之〉臨去，留二萬錢與潛，潛悉送酒家，稍就取酒。

O om. CL 。
尋］潯H。潛］淵明H。過］add.潯陽H。日…潛］日造淵明飲焉H；om.日日造N。邀］要N。坐］一坐N。潛，潛］淵明，淵明H。送］遣送H。
何法盛**晉中興書** ap.李善注 **文選**57，20a延之爲始安郡，道經尋陽，常飲淵明舍自晨達昏。及淵明卒，延之爲誄，極其思致。

〔P〕
嘗九月九日無酒，出宅邊菊叢中坐久，值弘送酒至，即便就酌，醉而後歸。

P om. C L。

無酒〕om. H。久〕久之HN；add. 滿手把菊，忽H。值〕逢N。後〕om.
H。

檀道鸞**續晉陽秋** ap. PTSC 155，12a；IWLC4，17b；CHC4，p.80；
PSLT1 ，27b；TPYL32，3a & 996，1b：陶淵明當九月九日無酒，
於宅邊菊叢內，摘盈把坐其側久，望見白衣人至，乃弘送酒也，即便就
酌，醉而後歸。

淵明〕潛IWLC，CHC， PSLT，TPYL32。當〕嘗IWLC；om. CHC，
PSLT ，TPYL。於〕出TPYL996；om. IWLC， PSLT，TPYL32。
宅〕om. TPYL996。邊〕add. 東籬下TPYL32。叢〕蘂TPYL32。內〕
中IWLC，CHC，TPYL；om. 菊叢內PSLT。盈〕菊盈PSLT。久〕久
之TPYL996；未幾TPYL32；om. 坐其側久PSLT。白〕一白TPYL
996。人〕om. IWLC。弘〕王弘IWLC，CHC， PSLT，TPYL。也〕
om. CHC， PSLT ，TPYL996。即〕om. PSLT。就〕om. PSLT。酌〕
飲 PSLT。醉〕om. CHC。後〕om. PSLT。歸〕om.醉而後歸TPYL
996。

〔Q〕
〈C其親朋好事，或載酒肴而往，潛亦無所辭焉，每一醉，
則大適融然。又不營生業，家務悉委之兒僕。未嘗有喜慍之
色。唯遇酒則飲，時或無酒，亦雅詠不輟。〉

〔R〕
〈C L嘗言夏月虛閒，高臥北窗之下，清風颯至，自謂羲皇
上人。〉

〔S〕
潛不解音聲，而畜素琴一張，無絃，每有酒適，輒撫弄以寄
其意。

潛〕淵明H；性C L。聲〕律H；om. C L。畜〕蓄H。素…絃〕無絃琴
一張H；om. 無絃N；素琴一張，絃徽不具C L。每…意〕om. 有H；每
朋酒之會，則撫而和之，曰，但識琴中趣，何勞絃上聲C L。

〔T〕

貴賤造之者，有酒輒設。潛若先醉，便語客，我醉欲眠，卿
可去。其真率如此。郡將候潛，值其酒熟，取頭上葛巾漉酒，
畢還復著之。

T om. C L。
潛〕淵明H。將〕add.嘗H。潛〕之H。值〕逢N。畢〕漉酒畢H。

〔U〕

〈H時周續之入廬山，事釋慧遠，彭城劉遺民亦遁迹匡山，
淵明又不應徵命，謂之潯陽三隱。後刺史檀韶苦請續之出州，
與學士祖企，謝景夷三人，共在城北講禮，加以讎校。所住
公廨，近於馬隊。是以淵明示其詩云…

宋書93，3b（周續之傳）：入廬山，事釋慧遠，時彭城劉遺民遁迹廬
山，陶淵明亦不應徵命，謂之尋陽三隱。

〔V〕

〈L時慧遠法師與諸賢結蓮社，以書招淵明，淵明曰，若許
飲則往。許之，遂造焉，忽攢眉而去。〉

〔W〕

潛弱年薄官，不潔去就之迹，自以曾祖晉世宰輔，恥復屈身
後代，自高祖王業漸隆，不復肯仕。

W om. C。
潛…迹〕om.HL；官字作宦N。自…輔〕自以晉世宰輔之後L。後〕異
L。自…仕〕宋高祖H；宋武帝N；om. L。

〔X〕

所著文章，皆題其年月。義熙以前，則書晉氏年號，自永初
以來，唯云甲子而已。

X om. HCL。

〔Y〕

與子書以言其志，并爲訓戒曰，…。又爲**命子詩**以貽之曰，…

Y om. H C L。

貽之曰…] om. 曰…N。

〔Z〕

潛，元嘉四年〈H N 將復徵命會〉卒，時年六十三。〈H N
L 世號靖節先生〉〈C 所有文集並行於世。〉

潛om. H C N L。元嘉] 以宋元嘉 C；宋元嘉 L。四年] 中 C。

〔ZA〕

〈H (after U) N 淵明妻翟氏亦能安勤苦，與其同志。〉〈N
夫耕於前，妻鋤於後云。〉

淵明] 其 N。亦…志] 志趣亦同，能安苦節 N。

[A] T'ao Ch'ien, courtesy-name Yüan-ming, (some say Yüan-ming, courtesy-name Yüan-liang)[1] was a native of Ch'ai-sang, Hsün-yang[2]. His great-grandfather K'an was Grand Marshal under the Chin. 〈C His grandfather Mao was Prefect of Wu-ch'ang.〉[3]

[B] Ch'ien in his youth had lofty aspirations. 〈HC He studied widely and was skilled in composition. The talents he revealed were uncommon. He relied on truth and was secure in himself.〉〈C He was honoured by his neighbours in his village.〉〈N Around his house were five willow trees and so〉 he wrote *The Biography of the Gentleman of the Five Willows* as an analogy of himself. [For translation see vol. 1, p. 208.] He described himself in this way and his contemporaries declared it a true record.

[C] His parent was old[4] and his family poor. He began his official career as Provincial Libationer,[5] but he could not bear official duties. After a short time he resigned and returned home. When the province called him to the post of Registrar, he did not accept. He supported himself by ploughing with his own hand, and as a result became emaciated and ill.

[D] 〈HN The Governor of Chiang-chou, T'an Tao-chi went to visit him and found that he had been lying wasted and hungry for several days. Tao-chi said: 'The wise man so lives in the world that if the empire has not the Way, he retires, but if it has, he comes forward. Now you have been born into an enlightened age, why do you afflict youself like this?' He replied: 'How dare I aspire to be thought wise? My ambition does not reach so far.' Tao-chi presented him with grain and meat, but he made signs for them to be taken away.⟩⁶

[E] Later he became Aide to the General of the Stabilization Army and to the Establishing Majesty General.⁷ He said to his relatives and friends: 'I should like with lute and song to support a "three-path" existence. Is it possible?'⁸ When the authorities heard of it, they appointed him Magistrate of P'eng-tse.⁹

[F] ⟨HN He did not take his family with him. He sent a servant for his sons and wrote to them: 'It is hard for you to provide for daily needs by yourselves. Now I am sending you this servant to aid you in the labour of gathering wood and drawing water. He too is a man's son and should be well treated.'⟩¹⁰

[G] In the public fields he ordered his subordinates to plant only glutinous rice. ⟨HC He said: 'It will be enough for me always to get drunk with wine.'⟩ When his wife and sons earnestly begged him to plant non-glutinous rice, then he had 2 *ch'ing* 50 *mou* planted with glutinous rice and fifty *mou* with non-glutinous rice.¹¹

[H] ⟨C By nature he thought little of high rank and was not subservient to high officials.⟩ ⟨H At the end of the year it happened that⟩ an Inspector, sent by the commandery, came to the district. His subordinates told him that he ought to tie his girdle and call on the Inspector. Ch'ien said with a sigh: 'I cannot for five pecks of rice bow before a country bumpkin.' The same day he untied his seal-ribbon and gave up the post.¹² He composed *Return Home!* ⟨N to give expression to his feelings.⟩ [For translation see vol. 1, pp. 191–94.]

[I] At the end of the I-hsi period [405–418] he was called to the post of Assistant Archivist, but did not accept.¹³

[J] ⟨C When he had given up ceremonial calls upon the officials of the province and the commandery, his fellow-villager Chang Yeh¹⁴ and his boon companions Yang Sung-ling¹⁵ and P'ang Tsun¹⁶ sometimes, when they had wine, invited him, and sometimes, when they had an invitation, took him with them to a drinking party. Even if he did not know the host, he was happy and made no objection. When he was drunk, he returned. He never went anywhere, going only to his farm and on excursions to Lu-shan. Governor Wang Hung¹⁷, who was Governor of [Chiang-]chou during the Yüan-hsi period, had a deep respect for him. Later he went personally to see him, but Ch'ien pleaded sickness and did not receive him. Afterwards he told someone: 'It is my nature not to associate with the world, but that with the excuse of sickness I can preserve my retirement is my good fortune; it is not pure ideals or a desire for fame. Surely I dare not think His Excellency Wang's disappointment a glory? To be deluded by the unworthy, this is what Liu Kung-kan thought invited criticism of the prince. The fault is not a slight one.'⟩[18]

[K] The Governor of Chiang-chou, Wang Hung, wished to make his acquaintance but was unsuccessful. Once when Ch'ien had gone to Lu-shan, Hung ordered Ch'ien's friend P'ang T'ung -chih[19] to take wine for a party and invite Ch'ien to it half-way [to Lu-shan] at Li-li[20]. Ch'ien had a bad foot and had a retainer and two sons carry him in a bamboo sedan. When he arrived, he was glad and they drank together. After a little while Hung came, and he still made no objection.

[L] ⟨C Ch'ien had no shoes. Hung asked his attendants to provide shoes for him. When the attendants asked for his shoe-measurements, Ch'ien stretched out his feet in the midst of the company and had them measure them.⟩[21]

[M] ⟨C Hung invited him to return to the city and enquired how he would travel. He replied: 'I have always had a bad foot and up till now I was riding in a bamboo sedan. I can still return by myself in it.' Then he had a retainer and two sons carry him. When he came to the city, he enjoyed the talk and laughter, but did not feel that there was anything to be envied in an elegant carriage.⟩[22]

[N] ⟨C Afterwards, Hung, whenever he wished to see him, sought for him among the woods and valleys. When his wine and grain ran short, he also sometimes supplied him.⟩[23]

[O] Before this, Yen Yen-chih had been Services Secretary to General of the Rear Liu Liu.[24] While he was at Hsün-yang, he had a deep friendship with Ch'ien. Later he became Prefect of Shih-an commandery[25], and passed through [Hsün-yang][26]. Daily he visited Ch'ien, and whenever he went, they always drank until they were drunk. ⟨HN Hung wished to invite Yen-chih to be his guest, but day after day he failed.[27] When Yen-chih⟩ was about to leave, he left 20,000 cash for Ch'ien. Ch'ien sent it all to the wineseller's and gradually obtained wine for it.

[P] On the ninth day of the ninth month he had no wine. He went out and sat for a long time among the chrysanthemum clumps beside his house. Hung happened to come with wine and they immediately poured it. Not until they were drunk, did Hung go home.[28]

[Q] ⟨C His friends and kindly persons sometimes came with wine and meats. Ch'ien on his part never refused them, and as soon as he was drunk, became very agreeable and genial. Further, he did not care about his livelihood and left all the household affairs to his sons and servants. He never wore looks of pleasure or anger. When he happened to have wine, he drank it. Sometimes he had no wine, and then he would hum continually without stopping.⟩[29]

[R] ⟨CL Once during the summer months, unoccupied, he reclined on a high pillow under the northern window. When a cool breeze suddenly came, he called himself a man of the remote times of the Emperor [Fu-]hsi.⟩[30]

[S] Ch'ien did not understand music, but he kept a plain lute without strings. Whenever there was a drinking party, he fingered it to express his thoughts.[31]

[T] Noble or humble, whoever came to see him, if he had wine, he always set it before them. If Ch'ien was the first to become drunk, he would say to his guest: 'I am drunk and wish to sleep; you, sir, may leave.' His frankness was like this. The Prefect visited Ch'ien. When the wine was heated, Ch'ien took the coarse cloth turban from his head to strain the wine, and when he had finished, put it on again.[32]

[U] ⟨H At this time Chou Hsü-chih had gone into Lu-shan to serve the monk Hui-yüan. Liu I-min of P'eng-ch'eng had also retired to K'uang[-lu] shan. Since Yüan-ming too did not accept appointment, they were called 'the Three Recluses of Hsün-yang'.[33] Later Governor T'an Shao earnestly requested Hsü-chih to take service in the province. Together with the scholars Tsu Ch'i and Hsieh Ching-i he expounded the *Rites* north of the city wall. They also collated texts. The official quarters in which they stayed was near the horse-lines. That is why Yüan-ming addressed to them his poem . . . [Quotes *To Secretary Chou, Tsu and Hsieh*, ll.7–8, 11–12, for which see vol. 1, p. 54]⟩.[34]

[V] ⟨L At the time the Master of the Doctrine [Hui-]yüan with various worthy men formed the Lotus Society. He sent a letter of invitation to Yüan-ming, who said: 'I shall go, if I am permitted to drink.' Hui-yüan gave permission and so he went to visit him. Suddenly he wrinkled his brow and left.⟩[35]

[W] Ch'ien in his youth held minor office and did not have a rigid stance towards public service. But since his great-grandfather had been a chief minister in the Chin period, he was ashamed to serve under a later dynasty. From Kao-tsu the imperial authority gradually increased, but he was no longer willing to serve.

[X] He put the date on all his writings. Up to the I-hsi period (405–418) he wrote the Chin year designation, but from the Yung-ch'u period (420–22) he used only the cyclical sign.[36]

[Y] He wrote to his sons to express his ideals and also to offer a caution to them. [For translation see vol.1, pp. 228–30.] He also composed the poem *Charge to My Son* to present to him. [For translation see vol. 1, pp. 26–29.]

[Z] Ch'ien in the fourth year of the Yüan-chia period (427) ⟨HN was again summoned to office[37] but⟩ died in his sixty-third year.[38] ⟨HN His posthumous name is Ching-chieh hsien-sheng.⟩ ⟨C His collected literary works are in circulation in the present day.⟩

[ZA] ⟨HN Yüan-ming's wife née Ti was also able quietly to endure toil and to share his ideals.⟩ ⟨N The husband ploughed in front, and the wife hoed behind.⟩[39]

Discussion

1. There is a curious and marked discrepancy between the versions of the biography with regard to T'ao's personal and courtesy-names, which has evoked much discussion. (A useful summary may be found in Chu Tzu-ch'ing's 'T'ao Yüan-ming nien-p'u chung chih wen-t'i', pp. 578–80.) From the discussion two points emerge that can be taken as certain: first, that in the Shen-ming of the *Nan shih*, Shen is only a substitution for Yüan, taboo on account of the personal name of T'ang Kao-tsu; secondly, since T'ao refers to himself in his biography of Meng Chia (p. 145) and in *In Sacrifice for My Sister Madame Ch'eng* (p. 158) as Yüan-ming, this must be a personal, not a courtesy-name. From here on the discussion becomes speculative. The main question is the relationship between the personal names Yüan-ming and Ch'ien. In the conversation between T'ao and T'an Tao-chi, who was Governor of Chiang-chou from the fifth month of 426 to the third month of 436, recorded by Hsiao T'ung and repeated in the *Nan shih* (see text [D]), T'ao refers to himself as Ch'ien. It may be presumed that Hsiao T'ung took this conversation from an existing source, since his practice elsewhere is to refer to T'ao as Yüan-ming. Whether this unknown source had recorded actual words of T'ao with accuracy must be open to question, when one takes account of the variation between Yüan-ming and Ch'ien in the surviving quotations of the now otherwise lost early histories of the Chin period. Thus Wu Jen-chieh's proposal (sub Yüan-chia 3), which Chu Tzu-ch'ing finally accepts, that T'ao used Ch'ien as a personal name during the Sung period (after 420) is founded not only on slight but probably unreliable evidence. It does not seem possible to go beyond a statement that T'ao probably used Ch'ien as a personal name during some period of his life.

2. Hsiao T'ung and the *Nan shih* follow the *Sung shu* in the statement that T'ao was a native of Ch'ai-sang but the *Chin shu* compilers for some reason omitted it. Ch'ai-sang was a hsien, established by Han and abolished by Sui.

Ch'ai-sang was also the name of a mountain; it is mentioned in the
Shan-hai-ching (5, 44a), where Kuo P'u (276–324) comments: 'It lies south of
Ch'ai-sang hsien, Hsün-yang and is joined to Lu-shan.' The hsien-town of
Ch'ai-sang was an important place from the third to the fifth century, but the
disappearance of the name from Sui onwards created uncertainty as to its
location among later writers of geographical and other works. This
uncertainty may partly have arisen from the extent of a hsien (as distinct from
the hsien-town) in this period, but it was probably especially caused by the
changes in the status of Ch'ai-sang during the Chin period. An indication of
this may be obtained from the late tenth century *T'ai-p'ing huan-yü chi* 111,
13a–b, which under Jui-ch'ang 瑞昌 hsien (100 *li* west of Te-hua = Hsün-yang
= present Kiukiang) states: 'Originally the locality of Ch'ih-wu ch'ang.
According to the *Wu shu*, in Sun Ch'üan's time there was a red crow seen
here, and so the place was first named. It was within the old limits of
Ch'ai-sang. According to the *Chou t'u-ching* (presumably the *Chiang-chou
t'u-ching*; an anonymous work of this title is mentioned in *Sung-shih
i-wen-chih*, p. 87) in the first year of the Chien-hsing period (313) of Chin a
commandery (chün) was established for the first time to administer the five
hsien. Hsün-yang, Ch'ai-sang, P'eng-tse, Shang-chia and Chiu-chiang, so
then Hsün-yang and Ch'ai-sang each had its own territory. Afterwards
Hsün-yang was included into Ch'ai-sang. Later Ch'ai-sang was abolished and
became Hsün-yang. Then Hsün-yang and Ch'ai-sang were combined in one
hsien but with separate names. At the beginning of the Wu-te period
(618–26) of T'ang the three hsien, Hsün-yang, P'eng-tse and Tu-ch'ang were
administered by Chiang-chou....' This statement is substantially supported
by *Chin shu* 15 (*Ti-li chih*), 7b: 'In the first year of the Yung-hsing period
(304) the two hsien Hsün-yang in Lu-chiang and Ch'ai-sang in Wu-ch'ang
were separated off and Hsün-yang commandery was established, coming
under Chiang-chou.' (Wu-ch'ang, according to the same source, was one of
the ten commanderies with which the province of Chiang-chou was formed in
291; the 313, Chien-hsing 1, of *T'ai-p'ing huan-yü chi* may be an error for 304,
Yung-hsing 1, as another Sung geographical work, the *Yü-ti kuang-chi* 24, 4a,
has the same date as the *Chin shu*.) *Chin shu* 15, 8b, also has: 'In the eighth
year of the I-hsi period (412) of the Emperor An's reign Hsün-yang hsien was
reduced and included in Ch'ai-sang hsien. Ch'ai-sang remained a
commandery.'
The town of Hsün-yang had originally been located north of the Yangtze. Tu
Yu's *T'ung-tien* 182, p. 967 states that it was moved from the area of Ch'i-
ch'un 蘄春 commandery (in modern Hupei) to its later position south of the
river (present Kiukiang) by Wen Ch'iao 溫嶠, Wen was Governor of Chiang-
chou from 326 until his death in 329. *T'ai-p'ing huan-yü chi* 111, 10a puts the
move in 326 (Ch'en Shun-yü, *Lu-shan chi* 1, p. 1026a gives an impossible 334,
but this is probably an error for 326, i.e. 咸和九年 in error for 咸和元年). Tu
Yu goes on to state that the Ch'u-ch'eng post station, south of Hsün-yang was

the former Ch'ai-sang hsien (and here hsien may be understood as the hsien-town). This is supported by the slightly later *Yüan-ho chün-hsien t'u-chih* (*c.* 815) of Li Chi-fu, which locates 'the old town' of Ch'ai-sang twenty *li* south-west of Hsün-yang (28, 6b).

From all of the above it may be concluded that Ch'ai-sang hsien extended west and south of present Kiukiang and the town of Ch'ai-sang lay on the north-western side of Lu-shan, probably not far from where the remains of the Hsi-lin and Tung-lin Buddhist temples, associated with T'ao's contemporary Hui-yüan, are situated. From Kuo P'u's comment to *Shan-hai-ching* it would be not unreasonable to conclude that the name Ch'ai-sang was also applied in the fourth century to a mountain in that same area. By the twelfth century, however, the name Ch'ai-sang had been transferred to the southern side of Lu-shan and here it can still be found today (or at least could at the time of my visit in 1956) in the small village of Ch'ai-sang ch'iao 橋. I suspect a mistaken association of T'ao Yüan-ming with southern Lu-shan was the cause of this transference and consequently the use of these later incorrect identifications of Ch'ai-sang in the arguments over the places where the poet lived is simply moving in a circle. (See further the discussion in 20 below.)

3. The statement that T'ao K'an (259–334) was the poet's paternal great-grandfather, which appears in all the biographies, seems not to have been doubted before it was disputed by Yen Yung, eldest son of the early Ch'ing classical scholar Yen Jo-chü (1636–1704), in his *Tso-fen chin-kao* (4a–5b), which was printed as an appendix to his father's *Ch'ien-ch'iu cha-chi*, Ch'ien Ta-hsin (1728–1804) attempted forcefully but not wholly logically to rebut Yen Yung in *Pa T'ao Yüan-ming shih-chi* (1788; contained in *Ch'ien-yen t'ang wen-chi* 31, 1a). Subsequently Fang Tung-shu (1772–1851) defended Yen Yung against Ch'ien Ta-hsin's criticisms in *Chao-mei chan-yen* 13, p. 356ff. The problem proves on investigation very difficult, and one may sympathize with Chu Tzu-ch'ing's decision after a detailed review of its discussion by the various critics that it was not finally soluble (op. cit., pp. 598–604).

If one considers the histories first, there is an immediate difficulty in the additional statement, which occurs only in the *Chin shu*, that the poet's grandfather was Mao, Prefect of Wu-ch'ang. For the biography of T'ao K'an in *Chin shu* 66 states (10b): 'K'an had seventeen sons; only Hung, Chan, Hsia, Ch'i, Ch'i, Pin, Ch'eng, Fan and Tai appear in the histories; the rest were all undistinguished.' To have been Prefect of Wu-ch'ang was certainly not 'undistinguished'. Thus were the compilers of the *Chin shu* guilty of an oversight in omitting Mao's name in the biography of T'ao K'an or was the name Mao incorrect? Li Kung-huan 1, 9b notes (although he does not accept the information) that a family register compiled by T'ao Mao-lin 茂麟 (tenth century) gave T'ao's grandfather as Tai 岱. T'ao Mao-lin's register (listed in the *Sung-shih i-wen-chih*, p. 77 as *T'ao-shih chia-p'u* in 1 chüan by T'ao Pa-lin 茇麟) has not survived, but the *Ku-chin hsing-shih shu pien-cheng* (presented to the throne in 1134) by Teng Ming-shih gives the same information (11, 6a), adding the title *yüan-wai san-ch'i* 員外散騎 (cf. the *san-ch'i shih-lang* of *Chin shu* 66). This poses the problem of whether the *Chin shu* biography of the poet was wrong in both the name and the official position of his grandfather and the Sung genealogies are correct or whether an attempt has been made in the genealogies to reconcile an apparent conflict in the *Chin shu*. Apart from the consideration of the general unreliability of such genealogies, T'ao's own words in the sixth stanza of *Charge to My Son* (p. 23) confirm that his grandfather held office as a prefect. In view of the manner of the compilation of the *Chin shu* from a large number of existing histories, not always very carefully, it seems quite probable that the compilers had some source for the statement that T'ao Mao, Prefect of Wu-ch'ang, was Yüan-ming's grandfather, but that they did not consider whether this was compatible with the other statement that T'ao K'an was his paternal great-grandfather, which they had most probably taken over from the *Sung shu* biography of the poet. A piece of circumstantial evidence favourable to Yüan-ming's grandfather having been Prefect of Wu-ch'ang is that his son, Yüan-ming's father, was married to Meng Chia's daughter (see *Biography of His Excellency Meng*, p. 145) and the Meng family lived in Wu-ch'ang. Since there is the poet's own statement in the same place that his maternal grandmother was a daughter of T'ao K'an, there is no question of his descent from K'an on the maternal side. In the much debated reference to descent from T'ao K'an on the paternal side, which occurs in the poem *To the Duke of Ch'ang-sha*, I have argued that the poet was a fifth, not a fourth, generation descendant (see p. 10 above). If my argument is accepted, there is no obstacle to his grandfather having been T'ao Mao, Prefect of Wu-ch'ang, since he would then have been a grandson not a son of T'ao K'an. On the other hand, all the biographies would have to be one generation out in his descent from K'an on the paternal side.

4. From Yen Yen-chih's *Elegy* (vol. 1, p. 245) it appears that T'ao's father had died before the poet took up his first appointment. In *Charge to My Son*, st. VI (p. 23) Yüan-ming refers to his father as deceased, but my own opinion (see p. 24) is that this poem cannot be dated so precisely (and thus perhaps not so early) as many critics have thought. Liang Ch'i-ch'ao (p. 40) suggested that 慈妣 'dear mother' in *In Sacrifice for My Sister Madame Ch'eng* (p. 158) might be an error for 慈考 'dear father' and that thus his father's death could be fixed in the poet's twelfth year ('My years were twice six'). While both Ku Chih (*nien-p'u*, 9a–10b) and Lu Ch'in-li (p. 230) accepted Liang's emendation, the arguments adduced do not justify the alteration of the text. There is a probable but imprecise reference to his father's death in *In Sacrifice for My Cousin Ching-yüan* (see p. 159). There is thus no means of dating the father's death, but it seems reasonable to understand 親老 here as referring to one parent only, the poet's mother who died in the winter of 401 (see vol.1, p. 236).

5. Provincial Libationer had during the Han and Three Kingdoms periods been simply a position of honour, but under the Eastern Chin it had become a minor post in the provincial administration (see Yen Keng-wang, *Wei Chin Nan-pei ch'ao ti-fang hsing-cheng chih-tu*, pp. 171–72). T'ao wrote in his poems that he lived in retirement 'for thirty years' (*Written in the Seventh Month of the Year Hsin-ch'ou*, p. 70) or until he was 'approaching thirty' (*Drinking Wine*, XIX, p. 89) so that if the traditional dating, which places his birth in 365, is followed, this appointment would need to be *c.* 393, the date which was proposed by Wu Jen-chieh and commonly followed. The Governor of Chiang-chou at this time was Wang Ning-chih 王凝之, second son of the famous calligrapher Wang Hsi-chih.

6. This passage was inserted at this point by Hsiao T'ung in his version of the biography very much out of chronology, since T'an Tao-chi did not become Governor of Chiang-chou until the fifth month of 426 (see *Sung shu* 5, 3a). Although Hsiao's source for this story is unknown, one may guess that it existed as a separate anecdote and that Hsiao placed it here on account of the sentence which now precedes it.

7. The problems of the identity of the General of the Stabilization Army and the Establishing Majesty General are fully discussed in the Additional Commentaries to *Written when Passing through Ch'ü-o* (pp. 67–68) and *Written in the Third Month of the Year I-ssu* (pp. 76–77). My suggestion is that these posts do not appear in the order in which T'ao held them but were merely arranged according to the ranking of these generals. If this is true, it is a significant illustration of the uncertainty of Shen Yüeh and the other compilers over the few data they had for the poet's life.

8. T'ao seems here to be represented as asking obliquely for a small post as a sinecure which would support him as 'a withdrawn scholar'. For 'lute and song' is probably a reference to *Lun-yü* 17, 4: 'When the Master went to the town of Wu, he heard the sound of lute and song.' Confucius' disciple Tzu-yu was warden of this small town of Wu 武. 'Three paths' had come into the terminology of 'withdrawal' from the story of Chiang Hsü 蔣詡, a Han official who retired rather than serve the usurper Wang Mang (AD 9–23). He made three paths to his hut and sought only the society of two other men who also refrained from taking office (see Additional Note 4 to *To My Sons, Yen and the Others*, p. 155). If this interpretation is correct, then, whether T'ao actually expressed himself in this way or not, — and on the whole I think that it is doubtful that he would have done so — an interesting sidelight is offered on fifth century attitudes which could thus accept 'retirement' being supported by its opposite, 'office'.

9. The Chin town of P'eng-tse was some way to the south-east of the present town of that name; it was situated ten miles east of the present town of Hu-k'ou 湖口, Kiangsi. The *Yüan-ho chün-hsien t'u-chih* 28, 7a states that 'the old town of P'eng-tse is forty-five *li* north of Tu-ch'ang 都昌. T'ao Ch'ien of Chin was magistrate of this town.' The poet's own account of his brief occupancy of the post of magistrate here for some eighty days between the eighth month and the eleventh month of 405 is to be found in the preface to *Return Home!* (p. 137).

10. This passage, inserted by Hsiao T'ung and copied by the *Nan shih*, seems rather to disagree with the words which immediately follow. For although 'he did not take his family with him', yet 'his wife and sons earnestly begged him to plant non-glutinous rice' in the public fields (i.e. the land from which the produce contributed to the magistrate's support). That he did not take his family with him, however, does seem to be borne out by the poet's own words in *Return Home!* (p. 137), where 'the children wait at the door', so that Hsiao T'ung or whoever first composed this (I do not think it can be accepted as literal fact) probably read T'ao's works more carefully than the compiler of the following anecdote. The formulation could have been suggested by T'ao's words in *To My Sons, Yen and the Others* (p. 153): 'You are young and the family is poor without servants. The labour of gathering wood and drawing water, when can it be escaped? The thought of it is always in my mind, but what is there to say?'

11. The poet's own statement in the preface to *Return Home!* ('the harvest of the public fields would be sufficient for making wine') was clearly responsible for the appearance of this anecdote, as Hsiao T'ung's small insertion underlines. The story was already present in T'an Tao-luan's *Hsü Chin yang-ch'iu*, as may be seen from the fragment preserved in *Pei-t'ang shu-ch'ao* 78, 9a. There is a very brief mention of T'an Tao-luan in *Nan shih* 72, 3b, which affords no precise date for his life: one can only conclude that the work was completed during the Sung period, i.e. before 479, and thus could have been a source for Shen Yüeh in the compilation of his biography of T'ao. Liu Chih-chi, *Shih-t'ung* 17, 1a stigmatizes T'an's work as one of the worst of the Chin histories. This story is certainly a clumsy invention, if one takes account of the poet's own statement that he was at P'eng-tse only from the eighth to the eleventh month (September to December) 405, i.e. not the rice-planting season. Even if T'an Tao-luan did not invent this anecdote, he did not consider it critically.

12. The account of how T'ao gave up his P'eng-tse appointment, which became one of the most commonly cited stories in Chinese literature, again is not confirmed by the preface to *Return Home!*, where the poet gives as his reason the death of his sister. Once again there is a source earlier than the *Sung shu*, in a fragment of Ho Fa-sheng's *Chin chung-hsing shu*, also preserved in *Pei-t'ang shu-ch'ao* 78, 9a. Ho Fa-sheng probably compiled his work during the later part of the Sung period. There is a reference to him in *Sung shu* 100, 14a as a Reviser of Documents in the Household of the Heir-apparent *c.* 455. The reference to him in the biography of Hsü Kuang 徐廣 (352–425) in *Nan shih* 33, 8b has no parallel in the *Sung shu* biography of Hsü Kuang (ch. 55) and seems likely to be erroneous (see discussion in Yao Chen-tsung, *Sui-shu ching-chi chih k'ao-cheng*, p. 209). It is not hard to see how T'ao's expressed reluctance for public service and his serving only for the sake of his belly (also in the preface to *Return Home!*) could have given rise to such an anecdote. It is noticeable that *Sung shu* and *Chin shu*, which include the text of *Return Home!*, omit the preface, presumably because the compilers were conscious that there was some contradiction.

The significance of the phrase *wu tou mi* attributed to T'ao in this apocryphal anecdote was debated in two issues (Nos 1 and 10) of *Li-shih yen-chiu* in 1957 by Miu Yüeh and Chang Chih-ming with many citations of supporting texts. The former argued that five pecks of rice represented the monthly consumption of a member of the gentry at this time in round figures. Thus T'ao would be saying 'I cannot for the sake of a full belly. . .' Chang Chih-ming, on the other hand, saw it as a contemporary cliché for a trifling amount, like the modern *wei liang-ko ch'ien* (爲兩個錢 'for two cash'). He compared the use of *wu tou mi* as a kind of standard fee by the religious Taoist T'ien-shih Tao sect (often called in consequence the Wu tou mi sect). The doubtfulness of these being T'ao's actual words renders the argument rather sterile for me, but I incline to Chang's interpretation.

13. Both the Hsiao T'ung and *Chin shu* biographies read 'Archivist' (*chu-tso-lang*). Yen Yen-chih in his *Elegy* (vol. 1, p. 245) also states that T'ao was called to the post of Archivist and follows this immediately with the statement that he died in 427. The Hsiao T'ung biography (followed by the *Nan shih*) also has that in 427 he 'was again called to office but died' (see section [Z]). One might argue from these various statements, as did Hung Liang-chi (*Hsiao tu-shu chai ssu-lu, shang*, 3b) that T'ao was twice called to archival posts, first at the end of the I-hsi period to Assistant Archivist and again in the last year of his life to Archivist. Yen Yen-chih's statement need, however, not refer to the end of the poet's life (although Hsiao T'ung, if this were his source, must have understood it to do so) and thus it becomes rather a matter of deciding which of the two readings is correct. If one bears in mind the possibility of the contamination of the texts by each other in transmission, too much weight need not be attached to the priority of Yen Yen-chih's text in date. The lower post has perhaps in itself the greater likelihood, and also the loss of a character in such a title is more likely than a deliberate addition. I therefore favour the reading 'Assistant Archivist'.

14. For Chang Yeh see Commentary to *At the End of the Year Answering a*

Poem by Attendant Chang (vol. 1, pp. 75–76).

15. For a discussion of the possible identity of Yang Sung-ling with the addressee of *To Chief of Staff Yang* see Commentary to that poem (vol. 1, pp. 73–74).

16. For P'ang Tsun see Commentary (vol. 1, pp. 22–23) and Additional Commentaries (pp. 15–17) to *In Reply to Aide P'ang*.

17. For Wang Hung (379–432), Governor of Chiang-chou (418–425), see Commentary to *Seeing off a Guest at General Wang's Banquet* (vol. 1, p. 70).

18. The reference is to the criticism by Liu Chen 劉楨 († 217; courtesy-name Kung-kan) of Ts'ao Chih (192–232) for his treatment of Hsing Yung 邢顒 († 223). Hsing Yung was appointed Assistant Superintendent of the Household (*chia-ch'eng* 家丞) to Ts'ao Chih during the period when he was Lord of P'ing-yüan 平原 (211–13). The short notice of Hsing Yung in *San-kuo chih, Wei shu* 12, 12b states: 'Yung guarded himself with the rites and was completely unbending. Because of this they [he and Ts'ao Chih] did not agree. The Private Secretary (*shu-tzu* 庶子) Liu Chen sent a letter of criticism to Chih, which read: "The Assistant Superintendent of the Household Hsing Yung is the most accomplished scholar of the northern region. In his youth he grasped high principles; he is profoundly quiet and tranquil; his words are few but his principles are many; he truly is a refined scholar. I certainly cannot couple myself with such a man or stand in the same company with him. Yet I have been especially courteously treated, while Yung on the contrary has been treated with indifference. I personally fear that those who observe it will say that your lordship makes the unworthy his intimates and is deficient in courtesy towards the worthy; he plucks the Private Secretary's spring flowers and forgets the Assistant Superintendent's autumn fruits. When a superior invites criticism, the fault is not slight. From this rebelliousness arises."''
Although no earlier source has survived for this *Chin shu* story, the words attributed to T'ao may be regarded as reasonably true in character.

19. P'ang T'ung-chih has generally been identified with P'ang Tsun of the *Chin shu* passage, inserted immediately before this.

20. Although there is no reference to Li-li (Chestnut Village) in any of T'ao's own surviving works, this place name, which appears almost incidentally in the *Sung shu* biography, was to become firmly implanted in the later traditions of the poet. Clearly a tradition associating T'ao with Li-li was in existence by the time of Po Chü-i, who in his poem *Visiting T'ao's Old Home* (written 816; see *Po Hsiang-shan shih-chi* 7, 1b–2a) speaks of:

Ch'ai-sang's old village,
Li-li's ancient hills and streams.

In his preface Po says: 'Now making an excursion to Lu-shan, I passed
through Ch'ai-sang and passed by Li-li. I thought of the man and visited his
home.' As has been seen in Note 2 above, Ch'ai-sang was located twenty *li*
south-west of Hsün-yang by Li Chi-fu in his *Yüan-ho chün-hsien t'u-chih*, a
work of almost exactly the same date as Po Chü-i's poem. Li-li was presumably
in the same area, i.e. on the north-west side of Lu-shan. By the beginning of
the Sung period, however, Li-li, like other places associated with the poet,
had been identified as being on the southern side of the mountain. Thus
T'ai-p'ing huan-yü chi 111, 5b–7b states: 'Li-li yüan [spring] is on the south of
the mountain.... By the side of the mountain stream is T'ao's
Drinking Stone.... Ch'ai-sang shan is near Li-li yüan. T'ao Ch'ien was a
native of this place.... T'ao's old home lies fifty *li* south-west of the *chou* (i.e.
Chiang-chou, Hsün-yang].... There is a poem *Visiting T'ao's Old Home* by
Po Chü-i of the T'ang.'
There is another reference to Li-li, which at first sight might seem to locate it
on the southern side of Lu-shan at a much earlier date and so confute my
argument. *T'ai-p'ing yü-lan* 41, 6b quotes a *Hsün-yang chi*: 'In T'ao Ch'ien's
Li-li there is now a flat stone like a whet-stone; its length and breadth are
more than ten feet. According to tradition, Ching-chieh hsien-sheng [T'ao]
slept on top of it when drunk. It is on the south side of Lu-shan.' Now the
Hsin T'ang shu bibliography (p. 163) records a *Hsün-yang chi* by Chang
Seng-chien 張僧鑒 in 2 chüan, and this was regarded by Wen T'ing-shih as a
work of the Chin period. He includes it in his *Pu Chin-shu i-wen chih* (p. 41)
and collects there some references to the author. There are in fact some
number of surviving quotations from *Hsün-yang chi* or Chang Seng-chien's
Hsün-yang chi: the earliest (*Hsün-yang chi*) are in Liu Chün's commentary to
Shih-shuo hsin-yü (C/A, 16b; C/B, 42a). But even if Chang's work were from
the Liu Sung rather than the Chin period, a quotation which refers to T'ao by
his posthumous name (and so must be later than 427), but more especially
uses the word 'tradition' seems very unlikely to have belonged to it. It may
have come from a later work of the same name (*T'ai-p'ing yü-lan* 717, 4a
contains a quotation headed 'Shan Ch'ien-chih 山謙之 *Hsün-yang chi*', but I
think that this is an error: Shan Ch'ien-chih is the author of the preceding
quotation from the *Wu-hsing chün chi* 吳興郡記) or from a revision of
Chang's work. In either case it is undatable, but is, I suspect from a period
very much later than Chin.
There is a loose and inaccurate quotation of the *Sung shu* version of section
[K] in *T'ai-p'ing yü-lan* 774, 4b.

21. There is a surviving source for this story included by the *Chin shu* in a
quotation of T'an Tao-luan's *Hsü Chin yang-ch'iu* to be found in *T'ai-p'ing
yü-lan* 697, 2b. This is slightly more extended than the present *Chin shu*

version: it adds that first 'Hung's attendants took off their shoes to give to him' and, at the end of the story, 'when the shoes arrived he put them on without hesitation'.

22. This section [M] from the *Chin shu* makes a rather more pointful use of the bad foot — bamboo sedan topic, which appears only incidentally in the *Sung shu* (section [K]). It may be imagined that this section existed as a separate anecdote, which was known to Shen Yüeh also, but he incorporated it into another story. The short *Lien-she kao-hsien chuan* version has the same: 'had a retainer and two sons carry him in a bamboo sedan' (in this case on visits to Lu-shan as in the *Sung shu* version), but places its statement after section [S] below.

23. Sections [K]–[N] of course follow consecutively in the *Chin shu* and it would have been possible to present [L], [M], [N] as one section. I believe, however, that [L] and [M] represent originally separate anecdotes inserted by the compilers at this point. One could easily imagine that [N] was the conclusion of [K] (in the *Chin shu* version).

24. Liu Liu was Governor of Chiang-chou from some time in 415, when he succeeded Meng Huai-yü 孟懷玉 (appointed 412) on the latter's death in office (see *Sung shu* 47, 3b), until his own death on 13 July 416 (see *Chin shu* 10, 8a).

25. Shih-an commandery is modern Kuei-lin 桂林, Kwangsi. Yen Yen-chih's banishment from the court to Shih-an has generally been dated 424 from the Sung *nien-p'u* compilers onwards to recent writers like Lu Ch'in-li (p. 245) and Chang Chih (p. 95). This date would seem at first sight to be secured by Yen Yen-chih's own *Chi Ch'ü Yüan wen* 祭屈原文 (*Wen-hsüan* 60, 34b): 'It was on a certain date in the fifth year of the House of Sung (i.e. 424) that the Governor of Hsiang-chou, Chang Shao 張邵 of Wu-chün, respectfully receiving the Emperor's command, set up his standard in ancient Ch'u.' Yen Yen-chih's biography in *Sung shu* 73 (1b) states that Yen wrote this piece for Chang Shao on his way to take up his appointment as Prefect of Shih-an. Ssu-ma Kuang, *Tzu-chih t'ung-chien* 120 (p. 3765) also placed Yen's banishment to Shih-an and that of Hsieh Ling-yün to Yung-chia 永嘉 in 424. The banishment of Yen and Hsieh was due, according to their respective biographies in the *Sung shu*, to their friendship with the Prince of Lu-ling, Liu I-chen 廬陵王義真, which aroused the hostility of Hsü Hsien-chih 徐羨之 and other powerful ministers.
According to *Sung shu* 3, 5a, however, Chang Shao (the SPPY ed. reads incorrectly Chang Chi 紀) was appointed Governor of Hsiang-chou, which, after being abolished in 417, was reformed out of ten commanderies of Ching-chou, on 12 March 422. Among Hsieh Ling-yün's surviving poems

there is *On the Sixteenth Day of the Seventh Month of the Third Year of Yung-ch'u* (= 19 August 422) *Going to My Commandery, I First Set Out from the Capital* (*Yung-ch'u san nien ch'i yüeh shih-liu jih chih chün ch'u fa tu* 永初三年七月十六日之郡初發都; see *Hsieh K'ang-lo shih chu*, p. 27). The first Sung emperor, Liu Yü died in the fifth month of 422 and was succeeded by his eldest son Liu I-fu 義符 (Shao-ti), but the reign title was not changed until the next year. The Prince of Lu-ling, the patron of Yen and Hsieh, had earlier (in the third month) been ordered to take up the governorship of Nan-Yü-chou (see *Sung shu* 3, 5a; the capital of Nan-Yü-chou was at Li-yang 歷陽, modern Ho-hsien 和縣, Anhui). The *Sung shu* biographies of Yen and Hsieh both state, without giving a precise date, that it was after the accession of Shao-ti that they were banished from the capital. Thus the cumulative evidence points to Yen Yen-chih's having left for Shih-an in the second half of 422, passing through Hsün-yang and Ch'ang-sha on his way there. It seems likely then that 'fifth year' in Yen's *Chi Ch'ü Yüan wen* should read 'third year' (i.e. there has been a graphic confusion of 三 with 五).

26. Hsün-yang is directly mentioned in Hsiao T'ung's version and also in the version of a fragment of Ho Fa-sheng's *Chin chung-hsing shu*.

27. Hsiao T'ung's embellishment of this story (repeated by the *Nan shih*) is historically possible since Wang Hung was still at this time Governor of Chiang-chou, but it looks rather like a doubling of Hung's attempts to meet T'ao Yüan-ming.

28. This episode has a source predating the *Sung shu* in T'an Tao-luan's *Hsü Chin yang-ch'iu*, from which it is quoted in early encyclopaedias no less than six times. It is worth noting that these six quotations of this short passage present nineteen small variations of text, which are eloquent testimony to the lack of exactness in such quotations. Many critics have connected T'ao's poem *Living in Retirement on the Ninth Day* with this story, but I rather doubt this association (see Commentary to the poem, vol. 1, pp. 44–45). The story became, however, one of the best remembered parts of the biography of the poet and an often recurring part of what I have called the furniture of Double Ninth poems (see my 'The Double Ninth Festival in Chinese Poetry'); a further early example not cited there may be found in Wang Wei's *Written by Chance*, Poem IV (*Ou-jan tso liu shou* 偶然作六首, *Wang Yu-ch'eng chi* 5, 3b). In these circumstances it is rather surprising that the compilers of the present *Chin shu* did not include it.

29. Although no version of section [Q] has survived in quotation from any of the early Chin histories, it has the appearance of having been compiled from one or more of them. It seems to have owed something originally to T'ao's own *Biography of the Gentleman of the Five Willows* (see p. 146).

30. This insertion in the *Chin shu* is taken with slight alteration from T'ao's own *To My Sons, Yen and the Others*, of which the *Sung shu* quotes the whole in section [Y] below.

31. The statement that T'ao did not understand music would seem at first sight to be contradicted by his own words in his poem *Written when Passing Through Ch'ü-o*:

> In my youth I stayed outside affairs;
> I set my love on 'lute and books'.

and in *To My Sons, Yen and the Others*, where he wrote: 'In my youth I studied lute and books.' 'Lute and books' is, however, a phrase which is part of the terminology of withdrawal (see the story of Wu-ling Tzu-chung, quoted in the Additional Notes to *In Reply to Aide P'ang* (pp. 17–18) so that it may be unnecessary to understand the reference to 'lute' literally. A circumstance which could be favourable to this statement of the biographies is the absence from T'ao's collected works of *yüeh-fu* such as are found in the surviving works of Hsieh Ling-yün, Yen Yen-chih and Pao Chao. It is true that there are in T'ao's collection three burial songs (*wan-ko*), a type of poem which is classified as *yüeh-fu*, but these are regular five-word poems and it is also probable that their correct title is *In Imitation of Burial Songs*.

32. This probably apocryphal story which Shen Yüeh included as an illustration of T'ao's uninhibited character is very vague, since neither the place nor the name of 'the Prefect' is given. For this reason one may suspect that Shen had no written source for it and that it was simply an anecdote generally current in literary circles.

33. 'At the time' shows Hsiao T'ung, in making his fairly long insertion at this point, to have once again had little regard for chronology. If 'at the time' had any particular reference, it should refer to some time in the governorship of Wang Hung at Hsün-yang (418–24), but any conjunction of T'ao Yüan-ming, Chou Hsü-chih and Liu I-min there would have occurred several years earlier. Hsiao T'ung uses the word 'later' in his next sentence, when he writes of the governorship of T'an Shao, who was in fact Wang Hung's predecessor in office (416–18). Liu I-min (personal name Ch'eng-chih 程之) probably died in 413. The date of his death is commonly given as 410 in accordance with the statement of the *Shih-pa hsien chuan* 十八賢傳 (contained in the *Lu-shan chi* of Ch'en Shun-yü, ch. 3; see *Taishō Tripitaka* 2095, vol. LI, p. 1039) that he died in I-hsi 6 in his fifty-seventh year. In what is said to be a revised version of this *Shih-pa hsien chuan* in the thirteenth century *Fo-tsu t'ung-chi*, chapter 26 (where the biography of T'ao Yüan-ming is also found) the same date is given but Liu is stated to have been in his fifty-ninth year, see *Taishō Tripitaka* 2035, vol. XLIX, p. 268. Nevertheless, the monk

Yüan-k'ang (studied in Ch'ang-an during the Chen-kuan period, 627–49) in his commentary to the *Chao lun* of Seng-chao (384–414) 僧肇, *Chao lun shu* 肇倫疏 (see *Taishō Tripitaka* 1859, vol. XLV, p. 181) quotes from an account of Liu I-min, written by Hui-yüan (334–416), the leader of the Lu-shan Buddhist community. Hui-yüan states that in I-hsi 9 (413) the Grand Commandant Liu (Yü) paid his respects to Liu I-min and also that Liu lived in the mountains for twelve years until his death. These twelve years are probably to be counted from 402, the year in which Hui-yüan with the monks and laymen of his White Lotus Society on 11 September took a vow together to be reborn in the Western Land. (Liu I-min composed the text of this vow, which is preserved in the biography of Hui-yüan in *Kao-seng chuan*, ch. 6. For a translation, see E. Zürcher, *The Buddhist Conquest of China*, I, p. 244.) The *Lu-shan chi* version of *Shih-pa hsien chuan* also records that Liu lived in the mountains altogether for twelve years. Another account of Liu in a letter of Hui-yüan, preserved in the *Kuang hung-ming chi* of Tao-hsüan (596–667), chapter 27 (*Taishō Tripitaka* 2103, vol. LII, p. 304) gives fifteen years as the period he lived in the mountains. If this is not the result of corruption in transmission, it could perhaps be that Hui-yüan was here counting from a different date. In this letter Hui-yüan says that Liu was Magistrate of Ch'ai-sang (the title by which T'ao Yüan-ming refers to him in two poems, see pp. 54 and 55) in the T'ai-yüan period (376–396) so that he may have retired to the mountains before 402. Liu I-min seems to have been the most earnest of the laymen in Hui-yüan's circle. The *Chao lun* includes a letter from him to Seng-chao, putting questions to the monk (for a translation, see Walter Liebenthal, *The Book of Chao*, pp. 86–95).

Chou Hsü-chih (377–423), who like Liu I-min took the vow which founded the White Lotus Society in 402, seems to have been rather a different type of man from Liu. His short biography in the *Shih-pa hsien chuan* (ap. *Lu-shan chi*, ch. 3, op. cit., p. 1040 and *Fo-tsu t'ung-chi*, ch. 26, loc. cit.) states that he was called by his contemporaries *t'ung-yin* 通隱, i.e. a 'retired scholar' who mixed with the world, and records the following anecdote: 'Someone asked Hsü-chih: "Why do you sometimes tread the royal court?" Hsü-chih said with a laugh: "He whose heart races to the high gate-tower [i.e. the imperial palace, symbol of public office] thinks rivers and lakes [i.e. retirement] a prison, but to him by whom feelings and attitudes are both forgotten, markets and courts are also simply caves."' Though this story may well be apocryphal, it illustrates clearly how the life of the hermit had come to be viewed in medieval China. Chou Hsü-chih is here represented as claiming that hermitage is a state of mind, not a matter of physical circumstances. T'ao would have gone a long way in agreement with him. Yet he retained something of the standpoint of the anonymous questioner in the conversation just quoted, as may be seen in his poem addressed to Chou, p. 44. Although Chou joined Hui-yüan's group and, according to his biography in *Sung shu* 93, 3b, did not take a wife, wore plain clothes and ate vegetarian food, he continued throughout his life to be highly regarded as a specialist in Confucian ritual. According to *Sung shu*, loc. cit., he had studied in his twelfth year under Fan Ning 范寧 (339–401), a famous Confucian scholar, who was at the time (388) Prefect of Yü-chang 豫章 (modern Nan-ch'ang, Kiangsi), the prefecture in which Chou lived.

Shen Yüeh follows the statement that Chou Hsü-chih entered Lu-shan to serve Hui-yüan with the remark that 'at this time Liu I-min of P'eng-ch'eng retired to Lu-shan. Since T'ao Yüan-ming also did not accept appointment, they were called "the Three Recluses of Hsün-yang"'. It is thus fairly certain that *Sung shu* is the source for Hsiao T'ung's insertion into his biography of T'ao. There is in fact no close indication of the time of the application of this title to the three men. There is an argument from silence that Chou remained in the Hsün-yang area from 402 until 416 or 417 (see Commentary to *To Secretary Chou, Tsu and Hsieh*, vol. 1, pp. 54–55). It is probable that Liu I-min and Chou Hsü-chih were both in Hsün-yang from 402 to 413 and during this period T'ao was away only during 404 (?) and 405. T'ao was probably in mourning for his mother 402–404 and was thus more properly to be called a "recluse" from 406 onwards and this is as far as one can reasonably go in attempting to define when this title was applied to the three men.

34. For a discussion of this episode, see Commentary to *To Secretary Chou, Tsu and Hsieh*, vol. 1, pp. 54–55.

35. This story, which is the only part of the *Lien-she kao-hsien chuan* account of T'ao not derived from the *Chin shu*, is certainly unhistorical, probably late in formulation and from a non-Buddhist hand. A closely similar version is quoted by Ho Meng-ch'un in his edition of the poet's works (1518) as from *Lu-fu tsa-chi* 廬阜雜記. I have failed to discover any bibliographical details of this work. The same passage is quoted from it by Mao Te-ch'i in his *Lu-shan chih* (preface date 1719) 12A, 14b–15a, but this could be taken from Ho Meng-ch'un's citation.

Although there is no early evidence to confirm or deny a personal encounter between Hui-yüan and T'ao, by the Northern Sung period Hui-yüan's friendly indulgence of the poet was an established tradition and has remained to this day. (In a recent book *Creativity and Taoism*, Chang Chung-yuan writes, p. 191: 'He was a good friend of Hui Yuan, the great fourth-century Buddhist, who broke the rules of the temple to entertain him with wine.') In 1080 the famous painter Li Kung-lin (1049–1106) painted a *Lien-she shih-pa hsien t'u* 蓮社十八賢圖 ('The Eighteen Worthies of the Lotus Society') and in the following year his cousin Li Yüan-chung 李元中 wrote a descriptive account of it (for text see *Lu-shan chih* 12A, 21b–25a). Here Li Yüan-chung wrote (22a): 'T'ao Ch'ien at this time had abandoned his office and was living at Li-li. He always came to the community, but sometimes when he had just come he wrinkled his brows and returned home. The Master

[Hui-]yüan was fond of him and wished to detain him but he could not.' And further: 'He [Hui-yüan] constantly ordered men to buy wine to induce Yüan-ming to come.' The similarity of this with the *Lien-she kao-hsien chuan* account will be noted.

In Li Yüan-chung's account of his cousin's painting there is mention also of the Taoist Lu Hsiu-ching 陸修靜 (406–477): 'Lu Hsiu-ching lived at the Chien-chi kuan and also constantly came to the community. He had excellent relations with [Hui-]yüan. Yüan himself lived at the Tung-lin [monastery] and never set foot beyond the Tiger Stream. One day while seeing off the Taoist Lu, he went unaware beyond the stream. They clasped each other and laughed.' This story is told to include T'ao Yüan-ming by Ch'en Shun-yü in his *Lu-shan chi*, chapter 1 (*Taishō Tripitaka* 2095, vol. LI, p. 1028): 'In the past when the Master [Hui-]yüan, in seeing off his guests, went beyond this (the Tiger Stream), the tiger always roared. Hence the name came about. At this time T'ao Yüan-liang was living at Li-li on the southern side of the mountain. Lu Hsiu-ching also was a scholar who possessed the Way. The Master [Hui-]yüan once was seeing off these two men and talking with them of the unity of the Way [of Buddhism and Taoism]. Unaware, he went beyond the stream, whereupon they laughed loudly together. In the present age a *San-hsiao t'u* [The Three Laughing] is transmitted.' The painting to which Ch'en Shun-yü referred was quite possibly a work by the tenth century painter of Buddhist and Taoist figures, Shih K'o 石恪, of which Su Shih wrote an appraisal (*tsan*) (see *Shu San-hsiao t'u hou*, *Su Tung-p'o chi*, *hsü-chi*, chapter 10 (13, p. 3); also quoted in Mao Te-ch'i's *Lu-shan chih* (12A, 38b). The unhistorical nature of this story is patent, when one considers that Lu Hsiu-ching was a boy of ten when Hui-yüan died and that it was not until some forty years later that he retired to Lu-shan. (For a biography of Lu Hsiu-ching see *Li-shih chen-hsien t'i-tao t'ung-chien* 24, 9a.) One could be tempted to think that the story of 'The Three Laughing' might be traced back into the T'ang period, for there is a poem by Li Po, *Taking Leave of the Monk of the Tung-lin* 別東林寺僧 (*Li T'ai-po ch'üan-chi* 15, 13a; probably written in 726):

> At the place where guests are seen off from the Tung-lin,
> The moon comes out and the white gibbons howl.
> Laughing, we part in the remoteness of Lu-shan;
> Why should he trouble to cross the Tiger Stream?

36. This statement by Shen Yüeh, which both Hsiao T'ung and the *Chin shu* omit, has provided the commentators and critics with a major topic for discussion, since it clearly does not agree with T'ao's works as transmitted. As Chu Tzu-ch'ing has shown in his detailed review of the discussion in 'T'ao Yüan-ming nien-p'u chung chih wen-t'i', section 3, many of the commentators and critics have increased the confusion by altering or misunderstanding Shen

Yüeh's remarks. I shall not go over this ground again but refer the reader to
Chu Tzu-ch'ing.
From the general usage of the Six Dynasties period it is probable that by
wen-chang Shen Yüeh intended T'ao's works as a whole, not simply his prose,
as Ch'ien Ta-hsin understood (see *Pa I-men tu-shu chi* 跋義門讀書記, ap.
Ch'ien-yen t'ang wen-chi 30, 14aff). There are in T'ao's transmitted works
twelve poems dated with cyclical signs and three 'prose' pieces: only one of
these, *In Sacrifice for Myself*, if the alternative date for *An Excursion to
Hsieh-ch'uan* (see pp. 41–42) is excluded, carries a Sung date. There are
three works in which year designations (*nien-hao*) appear and in one only of
these, *In Sacrifice for My Sister Madame Ch'eng*, does the *nien-hao* indicate
the date of composition. It is true, however, that nowhere does T'ao use a
Sung *nien-hao* and this is probably the main point that Shen Yüeh was seeking
to make. On the evidence of the transmitted works this would be as likely to
be fortuitous as deliberate, but Shen Yüeh was no doubt intending to
demonstrate T'ao's character. I think that we may agree with Chu Tzu-ch'ing
that Shen expressed himself carelessly. One is not justified in concluding from
his remarks that he had seen an edition of the poet's works, in which every
piece was dated, and one certainly cannot argue on from this, as T'ao Shu did,
that the edition which Shen had seen, was edited by T'ao Yüan-ming himself.

37. See Note 13 above.

38. The *Sung shu* states that T'ao died in 427 in his sixty-third year. Thus the
date of his birth would have been 365. In the *Wen hsüan* version of Yen
Yen-chih's *Elegy* (ch. 57, 22b) the age at which T'ao died is not given, but in
the version of the *Elegy* in the Tseng Chi and subsequent editions of T'ao's
collected works '63' has been inserted. It is thus probable that the *Sung shu*'s
statement of T'ao's age at the time of his death is primary and all others are
secondary to it.
Before modern times the dating of T'ao's life as 365–427 was called in
question only by the Southern Sung writer Chang Yin 張縯 in his critique of
Wu Jen-chieh's *nien-p'u, Wu-p'u pien-cheng* 吳譜辨證, quoted by Li
Kung-huan in his introductory general discussion at the beginning of his
edition of the collected works (8b). Chang Yin's study is noted in Ch'en
Chen-sun's *Chih-chai shu-lu chieh-t'i* 16, p. 438 as being in 1 chüan, but it now
survives only through quotation in Li Kung-huan's edition. Chang, adopting
the readings *hsin-ch'ou* = 401 and *wu-shih*, i.e. fifty years old in *An Excursion
to Hsieh-ch'uan*, calculated that T'ao was born in 352 and died in 427 in his
seventy-sixth year. His view appears to have gained no acceptance from later
commentators apart from Huang Chang 黃璋, a great-great-grandson of the
famous Huang Tsung-hsi (1610–95), mentioned by T'ao Shu (*nien-p'u
k'ao-i* A, 9b–10a).
The tendency of critics of modern times has been towards a reduction in the

length of T'ao Yüan-ming's life. The first to propose a later date for his birth appears to have been the Late Ch'ing scholar and educationalist Wu Ju-lun (1840–1903), who in a note to *Drinking Wine*, XIX in his anthology *Ku-shih ch'ao* calculated that the poet was in his twenty-ninth year in 405, since he refers the 'approaching "no doubts"' (i.e. thirty years old) of the fifth line of that poem to T'ao's giving up his post at P'eng-tse and retirement to the country. T'ao would thus have been in his fifty-first year at the time of his death in 427 and would have been born in 377.

This proposal by Wu Ju-lun seems to have attracted little notice. The revision of T'ao Yüan-ming's dates to 372–427 by Liang Ch'i-ch'ao (1873–1929), however, has gained wide acceptance, and these dates have appeared in many books without query as the indisputable dates of the poet. Liang's arguments, put forward in his *T'ao Yüan-ming* (1923), were in fact effectively criticized by Yu Kuo-en in his article 'T'ao Ch'ien nien-chi pien-i' 陶潛年紀辨疑 in the first number (devoted to T'ao Yüan-ming) of *Kuo-hsüeh yüeh-pao hui-k'an* (1928). A rival view was also expounded by Ku Chih in his *T'ao Ching-chieh nien-p'u* (1926). Ku adopted several of Liang's arguments but altered others to reach the conclusion that T'ao's dates should be 376–427, i.e. that he died in his fifty-second year.

The respective views of Liang and Ku were examined and rejected in favour of the traditional dating in 1933 by Chu Tzu-ch'ing in his 'T'ao Yüan-ming nien-p'u chung chih wen-t'i' (section 7). Nevertheless the 376–427 dating was taken up by two other writers, Lai I-hui in 'T'ao Yüan-ming sheng-p'ing shih-chi chi ch'i sui-shu hsin-k'ao' 陶淵明生平事蹟及其歲數新考 (*Ling-nan hsüeh-pao* VI, 1; 1937) and Lu Ch'in-li in 'T'ao Yüan-ming nien-p'u kao' 陶淵明年譜稿 (*Academia Sinica Bulletin* XX, 1; 1948).

In the last twenty years or so there has been a general return to the traditional dating in mainland China, while Li Ch'en-tung and others in Taiwan have kept to Liang Ch'i-ch'ao's alternative. In Japan, Suzuki Torao, Shiba Rokurō, Yoshikawa Kōjirō and others have all followed the traditional dating.

It is not in the end perhaps so very difficult to counter the arguments of those who have proposed to alter the traditional dates for T'ao's life, but it is far less easy to prove from statements in the poet's surviving writings that the dates which arise from the *Sung shu* are absolutely correct. Although Young Yong claims to have resolved the problem conclusively in his 'T'ao Yüan-ming nien-shou ying-wei liu-shih-san sui k'ao' 陶淵明年壽應爲六十三歲考 (*Hsin-ya shu-yüan hsüeh-shu nien-k'an* V; 1963), much of his argument is circumstantial and would have to be excluded in strict logic. The general fondness of Chinese poets for round figures, allusion and periphrastic expression must make the proving of a poet's exact age from the internal evidence of his own work difficult. There must indeed be many cases besides that of T'ao Yüan-ming where the statement of age at death in biographies in the dynastic histories would be equally hard to confirm with certainty. Unless

some obvious contradiction arises, such statements are generally accepted. I
think that we can presume that the *Sung shu*'s statement of T'ao's age at
death was unquestioningly accepted not only by the compilers of the later
histories but also generally by later writers and critics. Indeed, I consider that
it was probably this unquestioning acceptance which led an unknown editor to
suggest the emendation of *hsin-ch'ou* (401) to *hsin-yu* (421) in the preface to
An Excursion to Hsieh-ch'uan, when *wu-jih* (fifth day) in the first line of the
poem had accidently been corrupted into *wu-shih* (fifty years old), because, *as
everyone knew*, T'ao Yüan-ming was only in his thirty-seventh year in 401
(see Additional Commentary to *An Excursion to Hsieh-ch'uan,* pp. 41–43).
Chang Yin, however, took the opposite course of believing that the *Sung shu*
was incorrect and so began the doubting of the traditional dating.

Before leaving this problem it may be worthwhile to add a reference which I
think has not been brought into this discussion previously. Recently, in
reading the works of Yüan Chen (779–831) with a student I happened on the
poem *Returning to the Country* (*Kuei t'ien* 歸田 ; *Yüan-shih Ch'ang-ch'ing chi*
14, 5b) of which the first lines read:

> T'ao in his thirty-seventh year
> Hung up his seal-ribbon and went out of the capital's gate.
> I too am leaving in this present year . . .

(Yüan noted after the title that he was in his thirty-seventh year at the time,
i.e. 815.) At first sight this may seem to be an exciting new piece of evidence,
if one assumes that "T'ao chün' 陶君 is in fact T'ao Yüan-ming (the possibility
that it might be T'ao Hung-ching, 452–536, has to be considered but can be
dismissed since the latter is said to have retired to the mountains in 492, i.e.
his forty-first year). If T'ao Yüan-ming is intended, which date had Yüan
Chen in mind with his very precise 'thirty-seventh year'? Retirement from
office would generally in reference to T'ao suggest P'eng-tse and 405, but
P'eng-tse was not the capital. Yüan Chen's title calls to mind T'ao's series
Returning to Live in the Country, which has commonly been placed in 406
after T'ao's giving up office at P'eng-tse, but which I have argued (see vol. 1,
pp. 47–48) dates from after his return from *the capital* in 400. Did Yüan Chen,
pursuing a similar logic, think that this series was written in 401, T'ao's
thirty-seventh year by the *Sung shu's* dating? He must then have thought that
T'ao held some office in the capital, although now no positive statement of
this survives in any source. It is difficult to imagine that Yüan Chen had
approached T'ao's works in a spirit of scholarly inquiry and had researched
into the dates of the poems. It would be tempting to conclude that more
information was available to him than we now possess, and thus his poem
might be used as a piece of certain evidence. This, however, I regard as
improbable and would suggest that the solution may be that

    1) he accepted the *Sung shu*'s dating;

2) the works of T'ao Yüan-ming which he knew were very similar to the current version;

3) he was influenced in thinking that the *Returning to Live in the Country* series dated from 401 by the fact that they are followed by *An Excursion to Hsieh-ch'uan* which has this date in the preface.

If this view is correct, then this poem of Yüan Chen has no value as independent evidence for the traditional dating. In spite of this, Yüan could have been entirely accurate in his assumptions.

39. It seems certain that T'ao Yüan-ming married twice (for a full discussion of this question, see Additional Commentary to *Charge to My Son*, p. 24). If one could assume that the *Nan shih*'s addition to Hsiao T'ung's statement was anything more than a literary gloss, it would be possible to argue that the reference here is to T'ao's second wife, because his 'ploughing with his own hand' is likely to have begun after the death of his first wife. It has in fact been widely assumed that this wife, née Ti, was his second wife, but it must remain an assumption. The Ti family, which is still in the *T'ai-p'ing huan-yü chi* (111, 4a) listed as one of the three families of Hsün-yang (along with the T'aos and the Ch'iens 翟) produced four generations of recluses in the Eastern Chin period according to the biography of Ti T'ang 湯 in *Chin shu* 94, 11b–12a.

BIBLIOGRAPHY

(Section A contains editions of T'ao Yüan-ming's works and studies relating to the poet from all periods, arranged mainly by author; Section B contains the Chinese works cited in the commentaries and notes, arranged by title; Section C, the Western works cited, arranged by author.)

Abbreviations:

BMFEA	*Bulletin of the Museum of Far Eastern Antiquities*
CBH	*Chūgoku bungaku hō*
CHHP	*Ts'ing-hua hsüeh-pao*
CYYY	*Bulletin of the Institute of History and Philology, Academia Sinica*
JNCBRAS	*Journal of the North China Branch of the Royal Asiatic Society*
KHCPTS	*Kuo-hsüeh chi-pen ts'ung-shu* series
KHHTS	*Kuo-hsüeh hsiao ts'ung-shu* series
LSYC	*Li-shih yen-chiu*
SPPY	*Ssu-pu pei-yao*
SPTK	*Ssu-pu ts'ung-k'an*
TSCC	*Ts'ung-shu chi-ch'eng*
TT	*Taishō daizōkyō*
WYWK	*Wan-yu wen-k'u* series

A. T'ao Yüan-ming Editions, Commentaries and Studies

Chang Chih 張芝, *T'ao Yüan-ming ti chuan lun* 陶淵明的傳論 [Biographical Essay on T'ao Yüan-ming] (Shanghai, T'ang-ti 棠棣 ch'u-pan she, 1952; 3rd edn., 1953).

Chang Chih-ming 張志明 & Miao Yüeh 繆鉞, 'Tui-yü "T'ao Ch'ien pu wei wu-tou mi che-yao hsin-shih" ti shang-ch'üeh' 對於陶潛不為五斗米折腰新釋的商榷 [Discussion of 'A New Explanation of T'ao Ch'ien Not Bowing for Five Pecks of Rice'], *LSYC* 1957, 10, 87–93.

Chang P'u 張溥 (1602–41), *T'ao P'eng-tse chi* 陶彭澤集 [Works of Magistrate T'ao of P'eng-tse], in his *Han-Wei Liu-ch'ao pai-san ming-chia chi* 漢魏六朝百三名家集 [Hundred and Three Famous Writers of Han, Wei and the Six Dynasties]. (Shanghai, Sao-yeh shan-fang 掃葉山房 edn., 1917.)

Chang Yin 張縯, *Wu p'u pien-cheng* 吳譜辨證 [Critical Study of Wu (Jen-chieh's) Chronological Account of T'ao Yüan-ming], surviving only in quotations in Li Kung-huan (q.v.).

Ch'en Hang 陳沆 (1785–1826), *Shih pi-hsing chien* 詩比興箋 [Comments on Allegory and Metaphor in Poetry] (preface date 1854). Comments on 35 poems, mainly poems in series (Peking, Chung-hua shu-chü 中華書局, 1959).

Ch'en Li 陳澧 (1810–82), *T'ao Yüan-ming chi cha-chi* 陶淵明集札記 [Notes on the Works of T'ao Yüan-ming], edited by his great-grandson Ch'en Chih-mai 陳之邁 (Hong Kong, Lung-men shu-tien 龍門書店, 1974).

Ch'en Yin-k'o 陳寅恪 (1890–1969), '"T'ao-hua yüan chi" p'ang-cheng' 桃花源記旁證 [Circumstantial Evidence on *Peach-blossom Source*], *CHHP* XI, 1 (January, 1936), 79–88. Repr. in *T'ao Yüan-ming yen-chiu tzu-liao hui-pien* (q.v.), 338–47.

———, *T'ao Yüan-ming chih ssu-hsiang yü ch'ing-t'an chih kuan-hsi* 陶淵明之思想與清談之關係 [The Relationship between T'ao Yüan-ming's Thought and Pure Talk] (Peking, Harvard-Yenching Institute, 1945).

———, '*Wei shu Ssu-ma Jui chuan* Chiang-tung min-tsu t'iao shih-cheng chi t'ui-lun' 魏書司馬叡傳江東民族條釋證及推論 [Discussion and Conclusions about the References to Southern Tribes in the Biography of Ssu-ma Jui in the *Wei shu*], *CYYY* XI, 1, 1–25.

Ch'i I-shou 齊益壽, *T'ao Yüan-ming ti cheng-chih li-ch'ang yü cheng-chih li-hsiang* 陶淵明的政治立場與政治理想 [T'ao Yüan-ming's Political Position and Political Ideals], *Wen-shih ts'ung-k'an* 文史叢刊 no. 25 (Taipei, Taiwan National University, 1968).

Chu Tzu-ch'ing 朱自清 (1898–1948), 'T'ao Yüan-ming nien-p'u chung chih wen-t'i' 陶淵明年譜中之問題 [Problems in the Chronological Accounts of T'ao Yüan-ming), *CHHP* IX, 3 (July, 1934), 573–609. Repr. in *Chu Tzu-ch'ing wen-chi* 朱自清文集, 4 vols. (Peking, K'ai-ming shu-tien 開明書店, 1953), and in *T'ao Yüan-ming yen-chiu tzu-liao hui-pien* (q.v.).

Ch'u Wan-feng 儲皖峰, 'T'ao Yüan-ming "shu-chiu shih" pu-chu' 陶淵明述酒詩補注 [Supplementary Comments on T'ao Yüan-ming's Poem *Telling of Wine*], *Fu-jen hsüeh-chih* VIII, 1 (1939), 127–52.

Fang-Su (hsieh) pen T'ao chi 仿蘇（寫）本陶集, edition of T'ao's works in 10 chüan of which the original writing is supposed to have been that of Su Shih 蘇軾 (1037–1101). There are a number of Ch'ing editions all of which derive from the 1694 Chi-ku ko 汲古閣 reproduction of a Southern Sung edition with a colophon by Mao Chin's son Mao I 毛扆 (b. 1640, d. after 1710). For a discussion see Hashikawa Tokio, *T'ao-chi pan-pen yüan-liu k'ao*, 18b–21a and Kuo Shao-yü, 'T'ao-chi k'ao-pien', 39–41. This text is also reproduced in Ku Hao's *T'ao Yüan-ming chi chien-chu*.

Feng I 馮遠, 'Shih T'ao-shih "Mei hen mi so hui"' 釋陶詩《每恨靡所揮》 [Explaining T'ao's line 'Always I grieve to have no cup to raise'], *Wen-shih* 文史 I (Peking, Chung-hua shu-chü, 1962).

Fu Tung-hua 傅東華, *T'ao Yüan-ming shih* 陶淵明詩 [T'ao Yüan-ming's Poems], *Hsüeh-sheng kuo-hsüeh ts'ung-shu* 學生國學叢書 (Commercial Press, 1926; repr. in Hong Kong, 1959).

Fukunaga Mitsuji 福永光司, 'Tō Enmei no "shin" ni tsuite — Enmei no shisō to sono shūhen' 陶淵明の真について──淵明の思想とその周邊 [On 'Truth' in T'ao Yüan-ming — Yüan-ming's Thought and His Milieu], *Tōhō gakuhō* XXXIII (1963), 1–80.

Hashikawa Tokio 橋川時雄, *T'ao-chi pan-pen yüan-liu k'ao* 陶集版本源流攷 [Study of the Filiation of the Block-prints of T'ao's Works] (1931).

———, 'Tō Enmei bungaku no genryū o saguru' 陶淵明文學の源流を探る [Seeking Sources for T'ao Yüan-ming's Writing], *Jinbun kenkyū* V, 6 (June, 1954), 1–33.

Ho Ch'o 何焯 (1661–1722), *I-men tu-shu chi* 義門讀書記 [I-men's (Ho Ch'o's literary name) Notes on His Reading] (preface date 1769), in 58 chüan of which one is devoted to comments on poems of T'ao Yüan-ming.

Ho Meng-ch'un 何孟春 (1474–1536), *T'ao Ching-chieh chi* 陶靖節集 [Works of T'ao Ching-chieh], 10 chüan with commentary (1518).

Hsiao T'ung 蕭統 (501–531), *T'ao Yüan-ming chuan* 陶淵明傳 [Biography of T'ao Yüan-ming]. Printed in the Tseng Chi and many subsequent editions of T'ao's works.

Hsiao Wang-ch'ing 蕭望卿, *T'ao Yüan-ming p'i-p'ing* 陶淵明批評 [Criticism of (the Poems of) T'ao Yüan-ming] (K'ai-ming shu-tien, 1947; repr. in Hong Kong, T'ai-p'ing shu-chü, 1963).

Huang Chung-lun 黃仲崙, *T'ao Yüan-ming tso-p'in yen-chiu* 陶淵明作品研究 [Study of the Works of T'ao Yüan-ming] (Taipei, P'a-mi-erh (i.e. Pamir) shu-tien 帕米爾書店, 1969).

Ikkai Tomoyoshi 一海知義, 'Tō Enmei ni okeru kyokō to genjitsu' 陶淵明における虛構と現實 [Fiction and Reality in T'ao Yüan-ming], in *Yoshikawa hakase taikyū kinen Chūgoku bungaku ronshū* 吉川博士退休紀念中國文學論集, 189–208.

———, 'Monzen bankashi kō' 文選挽歌詩考 [Study of the Burial Songs in the *Wen-hsüan*], *CBH* XII, 19–48.

———, 'Sei Shin no shijin Chō Kyō ni tsuite' 西晉の詩人張協について [On the Western Chin Poet Chang Hsieh], *CBH* VII, 92–133.

———, *Tō Enmei* 陶淵明 [T'ao Yüan-ming]. *Chūgoku shijin senshū* 中國詩人選集 [Selected Works of Chinese Poets] (Iwanami 岩波, 1959).

———, *Tō Enmei, Bunshin chōryū* 陶淵明, 文心雕龍 [T'ao Yüan-ming, *Wen-hsin tiao-lung*], *Sekai koten bungaku zenshū* 世界古典文學全集 [Collected Works of World Classical

Literature] (Chikuma Shobō 筑摩書房, 1968).

Ku Chih 古直, *T'ao Ching-chieh nien-p'u* 陶靖節年譜 [Chronological Account of T'ao Yüan-ming], in his *Yü lou ts'ung-shu* 隅樓叢書 (1926). Repr. from his *Ts'eng-ping t'ang wu-chung* 層冰堂五種 (1935) as a supplement to *T'ao Ching-chieh shih chien* 陶靖節詩箋 (Taipei, Kuang-wen shu-chü 廣文書局, 1964).

———, *T'ao Ching-chieh shih chien* 陶靖節詩箋 [The Poems of T'ao Yüan-ming with Commentary], in his *Yü lou ts'ung-shu* (1926). Repr. from Ku's revised version, *T'ao Ching-chieh shih chien ting-pen* 定本 in his *Ts'eng-ping t'ang wu-chung* (1935) (Taipei, Kuang-wen shu-chü, 1964).

Ku Hao 顧鴞, *T'ao Yüan-ming chi chien-chu* 陶淵明集箋註 [The Works of T'ao Yüan-ming with Commentary] (Shanghai, Wen-jui lou 文瑞樓 lithograph, 1918).

Kuo Po-kung 郭伯恭, *Ko-yung tzu-jan chih liang ta shih-hao* 歌詠自然之兩大詩豪 [Two Great Nature Poets (T'ao Yüan-ming and Wang Wei)]. *KHHTS* (Shanghai, Commercial Press, 1936).

Kuo Shao-yü 郭紹虞, 'T'ao-chi k'ao-pien' 陶集考辨 [Investigation of (the Editions of) T'ao's Works], *Yen-ching hsüeh-pao* XX (December, 1936), 25–84.

Lai I-hui 賴義輝, 'T'ao Yüan-ming sheng-p'ing shih-chi chi ch'i sui-shu hsin-k'ao' 陶淵明生平事蹟及其歲數新考 [New Study of the Biography of T'ao Yüan-ming and His Age at Death], *Ling-nan hsüeh-pao* VI, 1 (March, 1937), 81–119.

Li Ch'en-tung 李辰冬, *T'ao Yüan-ming p'ing lun* 陶淵明評論 [Critical Discussion of T'ao Yüan-ming]. *Hsien-tai kuo-min chi-pen chih-shih ts'ung-shu* 現代國民基本知識叢書, 4th series (Taipei, Chung-hua wen-hua ch'u-pan shih-yeh wei-yüan-hui 中華文化出版事業委員會, 1956).

Li Kung-huan 李公煥, *Chien-chu T'ao Yüan-ming chi* 箋注陶淵明集 [Works of T'ao Yüan-ming with Commentary], 10 chüan. *SPTK* reprint of edition preserved in the Han-fen lou 涵芬樓. Li's edition, described in the *SPTK* catalogue as a Sung work, has been shown by Hashikawa Tokio in his discussion (*T'ao-chi pan-pen yüan-liu k'ao*, 21aff) to be Yüan.

Liang Ch'i-ch'ao 梁啟超, *T'ao Yüan-ming* 陶淵明. *KHHTS* (Shanghai, Commercial Press, 1923; repr. 1934).

Liao Chung-an 廖仲安, *T'ao Yüan-ming* 陶淵明. *Ku-tien wen-hsüeh chi-pen chih-shih ts'ung-shu* 古典文學基本知識叢書 (Peking, Chung-hua shu-chü, 1963).

Liu Li 劉履 (1317–79), *Hsüan-shih pu-chu* 選詩補註 [Selected Poems with Supplementary Comments], Ming print. Library of Congress Microfilms of Rare Books in the Peking National Library, no. 1641. Ch. 5 is devoted to T'ao Yüan-ming and contains 37 of his poems.

Liu Wen-tien 劉文典, 'Hsien-ch'ing fu' 閒情賦 [The *Fu*-poem *Quieting the Affections*], in *San-yü cha-chi* 三餘札記. 3 *ts'e* (Shanghai, Commercial Press, 1938), ch. 1, 2b–3b.

Lu Ch'in-li 逯欽立, '"Hsing-ying-shen shih" yü Tung-Chin chih fo-tao ssu-hsiang' 形影神詩與東晉之佛道思想 [The *Body, Shadow and Soul* Poem and Eastern Chin Buddhist and Taoist Thought], *CYYY* XVI, 1 (June, 1948), 211–28.

———, '"Lo-shen fu" yü "Hsien-ch'ing fu"' 洛神賦與閒情賦 [The *Fu*-poem *The Goddess of the Lo River* and the *Fu*-poem *Quieting the Affections*], *Hsüeh-yüan* 學原 II, 8 (December, 1948), 81–91.

———, '"Shu-chiu shih" t'i-chu shih-i' 述酒詩題注釋疑 [Investigation of Doubtful Points over the Title and Commentary to the Poem *Telling of Wine*], *CYYY* XVIII (1948), 361–74.

———, 'T'ao Yüan-ming nien-p'u kao' 陶淵明年譜稿 [Draft Chronological Account of T'ao Yüan-ming], *CYYY* XX, 1 (1948), 223–48.

Matsuzaki Meifuku 松崎明復, *Tō Enmei shū* 陶淵明集 [Works of T'ao Yüan-ming], 10 *kan*. With *San-Sha shi* 三謝詩 [Poems of the Three Hsiehs] in 1 *kan* as supplement (1840).

Miao Yüeh 繆鉞, 'T'ao Ch'ien pu wei wu-tou mi che-yao hsin-shih' 陶潛不為五斗米折腰新釋 [New Explanation of T'ao Ch'ien's Not Bowing for Five Pecks of Rice], *LSYC* 1957, 1, 79–85.

Ogawa Tamaki 小川環樹, 'Tō Enmei no banka' 陶淵明の挽歌 [T'ao Yüan-ming's Burial Songs], in *Kaze to kumo* 風と雲 (Asahi Shinbunsha 朝日新聞社, 1972), 340–44.

Ōyane Bunjirō 大矢根文次郎, *Tō Enmei kenkyū* 陶淵明研究 [Studies of T'ao Yüan-ming] (Waseda daigaku shuppanbu 早稲田大學出版部, 1967; 2nd edn., 1969).

P'an Ch'ung-kuei 潘重規, 'T'ao shih hsi-i' 陶詩析疑 [Resolution of Some Doubtful Points in T'ao's Poems], *CHHP* (new series) VII, 1 (August, 1968), 214–24.

Seitan 清潭, *Tō Enmei shū, Ō Ujō shū* 陶淵明集王右丞集 [T'ao Yüan-ming's Works, Wang Wei's Works], *Zoku Kokuyaku kanbun taisei* 續國譯漢文大成 (1929).

Shiba Rokurō 斯波六郎, *Chūgoku bungaku ni okeru kodokukan* 中國文學における孤獨感 [The Sense of Loneliness in Chinese Literature] (Iwanami, 1958).

———, *Tō Enmei shi chūyaku* 陶淵明詩注譯 [T'ao Yüan-ming's Poems with Commentary and Translation] (Tōmon Shobō 東門書房, 1951).

Suzuki Torao 鈴木虎雄, *Tō Enmei shi kai* 陶淵明詩解 [T'ao Yüan-ming's Poems with Explanations] (Kōbundō 弘文堂, 1948; 3rd edn., 1953).

T'an Chia-chien 譚家健, ' "*Tao-hua yüan chi*" cha-chi' «桃花源記» 札記 [Notes on *Peach-blossom Source*] in *T'ao Yüan-ming t'ao-lun chi* (q.v.), 151–59.

T'ang Ch'ang-ju 唐長孺, 'Tu "*T'ao-hua yüan chi* p'ang-cheng" chih-i' 讀«桃花源記旁證» 質疑 [Queries Raised in Reading 'Circumstantial Evidence on *Peach-blossom Source*'], in *Wei Chin Nan-pei ch'ao shih lun-ts'ung hsü-pien* 魏晉南北朝史論叢續編 [Collected Articles on the History of Wei, Chin and the Southern and Northern Dynasties, Supplementary Volume] (Peking, San-lien shu-tien 三聯書店, 1959), 163–74.

T'ang Han 湯漢 (c. 1198–1275), *T'ao Ching-chieh chi* 陶靖節集 [Works of T'ao Ching-chieh], (preface date 1241), 4 chüan, in *Pai-ching lou ts'ung-shu* 拜經樓叢書, compiled by Wu Ch'ien 吳騫 (1733–1813) (repr. in Shanghai, Po-ku chai 博古齋, 1922).

T'ao Shu 陶澍 (1779–1839), *Ching-chieh hsien-sheng chi* 靖節先生集, [Works of Master Ching-chieh]. 10 chüan, with *nien-p'u k'ao-i* 年譜考異 in 2 chüan, *SPPY* edn.; based on T'ao Shu's original *chi-chu* 集注 edn. of 1840.

T'ao wen ts'an 陶文殘, reprint of T'ang roll of *Kuei-ch'ü-lai tz'u*, dated 905, preserved in Japan, in *Chuan-hsi lu ts'ung-shu* 羹喜廬叢書 of Fu Yün-lung 傅雲龍 (Tokyo, 1889).

T'ao Yüan-ming shih-wen hui-p'ing 陶淵明詩文彙評 [Collected Comments on T'ao Yüan-ming's Poems and Prose], compiled by Pei-ching ta-hsüeh Chung-wen hsi wen-hsüeh shih chiao-yen shih chiao-shih wu liu chi ssu pan t'ung-hsüeh 北京大學中文系文學史教研室教師五六級四班同學 (Peking, Chung-hua shu-chü, 1961). Reissued as *T'ao Yüan-ming chüan* 陶淵明卷 vol. 2 (1962).

T'ao Yüan-ming t'ao-lun chi 陶淵明討論集 [Collection of Articles about T'ao Yüan-ming], compiled by *Wen-hsüeh i-ch'an* pien-chi pu 文學遺產編輯部 (Peking, Chung-hua shu-chü, 1961).

T'ao Yüan-ming yen-chiu tzu-liao hui-pien 陶淵明研究資料彙編 [Collection of Materials for the Study of T'ao Yüan-ming], compiled by Pei-ching ta-hsüeh Pei-ching shih-fan ta-hsüeh Chung-wen hsi chiao-shih t'ung-hsüeh 北京大學北京師範大學中文系教師同學 (Peking, Chung-hua shu-chü, 1962). This work was also issued as *T'ao Yüan-ming chüan*, vol. 1. Cf. *T'ao Yüan-ming shih-wen hui-p'ing* above.

Ting Fu-pao 丁福保 (1874–1952), *T'ao Yüan-ming shih chien-chu* 陶淵明詩箋注 [T'ao Yüan-ming's Poems with Commentary] (preface date 1927) (repr. in Taipei, I-wen yin-shu kuan, 1960).

Ting Yen 丁晏 (1794–1875), *Chin T'ao Ching-chieh nien-p'u* 晉陶靖節年譜 [Chronological Account of T'ao Yüan-ming of Chin] (1843), in Ting's *I-chih chai ts'ung-shu* 頤志齋叢書 (1862).

Tō Enmei shibun sōgō sakuin 陶淵明詩文綜合索引 [Concordance to the Poems and Prose of T'ao Yüan-ming], compiled by Horie Tadamichi 堀江忠道 (Kyoto, Ibundō shoten 彙文堂書店, 1976).

Ts'ao Tao-heng 曹道衡 'Kuan yü T'ao Yüan-ming ssu-hsiang ti chi-ko wen-t'i' 關於陶淵明思想的幾個問題 [On Some Problems in T'ao Yüan-ming's Thought]. *Wen-hsüeh i-ch'an tseng-k'an* 文學遺產增刊. 5th collection (Peking, Tso-chia ch'u-pan she 作家出版社, 1957).

Tseng Chi 曾集, *Sung-pen T'ao chi* 宋本陶集 [Sung edn. of T'ao's Works] (colophon date 1192). Facsimile reprint (1875). Also included in *Hsü ku-i ts'ung-shu* 繪古逸叢書 (1928).

Tsuru Haruo 都留春雄, *Tō Enmei* 陶淵明 [T'ao Yüan-ming]. *Chūgoku shibun sen* 中國詩文選 [Selected Works of Chinese Poetry and Prose], vol. 11 (Chikuma Shobō, 1974).

Tuan Hsi-chung 段熙仲, 'T'ao Yüan-ming shih-chi hsin-t'an' 陶淵明事迹新探 [New Researches into T'ao Yüan-ming's Biography], *Wen-hsüeh yen-chiu* 1957, 3, 99–103.

Urushiyama Matashirō 漆山又四郎, *Yakuchū Tō Enmei shū* 譯註陶淵明集 [T'ao Yüan-ming's Works with Translation and Comments], 2 vols. (Iwanami Bunko, 1928).

Wang Chih 王質 (1135–89), *T'ao Yüan-ming nien-p'u* 陶淵明年譜 [Chronological Account of T'ao Yüan-ming]. Repr. in Wu Chan-t'ai's *T'ao shih hui-chu* (q.v.) from Wang's *Shao T'ao lu* 紹陶錄. Also printed in *T'ao Yüan-ming yen-chiu tzu-liao hui-pien* (q.v.) as *Li-li p'u* 栗里譜 from T'ao Tsung-i 陶宗儀, *Nan-ts'un cho-keng lu* 南村輟耕錄, ch. 16.

Wang Kuei-ling 王貴苓, *T'ao Yüan-ming chi ch'i shih ti yen-chiu* 陶淵明及其詩的研究 [Study of T'ao Yüan-ming and His Poems]. *Wen-shih ts'ung-k'an* 文史叢刊, no. 18 (Taipei, Taiwan National University, 1966).

Wang Shu-min 王叔岷, *T'ao Yüan-ming shih chien-cheng kao* 陶淵明詩箋證稿 [A Draft Commentary on the Poems of T'ao Yüan-ming] (Taipei, I-wen yin-shu kuan, 1975).

Wang Yao 王瑤, *T'ao Yüan-ming chi* 陶淵明集 [T'ao Yüan-ming's Works] (Peking, Tso-chia ch'u-pan she, 1956).

Wen Ju-neng 溫汝能, *T'ao shih hui-p'ing* 陶詩彙評 [Collected Criticisms of T'ao's Poems] (preface date 1806). Sao-yeh shan-fang 掃葉山房 edn. (Shanghai, 1910).

Wu Chan-t'ai 吳瞻泰 (1657–1735), *T'ao shih hui-chu* 陶詩彙注 [Collected Comments on T'ao's Poems], in *Yün-nan ts'ung-shu* 雲南叢書, compiled by Ch'en Yung-ch'ang 陳榮昌 and others. Ta-Chung 大中 shu-chü edn. (1914. Shanghai, 1926).

Wu Jen-chieh 吳仁傑 (*chin-shih* 1244), *T'ao Ching-chieh hsien-sheng nien-p'u* 陶靖節先生年譜 [Chronological Account of T'ao Yüan-ming]. Repr. in Wu Chan-t'ai's *T'ao shih hui-chu* (q.v.); also printed in T'ao Yüan-ming yen-chiu tzu-liao hui-pien (q.v.) from Wu's edn.

Wu Shih-tao 吳師道 (Yüan period), *Wu Li-pu shih-hua* 吳禮部詩話 [Remarks on Poetry by Director of the Ministry of Rites Wu]. Extracts printed as a supplement to T'ang Han, *T'ao Ching-chieh chi* (q.v.).

Yang Hsi-min 楊希閔, *Chin T'ao Cheng-shih nien-p'u* 晉陶徵士年譜 [Chronological Account of T'ao, a Scholar Summoned by Chin], first printed in *Yü-chang hsien-hsien chiu-chia nien-p'u* 豫章先賢九家年譜 (1878). Repr. in *Shih-wu chia nien-p'u ts'ung-shu* 十五家年譜叢書 (Yang-chou ku-chi shu-tien 揚州古籍書店, 1958; repr. Kuang-ling ku-chi k'o-yin she 廣陵古籍刻印社, 1962).

Yang Lien-sheng 楊聯陞, 'Lun Tung-Chin Nan-ch'ao hsien-ling feng-lu ti piao-chun: T'ao Ch'ien pu wei wu-tou mi che-yao hsin-shih chih-i' 論東晉南朝縣令俸祿的標準：《陶潛不為五斗米折腰新釋》質疑 [On the Salary Standard of the District Magistrate of Eastern Chin and the Southern Dynasties: Questions Raised by 'New Explanation of T'ao Ch'ien's Not Bowing for Five Pecks of Rice'], *Tōyōshi kenkyū* XXI, 2 (September, 1962), 218–22.

Yoshikawa Kōjirō 吉川幸次郎, 'Kanjō no fu' 閑情の賦 [The *Fu*-poem *Quieting the Affections*], in collection of essays with the same title (Chikuma Shobō, 1957), 37–44.

———, *Tō Enmei den* 陶淵明傳 [Life of T'ao Yüan-ming] (Shinchōsha 新潮社, 1956).

———, 'Tō Enmei shi no kunko' 陶淵明詩の訓詁 [Explanation of (Some Points in) T'ao Yüan-ming's Poems], in *Shi to gekkō* 詩と月光 (Chikuma Shobō, 1964), 114–17.

Yoshioka Yoshitoyo 吉岡義豐, 'Kikyorai no ji ni tsuite' 歸去來の辭について [On *Return Home!*], *CBH* VI, 25–44.

———, 'Kikyorai no ji to bukkyō' 歸去來の辭と佛教 [*Return Home!* and Buddhism], *Ishihama sensei koki kinen Tōyōgaku ronsō* 石濱先生古稀紀念東洋學論叢 (Osaka, 1958), 610–22.

Young Yong 楊勇, *T'ao Yüan-ming chi chiao-chien* 陶淵明集校箋 [T'ao Yüan-ming's Works with Critical Evaluation of the Texts and Commentary] (Hong Kong, Ou Hin Kee Book Store 吳興記書局, 1971).

———, 'T'ao Yüan-ming "huan chiu-chü" shih k'ao-shih' 陶淵明還舊居詩考釋 [Explanation of T'ao Yüan-ming's Poem *Returning to My Old Home*], *Hsin-ya shu-yüan hsüeh-shu nien-k'an* VI (September, 1964), 271–96.

———, 'T'ao Yüan-ming nien-p'u hui-ting' 陶淵明年譜彙訂 [Collation of Chronological Accounts of T'ao Yüan-ming], *Hsin-ya hsüeh-pao* VII, 2 (1965), 215–304.

———, 'T'ao Yüan-ming nien-shou ying-wei liu-shih-san sui k'ao' 陶淵明年壽應為六十三歲考 [Inquiry into Whether T'ao Yüan-ming Died in His Sixty-third Year], *Hsin-ya shu-yüan hsüeh-shu nien-k'an* V (September, 1963), 139–63.

Yu Kuo-en 游國恩, 'T'ao Ch'ien nien-chi pien-i' 陶潛年紀辨疑 [Study of the Problems of the Chronology of T'ao Ch'ien], *Kuo-hsüeh yüeh-pao hui-k'an* I (1928), 236–42.

B. Chinese Works Cited

Chan-kuo ts'e 戰國策 [Strategies of the Warring States], in *SPTK* edn. with commentaries by Pao Piao 鮑彪 and Wu Shih-tao 吳師道. Trans. J.L. Crump, Jr, *Chan-kuo ts'e* (Oxford, Oxford University Press, 1970).

Chao lun 肇論 [The Discourses of (Seng-) chao], by Seng-chao 僧肇 (384–414), *TT*, no. 1858, XLV, 150–61. Trans. W. Liebenthal, *The Book of Chao*. Monumenta Serica Monograph XIII (Peking, The Catholic University of Peking, 1948).

Chao lun shu 肇論疏, commentary by Yüan-k'ang 元康 (7th cent.) to *Chao lun* of Seng-chao, *TT*, no. 1859, XLV, 161–200.

Chao-mei chan-yen 昭昧詹言 (first printed 1891), by Fang Tung-shu 方東樹 (1772–1851) (Peking, Jen-min wen-hsüeh ch'u-pan she 人民文學出版社, 1961).

Chi sheng-hsien ch'ün-fu lu 集聖賢羣輔錄 [Notes on Assembled Sages and Worthies and the Multitude of Aiding Ministers], ascribed to T'ao Yüan-ming and placed in ch. 9 and 10 of his works. Reference to *Ching-chieh hsien-sheng chi* 靖節先生集 with commentary by T'ao Shu, in *SPPY* edn.

Ch'i-chia Hou-Han shu 七家後漢書 [(Fragments of) Histories of the Later Han Dynasty by Seven Authors], compiled by Wang Wen-t'ai 汪文臺. Facsimile reprint of original edn. of 1882 (Taipei, Wen-hai ch'u-pan she, 1972).

(*Ch'ung-hsiu*) *Chiang-hsi t'ung-chih* (重修) 江西通志 [Revised General Gazetteer of Kiangsi Province], by Liu K'un-i 劉坤一 (1830–1902) and others (printed in 1880–81). The revision of the provincial gazetteer appeared under the name of Liu who was governor-general of Liang-Kiang at the time; the chief editor was Chao Chih-ch'ien 趙之謙 (1829–84).

Ch'ien-yen t'ang wen chi 薜研堂文集 [Prose Works of the Ch'ien-yen t'ang (name of Ch'ien's studio)], by Ch'ien Ta-hsin 錢大昕 (1728–1804), in *SPTK* edn.

Chih-chai shu-lu chieh-t'i 直齋書錄解題 [Notes on Books and Explanation of Titles in the Chih-chai (Ch'en's studio)], by Ch'en Chen-sun 陳振孫 (13th cent.), *TSCC*, nos. 44–48.

Chin chung-hsing shu 晉中興書 [History of the Restored Chin, i.e. Eastern Chin], by Ho Fa-sheng 何法盛 (5th cent.). Fragments collected by Huang Shih 黃奭 in his *Han-hsüeh t'ang ts'ung-shu* 漢學堂叢書 and by T'ang Ch'iu 湯球 in *Chiu-chia chiu Chin-shu chi-pen* 九家舊晉書輯本, printed in *Kuang-ya ts'ung-shu* 廣雅叢書. Reference given to original quotations.

Chin-lou-tzu 金樓子, works of Hsiao I 蕭繹 [Emperor Yüan 元 of Liang 508–554]. *Yung-lo ta-tien* text in 6 chüan, collated with *Chih pu-tsu chai ts'ung-shu* 知不足齋叢書 edn., by Hsieh Chang-t'ing 謝章鋌 (1820–1903). Facsimile reprint (Taipei, Shih-chieh shu-chü, 1960).

Chin shu 晉書 [History of the Chin Dynasty], by Fang Hsüan-ling 房玄齡 (578–648), Ch'u Sui-liang 褚遂良 and others, in *SPPY* edn.

Chin shu 晉書 [History of the Chin Dynasty] (presented to the throne in 340), by Wang Yin 王隱. Fragments collected by T'ang Ch'iu (see under *Chin chung-hsing shu*). Reference to original quotations.

Chin yang-ch'iu 晉陽秋 [Annals of Chin], by Sun Sheng 孫盛 (*c.* 302–373). Fragments collected by Huang Shih and T'ang Ch'iu (see under *Chin chung-hsing shu*). Reference to original quotations.

Chu-tzu p'ing-i 諸子平議 [Notes on the Various Philosophers] (1870), by Yü Yüeh 俞樾 (1821–1907), in *KHCPTS* (Shanghai, Commercial Press, 1935).

Chu-tzu yü-lei 朱子語類 [Classified Sayings of Master Chu], by Chu Hsi 朱熹 (1130–1200), compiled by Li Ching-te 黎靖德. Facsimile reprint of 1473 print, preserved in the National Central Library, 8 vols. (Taipei, Cheng-chung shu-chü 正中書局, 1962).

Ch'u-hsüeh chi 初學記 [Notes for First Studies], encyclopaedia compiled by Hsü Chien 徐堅 (659–729) and others, 3 vols. (Peking, Chung-hua shu-chü, 1962).

Ch'u-tz'u 楚辭 [The Songs of Ch'u], reference to *SPPY* edn. with supplementary commentary by Hung Hsing-tsu 洪興祖 (1090–1149). Trans. David Hawkes, *Ch'u Tz'u: The Songs of the South* (Oxford, Oxford University Press, 1959).

Chuang-tzu 莊子, reference to *Chuang-tzu pu-cheng* 補正, by Liu Wen-tien 劉文典 (Shanghai, Commercial Press, 1947). Trans. James Legge, *The Texts of Taoism* (Oxford, Oxford University Press, 1891); Burton Watson, *The Complete Works of Chuang Tzu* (New York, Columbia University Press, 1968).

Chung-kuo hsiao-shuo shih-lüeh 中國小說史略 [Historical Sketch of Chinese Fiction], by Lu Hsün 魯迅 (1881–1936), (first published 1923–24; revised edn., 1930; repr. Peking, Jen-min wen-hsüeh ch'u-pan she, 1952). Trans. Yang Hsien-yi 楊憲益 and Gladys Yang, *A Brief History of Chinese Fiction* (Peking, Foreign Languages Press, 1959).

Chung-kuo ku fang-chih k'ao 中國古方志考 [Study of Ancient Chinese Local Histories], by Chang Kuo-kan 張國淦 (Peking, Chung-hua shu-chü, 1962).

Chung-kuo ti-fang hsing-cheng chih-tu shih 中國地方行政制度史 [History of Local Administration in China] by Yen Keng-wang 嚴耕望. Part 2: *Wei Chin Nan-pei ch'ao ti-fang hsing-cheng chih-tu* 魏晉南北朝地方行政制度 [Local Administration in Wei, Chin and the Southern and Northern Dynasties]. The Institute of History and Philology, Academia Sinica, Monograph no. 45. 2 vols. (Taipei, 1963).

Chung-yung 中庸 [The Doctrine of the Mean], reference to chapter divisions as in James Legge, trans. *The Chinese Classics*, vol. I (repr. in Hong Kong, Hong Kong University Press, 1960).

Ch'üan Chin-shih, see *Ch'üan Han San-kuo Chin Nan-pei ch'ao shih*.

Ch'üan Chin-wen, see *Ch'üan shang-ku San-tai ch'in Han San-kuo Liu-ch'ao wen*.

Ch'üan Han San-kuo Chin Nan-pei Ch'ao shih 全漢三國晉南北朝詩 [The Complete Han, Three Kingdoms, Chin and Southern and Northern Dynasties Poems] (1916), compiled by Ting Fu-pao 丁福保 (1874–1952).

Ch'üan Han-wen, see *Ch'üan shang-ku San-tai Ch'in Han San-kuo Liu-ch'ao wen*.

Ch'uan Hou-Han wen, see *Ch'üan shang-ku San-tai Ch'in Han San-kuo Liu-ch'ao wen*.

Ch'üan Liang-shih, see *Ch'üan Han San-kuo Chin Nan-pei ch'ao shih*.

Ch'üan San-kuo wen, see *Ch'üan shang-ku San-tai Ch'in Han San-kuo Liu-ch'ao wen*.

Ch'üan shang-ku San-tai Ch'in Han San-kuo Liu-ch'ao wen 全上古三代秦漢三國六朝文 [The Complete Prose of High Antiquity, the Three Dynasties, Ch'in, Han, the Three Kingdoms and the Six Dynasties] (first printed 1893), compiled by Yen K'o-chün 嚴可均 (1762–1843). Facsimile reprint. 4 vols. (Peking, Chung-hua shu-chü, 1958).

Ch'üan Sung wen, see *Ch'üan shang-ku San-tai Ch'in Han San-kuo Liu-ch'ao wen*.

Erh-ya 爾雅 [Vocabulary of the Classics], reference to *Erh-ya yin-te*. Harvard-Yenching Institute Sinological Index Series, Supplement 18 (June, 1941).

Fa-yen 法言 [Model Words], by Yang Hsiung 揚雄 (53 BC–AD 18), in *SPTK* edn.

Feng-su t'ung-i 風俗通義 [General Principles for (Reforming) Customs] (AD 175), by Ying Shao 應劭. Reference to *Index du Fong sou t'ong yi* (Peking, Centre Franco-Chinois d'Études Sinologiques, November 1943).

Fo-tsu t'ung-chi 佛祖統紀 [Record of the Lineage of the Buddha and Patriarchs] (compiled in period 1258–69), by Chih P'an 志磐, *TT*, no. 2035, XLIX, 129–475.

(*Ch'ien*) *Han chi* (前) 漢紀 [Record of the Former Han Dynasty], by Hsün Yüeh 荀悅 (148–209), in *SPTK* edn.

Han-Chin ch'un-ch'iu 漢晉春秋 [Annals of Han and Chin], by Hsi Tso-ch'ih 習鑿齒 († 384). Fragments collected by Huang Shih and T'ang Ch'iu (see under *Chin chung-hsing shu*). Reference to original quotations.

Han-Fei-tzu 韓非子, reference to *Han-Fei-tzu chi-shih* 集釋, by Ch'en Ch'i-yu 陳奇猷. 2 vols. (Peking, Chung-hua shu-chü, 1958). Trans. W.K. Liao, *The Complete Works of Han Fei Tzu*. 2 vols (London, Probsthain, 1939).

Han-shih wai-chuan 韓詩外傳 [Outer Commentary to the Han School Version of the *Book of Songs*], by Han Ying 韓嬰 (2nd cent. BC), in *SPTK* edn. Trans. J.R. Hightower, *Han Shih Wai Chuan: Han Ying's Illustrations of the Didactic Application of the Classic of Songs* (Cambridge, Harvard University Press, 1952).

Han shu 漢書 [The History of the Former Han Dynasty], by Pan Ku 班固 (AD 32–92), in *SPPY* edn. Partial trans. H.H. Dubs, *The History of the Former Han Dynasty*. 3 vols. (Baltimore, Waverly Press, 1938–55); Burton Watson, *Courtier and Commoner in Ancient China* (New York, Columbia University Press, 1974).

Han-Wei yüeh-fu feng chien 漢魏樂府風箋 [*Yüeh-fu* songs of Han and Wei with Commentary], by Huang Chieh 黃節 (Peking, Peking University, 1936).

Han Wu-ti nei-chuan 漢武帝內傳 [Inner History of the Emperor Wu], ascribed to Pan Ku 班固 (AD 32–92) but 4th cent. or later, in *Lung-wei pi-shu* 龍威秘書 (1794) of Ma Chün-liang 馬俊良.

Hou-Han shu 後漢書 [The History of the Later Han Dynasty], by Fan Yeh 范曄 (398–445), in *SPPY* edn.

Hou-Han shu pu-chu 後漢書補注 [Supplementary Commentary to the *History of the Later Han Dynasty*] (first printed 1804), by Hui Tung 惠棟 (1697–1758) in *Yüeh-ya t'ang ts'ung-shu* 粵雅堂叢書 (1851) of Wu Chung-yüeh 伍崇曜 (1810–63).

Hsi-ching tsa-chi 西京雜記 [Miscellaneous Records of the Western Capital], ascribed to Liu Hsin 劉歆 (*c.* 46 BC–AD 23) and also to Ko Hung 葛洪 (283–343), but probably by Wu Chün 吳均 (469–520), in *Lung-wei pi-shu* 龍威秘書 (1794) of Ma Chün-liang 馬俊良.

Hsi K'ang chi 嵇康集 [Collected Works of Hsi K'ang (223–62)], edited by Lu Hsün 魯迅 (1881–1936) (Peking, Wen-hsüeh ku-chi k'an-hsing she 文學古籍刊行社, 1956). Partial trans. Donald Holzman, *La Vie et la Pensée de Hi K'ang* (Leiden, E.J. Brill, 1957).

Hsiao-ching 孝經 [The Classic of Filial Piety], in *SPTK* edn.

Hsiao tu-shu chai ssu-lu 晚讀書齋四錄 [Four Studies from the Reading at Dawn Studio], by Hung Liang-chi 洪亮吉 (1746–1809), in *Hung Pei-chiang hsien-sheng i-chi* 洪北江先生遺集 (printed by his great-grandson Hung Yung-ch'in 用勲, 1877–79). Facsimile reprint. 18 vols. (Taipei, Hua-wen shu-chü, 1969).

Hsieh K'ang-lo shih chu 謝康樂詩注 [Poems of Hsieh Ling-yün 謝靈運 (385–433) with Commentary] (first published 1924), by Huang Chieh 黃節 (Peking, Jen-min wen-hsüeh ch'u-pan she, 1958). Trans. J.D. Frodsham, *The Murmuring Stream*. 2 vols. (Kuala Lumpur, University of Malaya Press, 1967).

Hsin-hsü 新序 [New Preface], by Liu Hsiang 劉向 (79–8 BC), in *SPTK* edn.

Hsin T'ang-shu i-wen-chih 新唐書藝文志 [Bibliographical Treatise of the New T'ang History] (ch. 57–60 of *Hsin T'ang-shu*). Reference to *T'ang-shu ching-chi i-wen ho-chih* 唐書經籍藝文合志 (Shanghai, Commercial Press, 1956).

Hsü Chin yang-ch'iu 續晉陽秋 [Annals of Chin Continued], by T'an Tao-luan 檀道鸞 (5th cent.). Fragments collected by Huang Shih and T'ang Ch'iu (see under *Chin chung-hsing shu*). Reference to original quotations.

Hsün-tzu 荀子, reference to *Hsün-tzu chi-chieh* 集解 (1891), by Wang Hsien-ch'ien 王先謙 (1842–1918), in *Chu-tzu chi-ch'eng* 諸子集成, vol. 2 (Peking, Chung-hua shu-chü, 1954). Trans. H.H. Dubs, *The Works of Hsün-tze* (London, Probsthain, 1930); Burton Watson, *Hsün Tzu: Basic Writings* (New York, Columbia University Press, 1963).

Huai-nan-tzu 淮南子 (*Huai-nan hung-lieh chieh* 淮南鴻烈解), in *SPTK* edn. Partial trans. Evan Morgan, *Tao the Great Luminant* (London, Kegan Paul, preface date 1933).

Hung-ming chi 弘明集 [Great Knowledge Collection] (compiled *c*. 515), by Seng-yu 僧佑 , *TT*, no. 2102, LII, 1–96.

I-ching 易經 [The Book of Changes], reference by hexagrams and commentaries as in *Chou-i yin-te*. Harvard-Yenching Institute Sinological Index Series, supplement 10 (October, 1935). Trans. James Legge, *The Texts of Confucianism*, Part II (Oxford, Oxford University Press, 1882); Richard Wilhelm, *The I Ching or Book of Changes*, rendered into English by Cary F. Baynes. 2 vols. (London, Routledge and Kegan Paul, 1951).

I Chou shu 逸周書 ['Lost' Documents of Chou], in *SPPY* edn., based on the *Pao-ching t'ang ts'ung-shu* 抱經堂叢書 edn. of Lu Wen-ch'ao 盧文弨 (1717–96).

I-chou shuang-chi 藝舟雙楫, by Pao Shih-ch'en 包世臣, (1775–1855), in his *An-wu ssu-chung* 安吳四種 (1846), Chu-ching t'ang 注經堂 block print, 1872.

I-wen lei-chü 藝文類聚 [Classified Extracts from Literature], compiled by Ou-yang Hsün 歐陽詢 (557–641) and others. Facsimile of Sung edn., 16 *ts'e* (Peking, Chung-hua shu-chü, 1959), and in 2 vols. (Taipei, Hsin-hsing shu-chü, 1960).

Jih-sun chai pi-chi 日損齋筆記 [Notes from the Daily Declining Studio], by Huang Chin 黃溍 (1277–1357), in *Shou-shan ko ts'ung-shu* 守山閣叢書 of Ch'ien Hsi-tso 錢熙祚 (1801–44).

Juan Pu-ping yung-huai shih-chu 阮步兵詠懷詩註 [Poems of Juan Chi 阮籍 (210–265) with Commentary], by Huang Chieh 黃節 (Peking, Jen-min wen-hsüeh ch'u-pan she, 1957). Trans. Donald Holzman, *Poetry and Politics: the Life and Works of Juan Chi* (Cambridge, Cambridge University Press, 1976).

Kao-seng chuan 高僧傳 [Lives of Eminent Monks], by Hui-chiao 慧皎 (497–554), *TT*, no. 2059, L, 322–423.

Kao-shih chuan 高士傳 [Lives of Recluses], by Huang-fu Mi 皇甫謐 (215–82), in *SPPY* edn.

Ku-chin chu 古今註 [Comments on Matters Old and New], by Ts'ui Pao 崔豹 (*fl.* late 3rd-early 4th cent.). Reference to *Ku-chin chu, Chung-hua ku-chin chu, Su-shih yen-i* 中華古今注, 蘇氏演義 with 4-corner index (Shanghai, Commercial Press, 1956).

Ku-chin hsing-shih-shu shu pien-cheng 古今姓氏書辯證 [Critical Study of Ancient and Modern Works on Surnames] (1134), by Teng Ming-shih 鄧名世, in *Shou-shan ko ts'ung-shu* 守山閣叢書 of Ch'ien Hsi-tso 錢熙祚 (1801–44).

Ku hsiao-shuo kou-ch'en 古小說鉤沉 [Ancient Fiction Dredged from the Depths], by Lu Hsün 魯迅 (1881–1936), in *Lu Hsün san-shih nien chi* 三十年集 (1937).

Ku-shih shih-chiu shou 古詩十九首 [*Nineteen Old Poems*], in *Wen-hsüan*, ch. 28. Reference by number. Partial trans. Arthur Waley, *Chinese Poems* (London, Allen and Unwin, 1946).

Ku-wen yüan 古文苑 [Garden of Old-style Prose], compiler unknown. Commentary by Chang Chiao 章焦 (13th cent.), in *SPTK* edn.

Kuang hung-ming chi 廣弘明集 [Extended Great Knowledge Collection], compiled by Tao-hsüan 道宣 (596–667), *TT*, no. 2103, LII, 97–362.

Kung-yang chuan 公羊傳 [Kung-yang Commentary (to *Spring and Autumn Annals*)]. Reference by the years of the dukes of Lu.

Kung-yang i-shu 公羊義疏 [Additional Commentary to the *Kung-yang (chuan)*], by Ch'en Li 陳立 (1809–69), in *SPPY* edn., based on the text printed in the *Huang-Ch'ing ching-chieh hsü-pien* 皇清經解續編 (1886–88).

K'ung-ts'ung-tzu 孔叢子, ascribed to K'ung Fu 孔鮒 (1st cent. BC), in *SPTK* edn.

K'ung-tzu chia-yü 孔子家語, in *SPTK* edn. Partial trans. R.P. Kramers, *K'ung Tzu Chia Yü: the School Sayings of Confucius* (Leiden, E.J. Brill, 1949).

Kuo-yü 國語 [Discourse of the States], in *SPPY* edn., based on the recut Northern Sung edn. of 1023–33. Printed in *Shih-li chü Huang-shih ts'ung-shu* 士禮居黃氏叢書 of Huang P'i-lieh 黃丕烈 (1763–1825).

Lao-tzu 老子. Reference by chapters (章). Trans. Arthur Waley, *The Way and its Power* (London, Allen and Unwin, 1934); J.J.L. Duyvendak, *Tao Te Ching* (London, John Murray, 1954).

Lao-tzu chiao-ku 老子校詁 [Critical Examination of the Text of *Lao-tzu*], by Chiang Hsi-ch'ang 蔣錫昌 (Shanghai, Commercial Press, 1937).

Li-chi 禮記 [*Record of the Rites*], in *SPPY* edn. Trans. James Legge, *The Li Ki*. 2 vols. (Oxford, Oxford University Press, 1885).

Li-shih chen-hsien t'i-tao t'ung-chien 歷世真仙體道通鑑 [General Record of True Immortals Embodying the Tao Throughout the Ages], by Chao Tao-i 趙道一 (Yüan period), in *Tao-ts'ang* 道藏, *ts'e* 139–48 (I-wen yin-shu kuan reprint, 1962).

Li-tai ming-hua chi 歷代名畫記 [Record of Famous Paintings Through the Ages] (completed 847), by Chang Yen-yüan 張彥遠. *Chung-kuo mei-shu lun-chu ts'ung-k'an* 中國美術論著叢刊 series (Peking, Jen-min mei-shu ch'u-pan she, 1963).

Li T'ai-po ch'üan-chi 李太白全集 [Complete Works of Li Po (701–762)], with commentary by Wang Ch'i (18th cent.), in *SPPY* edn. Partial trans. Obata Shigeyoshi 小畑薰良, *The Works of Li Po* (Tokyo, 1935; New York, Paragon Book Reprint Corporation, 1965); Arthur Waley, *The Poetry and Career of Li Po* (London, Allen and Unwin, 1950).

Liang Chao-ming t'ai-tzu wen-chi 梁昭明太子文集 [Collected Works of Hsiao T'ung 蕭統 (501–531)], in *SPTK* edn.

Lieh-hsien chuan 列仙傳 [Lives of Immortals], ascribed to Liu Hsiang 劉向 (79–8 BC). Reference to *Le Lie-sien tchouan*, translated and annotated by M. Kaltenmark (Peking, Centre d'Études Sinologiques de Pékin, 1953).

Lieh-nü chuan 列女傳 [Lives of Eminent Women], by Liu Hsiang 劉向 (79–8 BC), in *SPTK* edn.

Lieh-tzu 列子, reference to *Lieh-tzu chi-shih* 集釋, by Yang Po-chün 楊伯峻 (Shanghai, Lung-men lien-ho shu-chü, 1958). Trans. A.C. Graham, *The Book of Lieh-tzu* (London, John Murray, 1960).

Lieh-tzu pu-cheng 列子補正 [Supplementary Commentary to *Lieh-tzu*], by Wang Shu-min 王叔岷. Academia Sinica, Institute of History and Philology, Monograph no. 31 (Shanghai, Commercial Press, 1948).

Lien-she kao-hsien chuan 蓮社高賢傳 [Lives of Worthies of the White Lotus Society], ascribed to an anonymous Chin period author. Reference to versions in *Lu-shan chi* (q.v.), 1039–42 and *Fo-tsu t'ung-chi* (q.v.), 265–71.

Lu-shan chi 廬山記 [Record of Lu-shan], by Ch'en Shun-yü 陳舜俞 († 1074), *TT*, no. 2095, LI, 1024–52.

Lu-shan chi-lüeh 廬山記略 [Draft Record of Lu-shan], by Hui-yüan 慧遠 (334–416), in *Shou-shan ko ts'ung-shu* 守山閣叢書 of Ch'ien Hsi-tso 錢熙祚 (1801–44).

Lu-shan chih 廬山志 [Treatise on Lu-shan] (preface date 1719), by Mao Te-ch'i 毛德琦.

Lu Shih-heng shih chu 陸士衡詩註 [Poems of Lu Chi 陸機 (261–303) with Commentary], by Hao Li-ch'üan 郝立權 (Peking, Jen-min wen-hsüeh ch'u-pan she, 1958).

Lü-shih ch'un-ch'iu 呂氏春秋 [Master Lü's Annals], in *SPTK* edn. Trans. Richard Wilhelm, *Frühling und Herbst des Lü Bu We* (Jena, Eugen Diederichs, 1928).

Lun-heng 論衡 [Evaluation of Views], by Wang Ch'ung 王充 (AD 27–97), in *SPPY* edn. Trans. Alfred Forke, *Lun-heng: Philosophical Essays of Wang Ch'ung*. 2 vols. (1907; 2nd edn., New York, Paragon Book Gallery, 1962).

Lun-yü 論語 [The Sayings of Confucius]. Reference to chapter divisions as in James Legge, trans., *The Chinese Classics*, vol. I (repr. in Hong Kong, Hong Kong University Press, 1960); also trans. Arthur Waley, *The Analects of Confucius* (London, Allen and Unwin, 1939).

Lun-yü chi-chieh i-shu 論語集解義疏 [Additional Commentary to the Collected Explanations of the Sayings of Confucius by Ho Yen 何晏 († 249)], by Huang K'an 皇侃 (488–545), *TSCC*, nos. 481–84.

Meng-tzu 孟子. Reference to chapter divisions as in James Legge, trans., *The Chinese Classics*, vol. II (repr. in Hong Kong, Hong Kong University Press, 1960).

Mu t'ien-tzu chuan 穆天子傳 [Account of Emperor Mu], in *SPPY* edn., based on the *P'ing-chin kuan ts'ung-shu* 平津館叢書 edn. (1806) with collation notes by Hung I-hsüan 洪頤煊 (1765–1837). Trans. Cheng Te-k'un, 'Travels of the Emperor Mu', *JNCBRAS* LXIV (1933) and LXV (1934).

Nan shih 南史 [The History of the Southern Dynasties], by Li Yen-shou 李延壽 († c. 679), in *SPPY* edn.

Pai-ching lou shih-hua 拜經樓詩話 [Remarks on Poetry from the Tower of Honouring the Classics] (preface date 1797), by Wu Ch'ien 吳騫 (1733–1813), in his *Pai-ching lou ts'ung-shu* 叢書 (repr. in Shanghai, Po-ku chai 博古齋, 1922).

Pao-p'u-tzu 抱樸子, by Ko Hung 葛洪 (283–343), in *Chu-tzu chi-ch'eng* 諸子集成. Vol. 8 (Peking, Chung-hua shu-chü, 1954).

Pao Ts'an-chün shih chu 鮑參軍詩註 [Poems by Pao Chao 鮑照 (c. 420–66) with Commentary], by Huang Chieh 黃節 (Peking, Jen-min wen-hsüeh ch'u-pan she, 1957).

Pei-t'ang shu-ch'ao 北堂書鈔 [Extracts from the Northern Hall (of the Sui Imperial Library)], encyclopaedia compiled by Yü Shih-nan 虞世南 (558–638). Facsimile reprint of K'ung Kuang-t'ao 孔廣陶 edn. of 1888. 2 vols. (Taipei, Wen-hai ch'u-pan she, 1962).

Po Hsiang-shan shih-chi 白香山詩集 [Collected Poems of Po Chü-i 白居易 (772–846)], in *SPPY* edn., based on the I-yu ts'ao-t'ang 一隅草堂 block print of Wang Li-ming 注立名 of 1703. Partial trans. Arthur Waley, *Chinese Poems* (London, Allen and Unwin, 1946) and *The Life and Times of Po Chü-i* (London, Allen and Unwin, 1949); Howard S. Levy, *Translations from Po Chü-i's Collected Works*. 2 vols. (New York, Paragon Book Reprint Corporation, 1971).

Po-shih liu-t'ieh shih-lei chi 白事六帖事類集, compiled by Po Chü-i (772–846). Facsimile reprint of a Sung edition in the collection of Fu Tseng-hsiang 傅增湘. 2 vols. (Taipei, Hsin-hsing shu-chü, 1969).

Pu Chin-shu i-wen chih 補晉書藝文志 [Bibliographical Treatise to Supplement the *Chin shu*], compiled by Wen T'ing-shih 文廷式 (1856–1904), in *Erh-shih-wu shih pu-pien* 二十五史補編,

vol. 3 (Shanghai, Chung-hua shu-chü edn., 1955).

San-fu chüeh-lu 三輔決錄 [Definitive Notes on the Three Supporting Areas (of the Capital Ch'ang-an)], by Chao Ch'i 趙岐 († 201) with commentary by Chih Yü 摰虞 (Chin period). Fragments collected by Chang Shu 張澍 in his *Erh-yu t'ang ts'ung-shu* 二酉堂叢書 (1821).

San-kuo chih 三國志 [The History of the Three Kingdoms], by Ch'en Shou 陳壽 (233–297), in *SPPY* edn.

Shan-hai-ching 山海經 [The Book of Hills and Seas]. Reference to *Shan-hai-ching chien-shu* 箋疏, by Hao I-hsing 郝懿行 (1757–1825), in *SPPY* edn.

(Tsu-pen) Shan-hai-ching t'u-tsan (足本) 山海經圖贊 [Restored Text of the Appraisals to the Illustrations in the Book of Hills and Seas), edited by Chang Tsung-hsiang 張宗祥 (Shanghai, Ku-tien wen-hsüen ch'u-pan she 古典文學出版社, 1958).

Sheng-hsien kao-shih chuan 聖賢高士傳 [Lives of Sages, Worthies and Recluses], by Hsi K'ang 嵇康 (223–62). Fragments collected by Yen K'o-chün in *Ch'üan San-kuo wen* (q.v.).

Shih-chi 史記 [Historical Records], by Ssu-ma Ch'ien 司馬遷 (145–86 BC), reference to *Shiki kaichū kōshō* 史記會注考證 (1934), by Takigawa Kametarō 瀧川龜言. Facsimile reprint. 10 vols. (Peking, Wen-hsüeh ku-chi k'an-hsing she, 1955). Partial trans. Édouard Chavannes, *Les Mémoires Historiques de Se-ma Ts'ien*. 5 vols. (Paris, E. Leroux, 1895–1905). Reprinted with additional 6th vol. (Paris, Maisonneuve, 1967–69); Burton Watson, *Records of the Grand Historian of China*. 2 vols. (New York, Columbia University Press, 1961).

Shih-chi 詩紀 [The Record of Poetry], compiled by Feng Wei-no 馮惟訥 (†1572), printed in the Wan-li period (1573–1619).

Shih-chia chai yang-hsin lu 十駕齋養新錄 [Notes of Newly Nurtured Thoughts from the Ten Carriage Studio], by Ch'ien Ta-hsin 錢大昕 (1728–1804), in *SPPY* edn.

Shih-ching 詩經 [*The Book of Songs*]. Reference by numbers (1–305). Trans. Arthur Waley, *The Book of Songs* (London, Allen and Unwin, 1937); Bernhard Karlgren, *The Book of Odes* (Stockholm, Museum of Far Eastern Antiquities, 1950).

Shih-liu kuo ch'un-ch'iu chi-pu 十六國春秋輯補 [Supplement to the Fragments of the Annals of the Sixteen States], by T'ang Ch'iu 湯球. Printed in *Kuang-ya shu-chü ts'ung-shu* 廣雅書局叢書 (1895). Reprinted in *KHCPTS* (Commercial Press, 1958).

Shih-ming 釋名 [Explaining Names], lexicon compiled by Liu Hsi 劉熙 (Later Han period). Reference to *Shih-ming shu-cheng pu* 疏證補 (printed 1896), by Wang Hsien-ch'ien 王先謙 (1842–1918). 2 vols. *WYWK* (Shanghai, Commercial Press, 1937).

Shih-pen 世本 [Genealogies] (compiled *c*. 234–228 BC), with commentary by Sung Chung 宋衷 (Han period). Fragments collected by Ch'in Chia-mo 秦嘉謨 and others in *Shih-pen pa-chung* 八種 (Shanghai, Commercial Press, 1957).

Shih-pa hsien chuan 十八賢傳 [Lives of the Eighteen Worthies], see *Lien-she kao-hsien chuan*.

Shih san-chia i chi-shu 詩三家義集疏 [Collected Additional Commentary on the Three Schools Versions of the *Book of Songs*] (1915), by Wang Hsien-ch'ien 王先謙 (1842–1918). Facsimile reprint (Taipei, Shih-chieh shu-chü, 1957).

Shih-shuo hsin-yü 世說新語 [The Tales of the World Newly Told], by Liu I-ch'ing 劉義慶 (403–444), with commentary by Liu Chün 劉峻 (462–521), in *SPTK* edn. Trans. Richard B. Mather, *Shih-shuo Hsin-yü, A New Account of Tales of the World* (Minneapolis, University of Minnesota Press, 1976).

Shih-t'ung 史通 [Generalities on History], by Liu Chih-chi 劉知幾 (661–721), in *SPTK* edn.

Shu-ching 書經 [*The Book of Documents*]. Reference to (*Chien-pen tsuan-t'u chung-yen chung-i hu-chu tien-chiao*) *Shang-shu* (監本纂圖重言重意互注點校) 尚書, in *SPTK* edn.

Shu-i chi 述異記 [Description of Marvels], ascribed to Jen Fang 任昉 (460–508), in *Lung-wei pi-shu* 龍威秘書 (1794) of Ma Chün-liang 馬俊良.

Shui-ching chu 水經注 [Commentary to the Book of Rivers], by Li Tao-yüan 酈道元 († 527), in *KHCPTS* (repr. in Peking, 1958).

Shuo-wen, see *Shuo-wen chieh-tzu*.

Shuo-wen chieh-tzu 說文解字 [Expounding Writing and Explaining Characters] (AD 121), dictionary compiled by Hsü Shen 許慎. Reference to Chung-hua shu-chü reprint (with index) of 1873 edn. by Ch'en Ch'ang-chih 陳昌治 (Peking, 1963).

Shuo-yüan 說苑 [Garden of Stories], by Liu Hsiang 劉向 (79–8 BC), in *SPTK* edn.

Shuo-yüan chiao-pu 說苑校補 [Supplementary Textual Notes on the *Shuo-yüan*], by Lu Wen-ch'ao 盧文弨 (1717–96), contained in his *Ch'ün-shu shih-pu* 羣書拾補. 3 vols., in *KHCPTS* (Shanghai, 1937).

Sou-shen hou-chi 搜神後記 [Later Records of Searching for Spirits], ascribed to T'ao Ch'ien, in *Chin-tai pi-shu* 津逮秘書, compiled by Mao Chin 毛晉 (1599–1659) (repr. in Shanghai, Po-ku chai 博古齋, 1922).

Ssu-k'u ch'üan-shu tsung-mu t'i-yao 四庫全書總目提要 [Catalogue of the Complete Library in Four Divisions] (1782). 40 vols, in *WYWK* (Shanghai, Commercial Press, 1931).

Su-shuo 俗説 [Popular Tales], by Shen Yüeh 沈約 (441–513). Fragments collected by Ma Kuo-han 馬國翰 (1794–1857) in his *Yü-han shan-fang chi-i shu* 玉函山房輯佚書 (1883) and by Lu Hsün 魯迅 (1881–1936), in his *Ku hsiao-shuo kou-ch'en* (q.v.). Reference to original quotations.

Su Tung-p'o chi 蘇東坡集 [Collected Works of Su Shih 蘇軾 (1037–1101)], 3 vols. in *KHCPTS* (repr. in Shanghai, 1958).

Sui-shu ching-chi chih 隋書經籍志 [Bibliographical Treatise of the *Sui shu*, ch. 32–35], compiled by Chang-sun Wu-chi 長孫無忌 and others (completed 656) (Shanghai, Commercial Press, 1955, with four-corner index).

Sui-shu ching-chi chih k'ao-cheng 隋書經籍志考證 [Critical Study of the Bibliographical Treatise of the *Sui shu*], by Yao Chen-tsung 姚振宗, in *Erh-shih-wu shih pu-pien* 二十五史補編, vol. 4 (Shanghai, Chung-hua shu-chü edn., 1955).

Sung-shih i-wen-chih 宋史藝文志 [Bibliographical Treatise of the *Sung shih*, ch. 155–62] (compiled 1343–45), by T'o T'o 脱脱 and others. Printed with *Sung-shih i-wen-chih pu* 補 and *Sung-shih i-wen-chih fu-pien* 附編, with a four-corner index (Shanghai, Commercial Press, 1957).

Sung shu 宋書 [The History of Sung, AD 420–79], compiled by Shen Yüeh 沈約 (441–513), in *SPPY* edn.

T'ai-p'ing huan-yü chi 太平寰宇記 [The T'ai-p'ing (= AD 976–83) Record of the World], by Yüeh Shih 樂史 (930–1007), in Chin-ling shu-chü 金陵書局 edn. (1882).

T'ai-p'ing yü-lan 太平御覽 [The T'ai-p'ing Imperial Encyclopaedia] (983), compiled by Li Fang 李昉 (925–996) and others, in *SPTK san pien* facsimile of Sung edn. supplemented from various copies preserved in Japan. 12 vols. (Taipei, Hsin-hsing shu-chü, 1959).

Teng-hsi-tzu 鄧析子, reference to Wang K'ai-luan 王愷鑾, *Teng-hsi-tzu chiao-cheng* 校正, *KHHTS* (Shanghai, Commercial Press, 1935). Trans. H. Wilhelm, 'Schriften und Fragmente zur Entwicklung der staatsrechtlichen Theorie in der Chou-zeit', *Monumenta Serica* XII (1947), 41–96.

Ti-wang shih-chi 帝王世紀 [Genealogical Records of Emperors and Kings], by Huang-fu Mi 皇甫謐 (215–82). Reference to Hsü Tsung-yüan 徐宗元, *Ti-wang shih-chi chi-ts'un* 輯存 (Peking, Chung-hua shu-chü, 1964).

Ts'ao Ts'ao chi 曹操集 [The Works of Ts'ao Ts'ao (155–220)], compiled and published by Chung-hua shu-chü (Peking, 1959). 2nd edn. with revisions and additions (1962).

Ts'ao Tzu-chien shih-chu 曹子建詩註 [The Poems of Ts'ao Chih (192–232) with Commentary] (first published 1930) by Huang Chieh 黃節 (Peking, Jen-min wen-hsüeh ch'u-pan she, 1957). Partial trans. George W. Kent, *Worlds of Dust and Jade* (New York, Philosophical Library, 1969).

Tso-chuan 左傳. Reference by years of dukes of Lu. Trans. James Legge, *The Chinese Classics*, vol. 5 (repr. in Hong Kong, Hong Kong University Press, 1960).

Tso-fen chin-kao 左汾近稿 [Recent Drafts of Tso-fen (Yen's literary name)], by Yen Yung 閻詠, son of Yen Jo-chü 閻若璩 (1636–1704). Printed as an appendix to his father's *Ch'ien-ch'iu cha-chi* 潛邱劄記, (Chüan-hsi t'ang 眷西堂, block print, 1744).

Tu shih 杜詩, the poems of Tu Fu 杜甫 (712–770). Reference to *Tu shih yin-te*. Harvard-Yenching Institute Sinological Index Series, Supplement 14. 3 vols. (Peking, 1940). Partial trans. William Hung, *Tu Fu: China's Greatest Poet* (Cambridge, Harvard University Press, 1952); A.R. Davis, *Tu Fu* (New York, Twayne, 1971).

Tung-kuan Han-chi 東觀漢記 [The Eastern Pavilion Record of Han], by Liu Chen 劉珍 (*fl.* early 2nd cent.) and others, in *SPPY* edn., based on the Sao-yeh shan-fang 掃葉山房 edn. (1795).

Tung-p'o t'i-pa 東坡題跋 [Colophons by Su Shih 蘇軾 (1037–1101)], in *Chin-tai pi-shu* 津逮祕書, compiled by Mao Chin 毛晉 (1599–1659) (repr. in Shanghai, Po-ku chai 博古齋, 1922).

Tung-p'o yüeh-fu chien 東坡樂府箋 [The *Tz'u*-poems of Su Shih], edited by Lung Yü-sheng 龍榆生. 2 *ts'e* (Shanghai, Commercial Press, 1936; repr., 1958).

T'ung-tien 通典 [The Comprehensive Statutes], compiled by Tu Yu 杜佑 (735–812), in *Shih t'ung* 十通 (Shanghai, Commercial Press, 1935–36).

Tzu-chih t'ung-chien 資治通鑑 [Comprehensive History to Aid Government], by Ssu-ma Kuang 司馬光 (1019–86). 10 vols. (Peking, Ku-chi ch'u-pan she, 1956).

Wang Ching-kung shih-wen Shen-shih chu 王荊公詩文沈氏注 [Comments of Shen Ch'in-han 沈欽韓 (1775–1832) on the Poetry and Prose of Wang An-shih 王安石 (1021–86)], being Shen's *Wang Ching-kung shih-chi Li Pi chu kan-wu pu-cheng* 王荊公詩集李壁注勘誤補正 and *Wang Ching-kung wen-chi chu* 王荊公文集注, compiled by Shanghai Chung-hua shu-chü (1959).

Wang Yu-ch'eng chi 王右丞集 [Collected Works of Wang Wei 王維 (699/701–759/761)], with commentary by Chao Tien-ch'eng 趙殿成 (1683–1756), in *SPPY* edn. Partial trans. G.W. Robinson, *Poems of Wang Wei* (Penguin Books, 1973).

'Wei Chin Nan-ch'ao ti-fang cheng-fu shu-tso k'ao' 魏晉南朝地方政府屬佐考 [Study of Subordinates in Local Government in Wei, Chin and the Southern Dynasties], by Yen Keng-wang 嚴耕望, *CYYY* XX, 1 (1950), 445–538.

Wei Chin Nan-pei ch'ao ti-fang hsing-cheng chih-tu, see *Chung-kuo ti-fang hsing-cheng chih-tu shih*.

Wei-lüeh 魏略 [Outline History of Wei AD 220–65], by Yü Huan 魚豢 (3rd cent.). Fragments collected by Chang Peng-i 張鵬一 and printed in his *Kuan-lung ts'ung-shu* 關隴叢書 (1924). Facsimile repr. (Nagoya, Saika shorin 采華書林, 1972).

Wei shu 魏書 [The History of Wei AD 386–535], compiled by Wei Shou 魏收 (506–72), in *SPPY* edn.

Wei-shu t'ung-k'ao 偽書通考 [Study of Forged Books], by Chang Hsin-ch'eng 張心澂 (Shanghai, Commercial Press, 1939). Revised edn. 2 vols. (1957).

Wei Wu-ti Wei Wen-ti shih chu 魏武帝魏文帝詩注 [Poems of Ts'ao Ts'ao 曹操 (155–220) and Ts'ao P'i 曹丕 (186–226) with Commentary], by Huang Chieh 黃節, with appendix *Wei Ming-ti* [= Ts'ao Jui 曹睿 (204–239)] *shih chu* 魏明帝詩注 (Peking, Jen-min wen-hsüeh ch'u-pan she, 1958).

Wen-chang yüan-ch'i 文章緣起 [The Origins of Literary Genres], ascribed to Jen Fang 任昉 (460–508), in *Hsüeh-hai lei-pien* 學海類編 (first printed 1834), compiled by Ts'ao Jung 曹溶 (1613–85), vol. 4 (repr. in Taipei, Wen-hai ch'u-pan she, 1965).

Wen-hsin tiao-lung 文心雕龍, by Liu Hsieh 劉勰 (c. 466–505). Reference to *Wen-hsin tiao-lung chu* 註, by Fan Wen-lan 范文瀾. 2 vols. (Peking, Jen-min wen-hsüeh ch'u-pan she, 1958). Trans. Vincent Yu-chung Shih, *The Literary Mind and the Carving of Dragons* (New York, Columbia University Press, 1959).

(Liu ch'en chu) Wen-hsüan (六臣註) 文選 [The Anthology of Literature with Commentary by the Six Ministers], compiled by Hsiao T'ung 蕭統 (501–31) with commentary by Li Shan 李善, Lü Yen-chi 呂延濟, Liu Liang 劉良, Chang Hsien 張銑, Li Chou-han 李周翰 and Lü Hsiang 呂向, in *SPTK* repr. of Sung edn. Unless otherwise indicated reference to *Wen-hsüan* is to this edn.

Wen-hsüan 文選, compiled by Hsiao T'ung, with commentary by Li Shan, re-cut print of 1181 edn., with *k'ao-i* (examination of variants) under the name of Hu K'o-chia 胡克家 (1757–1816); actually by Ku Kuang-ch'i 顧廣圻 (1776–1835), (1809, repr. in Taipei, I-wen yin-shu kuan, 1971).

Wen-kuan tz'u-lin 文館詞林 [The Hall of Literature and the Grove of Words] (658), anthology compiled in 1,000 chüan, of which 27 have been wholly or partially preserved, by Hsü Ching-tsung 許敬宗 (592–672) and others. Reference to *Wen-kuan tz'u-lin ts'an erh-shih-san chüan* 殘二十三卷 (1914), in *Shih-yüan ts'ung-shu* 適園叢書, compiled by Chang Chün-heng 張鈞衡 See also (*Ei Kōjin hon*) *Bunkan shirin* 影弘仁本文館詞林 (Tokyo, Koten Kenkyūkai 古典研究會, 1969).

Wu-ling chi 武陵記 [Record of Wu-ling], by Huang Min 黃閔. Fragments collected by Ch'en Yün-jung 陳運溶 in his *Lu-shan ching-she ts'ung-shu* 麓山精舍叢書 (1900). Repr. as appendix to *Han-T'ang ti-li shu ch'ao* 漢唐地理書鈔 (Peking, Chung-hua shu-chü, 1961).

Yen-shih chia-hsün 顏氏家訓, by Yen Chih-t'ui 顏之推 (531–91), in *SPPY* edn. Trans. Teng Ssu-yü, *Family Instructions for the Yen Clan*. *T'oung Pao* Monographie IV (Leiden, E.J. Brill, 1968).

Yen-t'ieh lun 鹽鐵論, by Huan K'uan 桓寬 (1st cent. BC). Reference to *Yen-t'ieh lun chiao-chu* 校注, by Wang Li-ch'i 王利器 (Shanghai, Ku-tien wen-hsüeh ch'u-pan she, 1958). Partial trans. Esson M. Gale, *Discourses on Salt and Iron*. Sinica Leidensia, vol. II (Leiden, E.J. Brill, 1931). Repr. with addition of trans. of ch. 20–28 originally published in *JNCBRAS* LXV (1934) (Taipei, Ch'eng-wen Publishing Company, 1967).

Yü-t'ai hsin-yung 玉臺新詠 [New Songs from the Jade Terrace], compiled by Hsü Ling 徐陵 (507–83), in *SPPY* edn.

Yü-ti kuang-chi 輿地廣記 [Extensive Account of the World], by Ou-yang Min 歐陽忞 (fl. early 12th cent.), with notes by Huang P'i-lieh 黃丕烈 (1763–1825). Printed in his *Shih-li chü Huang-shih ts'ung-shu* 士禮居黃氏叢書 (repr. in Shanghai, Po-ku chai 博古齋, 1922).

Yüan-ho chün-hsien t'u-chih 元和郡縣志 [Treatise with Maps of the Commanderies and Districts of the Yüan-ho Period AD 806–820], by Li Chi-fu 李吉甫 (758–814) in *T'ai-nan ko ts'ung-shu* 岱南閣叢書, compiled by Sun Hsing-yen 孫星衍 (1753–1818) (repr. in Shanghai, Po-ku chai 博古齋, 1924).

Yüan-shih Ch'ang-ch'ing chi 元氏長慶集 [Collected Works of Yüan Chen 元稹 (779–831)], in *SPTK* edn.

Yüeh-fu shih chi 樂府詩集 [Collection of *Yüeh-fu* Poems], compiled by Kuo Mao-ch'ien 郭茂倩 (fl. late 11th cent.), in *SPTK* edn.

Yung-lo ta-tien 永樂大典 [The Yung-lo (AD 1403–1425) Encylopaedia], compiled 1403–1407. Surviving chüan in 202 *ts'e* (Peking, Chung-hua shu-chü, 1960).

C. Western Works Cited

Bodde, Derk, *Statesman, Patriot, and General in Ancient China: Three Shih-chi Biographies of the Ch'in Dynasty (255–206 BC)* (New Haven, American Oriental Society, 1940).

Chang Chung-yuan, *Creativity and Taoism; A Study of Chinese Philosophy, Art, and Poetry* (New York, The Julian Press, 1963).

Davis, A.R., 'The Double Ninth Festival in Chinese Poetry' in Chow Tse-tsung (ed.), *Wen-lin: Studies in the Chinese Humanities* (Madison, University of Wisconsin Press, 1968), 45–64.

———, 'The Fortunate Banishment; Liu Tsung-yüan in Yung-chou', *Journal of the Oriental Society of Australia* IV, 2 (December, 1966), 38–48.

———, *Tu Fu* (New York, Twayne, 1971).

Dubs, H.H., *The History of the Former Han Dynasty*. 3 vols. (Baltimore, Waverly Press, 1938–55).

Hightower, J.R., 'The Fu of T'ao Ch'ien', *Harvard Journal of Asiatic Studies* XVII (1954), 169–230.

———, *The Poetry of T'ao Ch'ien* (Oxford, Oxford University Press, 1970).

———, 'T'ao Ch'ien's "Drinking Wine" Poems' in Chow Tse-tsung (ed.), *Wen-lin: Studies in the Chinese Humanities* (Madison, University of Wisconsin Press, 1968), 3–44.

Karlgren, Bernhard, 'Glosses on the Kuo Feng Odes', *BMFEA* XIV (1942), 71–247; 'Glosses on the Siao Ya Odes', *BMFEA* XVI (1944), 25–169; 'Glosses on the Ta Ya and Sung Odes', *BMFEA* XVIII (1946), 1–198.

———, 'Legends and Cults in Ancient China', *BMFEA* XVIII (1946), 199–365.

Liebenthal, W., *The Book of Chao*. Monumenta Serica Monograph XIII (Peking, The Catholic University of Peking, 1948).

———, 'The Immortality of the Soul in Chinese Thought', *Monumenta Nipponica*, VIII (1952), 327–97.

Maspero, Henri, 'Le Roman historique dans la litterature chinoise de l'Antiquite' in *Mélanges posthumes sur les religions et l'histoire de la Chine* III. Publications du Musee Guimet, Bibliothèque de Diffusion, LIX (Paris, 1950).

Rogers, Michael. C., *The Chronicle of Fu Chien: a Case of Exemplar History*. Chinese Dynastic Histories Translations, no. 10 (University of California Press, 1968).

Waley, Arthur, *Chinese Poems* (London, Allen and Unwin, 1946).

———, *The Life and Times of Po Chü-i (AD 772–846)* (London, Allen and Unwin, 1949).

Watson, Burton, *Chinese Rhyme-prose: Poems in the Fu Form from the Han and Six Dynasties Periods* (New York, Columbia University Press, 1971).

Whitaker, K.P.K., 'Some Notes on the Background and Date of Tsaur Jyr's Poem on the Three Good Courtiers', *Bulletin of the School of Oriental and African Studies*, XVIII, 303–11.

Zürcher, E., *The Buddhist Conquest of China: The Spread and Adaptation of Buddhism in Early Medieval China*. Sinica Leidensia XI. 2 vols. (Leiden, E.J. Brill, 1959).

INDEX

27677051R00129

Printed in Great Britain
by Amazon